Jennifer Ho

Leisure and Recreation Studies
*Series Editors*: Stanley Parker and Sarah Gregory

5 Politics and Leisure

Leisure and Recreation Studies

1. LEISURE IDENTITIES AND INTERACTIONS
   *by John R. Kelly*

2. LEISURE AND WORK
   *by Stanley Parker*

3. YOUTH AND LEISURE
   *by Kenneth Roberts*

4. LEISURE AND THE FUTURE
   *by A. J. Veal*

# Politics and Leisure

## John Wilson
*Duke University*

Boston
**UNWIN HYMAN**
London   Sydney   Wellington

© John Wilson, 1988
This book is copyright under the Berne Convention. No reproduction without permission. All rights reserved.

Allen & Unwin, Inc.,
8 Winchester Place, Winchester, Mass. 01890, USA

Published by the Academic Division of
**Unwin Hyman Ltd**
15-17 Broadwick Street, London W1V 1FP, UK

Allen & Unwin (Australia) Ltd,
8 Napier Street, North Sydney, NSW 2060, Australia

Allen & Unwin (New Zealand) Ltd in association with the
Port Nicholson Press Ltd,
60 Cambridge Terrace, Wellington, New Zealand

First published in 1988

**Library of Congress Cataloging-in-Publication Data**

Wilson, John, 1942-
  Politics and leisure / John Wilson.
  p. cm.—(Leisure and recreation studies : 5)
  Bibliography: p.
  Includes index.
  ISBN 0-04-301265-5 (alk. paper). ISBN 0-04-301266-3 (pbk. : alk. paper)
  1. Political science.   2. Leisure.   I. Title.   II. Series.
  JA71.W465 1988
  306'.2—dc19                                                    87-21154
                                                                      CIP

**British Library Cataloguing in Publication Data**

Wilson, John, *1942–*
  Politics and Leisure.
  (Leisure and recreation studies; 5).
  1. Leisure—Political aspects
  I. Title    II. Series
  306'.48    GV14
  ISBN 0-04-301265-5
  ISBN 0-04-301266-3 Pbk

Set in 10 on 11 point Bembo by Columns of Reading
and printed in Great Britain by Billing and Son,
London and Worcester

# Contents

| | | |
|---|---|---|
| 1 | Politics and Leisure | page 1 |
| | What Is Leisure? | 1 |
| | What Is Politics? | 5 |
| | The Relationship between Politics and Leisure | 11 |
| | Leisure's Impact on Politics | 14 |
| | Looking Ahead | 18 |
| 2 | The Control of Leisure | 21 |
| | The Politics of Time and Space | 21 |
| | From Repression to Cooptation | 27 |
| | Leisure Professionals | 33 |
| | The Mass Media | 36 |
| | Sports | 41 |
| | Sexuality | 44 |
| | Politics and the Market | 51 |
| 3 | Resistance | 56 |
| | Class | 61 |
| | Gender | 69 |
| | Race | 73 |
| | Cooptation | 76 |
| 4 | Leisure in the Liberal State: the United States | 78 |
| | The Entitlement to Free Time | 80 |
| | Leisure Services in a Liberal State | 81 |
| | Politics and Amateur Sports | 85 |
| | Government and the Sports Business | 88 |
| | The Market and the State | 97 |
| 5 | Leisure in the Welfare State: the United Kingdom | 101 |
| | The Entitlement to Free Time | 102 |
| | The Political Organization of Leisure Services | 104 |
| | The Government and Leisure Policy | 115 |
| | Can Leisure be Administered? | 119 |
| 6 | Leisure in Totalitarian Regimes | 121 |
| | Leisure in Communist Countries | 121 |

|   |   |   |
|---|---|---|
| Similarities and Differences | page | 138 |
| Leisure in Fascist Regimes | | 140 |
| Consent Denied | | 148 |

7 Leisure and Nationalism     149

|   |   |
|---|---|
| Achieving Nationhood | 150 |
| Sport and the World System of Exchange | 154 |
| The World Order of Sport as a Political System | 161 |
| Sport, National Integration and Disintegration | 165 |
| The Relationship between National and International Organizations | 170 |

8 Conclusion: The Future of Politics and Leisure     174

References     190

Index     198

# 1
# Politics and Leisure

In this opening chapter, I shall introduce the major concepts and ideas to be used in the book and explain how they will be used. 'Politics' and 'leisure' are words with deceptively obvious meanings. Actually each has many meanings, not only in everyday speech but also in the social sciences. I need to indicate how I shall be using them. A second problem is that we do not usually associate politics and leisure. Rather, we think of them as completely separate spheres. I therefore need to explain how they are related.

## What Is Leisure?

Leisure is notoriously difficult to define. Some sociologists treat it as a portion of one's time. Others regard it as a quality of experience unconfined to particular times. It is generally agreed that attempts to list all 'leisure' activities do not help much, because almost any activity can be a leisure activity if the right attitude of mind is adopted toward it. Nor should we be misled by the enormous popularity of commercialized entertainment or the prestige of the 'high culture' world of museums and galleries when trying to decide what leisure is. At the heart of most people's leisure are informal and everyday things like playing with the children or pets, chatting with friends, pottering about in the garden, keeping one eye on the television, browsing in shops, or simply daydreaming. The more public part of the leisure world—theme parks, vacation spots, cinemas, libraries, fairs, sports stadiums and playing fields—are only the tip of the iceberg. Another difficulty in drawing a boundary around leisure is that much of our leisure occurs in the interstices of other social institutions; we might read a novel on the way to work, play squash on our lunch break, play with the children while taking the dog for a walk, gossip on our way to the shops, play softball with our church group. All this makes distinguishing leisure from other activities extremely difficult. Much overlapping and merging occurs, and much depends on the attitude taken toward an activity by the individual or group.

*Leisure and Freedom*

We should not abandon the attempt to define leisure simply because exceptions to any definition we agree upon will always be found. Leisure is essentially 'autotelic' activity. In other words, it is chosen primarily for its own sake. 'If there are sanctions applied for failure to participate in a given activity, it is not leisure because it is not freely chosen' (Lane, 1978, p. 149). Leisure is thus to be distinguished from whatever has to be done, it is voluntary, and the motivation is intrinsic. Of course, each of these elements in the definition is subject to modification in the real world. It is often impossible to decide what is absolutely necessary as opposed to something that is discretionary. For example, how clean does the car really have to be to prevent rust and deterioration? We can all agree that leisure must be free, but what kind of freedom do we have in mind? We must distinguish between freedom from compulsion (play is hardly something we can be forced to do) from freedom in the broader social and political sense. We can certainly define leisure as free in the first sense but it is not so clear that leisure could ever be free of social or political constraint. Specific leisure activities might be freely chosen, but the choice is always made within social and cultural constraints. For example, we can choose what we read, but not every kind of reading material is widely available. Finally, although we all have a fairly good idea of when we are doing something for its own sake, just for fun, much of what we do, such as jogging, contains both intrinsic and extrinsic motivations, and we ourselves are not sure where one begins and the other leaves off. None of these 'real world' problems with our definition, however, should be allowed to obscure our view of the one essential and universal feature of leisure, that it is autotelic or instrinsically motivated. 'All people experience the two states of existence, one that asks no question of objectives beyond itself, the other that is stimulated and sustained by the goal that exists outside the behavior' (Blanchard and Cheska, 1985, p. 40). No matter how much our free time becomes encrusted within activities which have some ulterior purpose—military preparation, rehabilitation for work, child-minding, impression-management—it will have at its core a leisurely component if it is energized and directed in part 'for its own sake.' The desire to protect, reproduce and distill this essentially autotelic experience without at the same time sacrificing its spontaneity and freedom is part of the dialect of leisure.

*Leisure Ideologies*
The concepts of social science, so often drawn from everyday speech, are frequently weighted down with political assumptions which limit their usefulness in research and analysis. In thus defining leisure I have tried to eliminate as much of this political bias as possible, because the relation of leisure to politics is the subject of the book. Nevertheless, it is as well to be aware of the ideological freight the concept of leisure carries in our culture. Simply to define leisure as time 'left over' from work in which people seek self-fulfillment means making a number of covert assumptions about what social life is 'really' like, none of which stand up to historical scrutiny. One of these assumptions is that the boundary between work and leisure is fixed and clearly marked. Another is that work is primary and leisure secondary. Most of us also assume that leisure needs are principally geared to the improvement of the self. As assumptions about the part played by leisure in social life, each is false. Before people started working in factories, fields and offices for hourly wages it was very difficult to separate work time from non-work time, as it still is today for the self-employed or for housewives. If we drop all reference to work and simply describe leisure as 'non-obligated time' we discover that few people living in the eighteenth century would have enjoyed any 'leisure' at all. Most would have had 'sports' and 'pastimes' which were organized, communal activities and hence more or less obligatory occasions. Leisure, in the sense of non-obligated time, would have been considered 'idleness' on the part of any group except the aristocracy. The definition of leisure as time 'left over' from work implies that work comes first and leisure is the residue. This, too, is an assumption that history questions. The idea that hard work is good and play is bad is Puritanical. As that world-view has begun to fade, so too has the idea of the work ethic, to be replaced by a 'fun ethic' in conformity to which people feel the 'duty' to have a good time. If work comes to be seen as a necessary inconvenience, a return in many ways to the morality of the Middle Ages, then we should not see leisure as a left-over. Finally, the idea that leisure is by definition devoted to the pursuit of self-fulfillment contains a bias toward a more individualistic conception of the good life. But not all societies have exalted the pursuit of individual happiness in preference to, or at the cost of, the common good. Not all societies are as inclined as modern capitalist societies to define happiness in terms of the gratification of the individual consumer.

It is not possible, nor is it necessarily desirable, to eliminate all traces of such ideological biases from our treatment of leisure. As we shall see, virtually any sociological analysis of the relation between politics and leisure contains its class and gender biases. All we can hope for is to be cognizant of them and to draw our conclusions about politics and leisure fully conscious of the starting point from which we began. These sociological and ideological problems of defining leisure are very similar to those presented by an institution like religion, another human activity that has proven difficult to define precisely. It might be instructive to draw out the parallels. Like leisure, religion is not 'contained' in any set of activities; no list of practices or beliefs could hope to be exhaustive. Like modern leisure, modern religion is somewhat misleading because it has become highly organized; the churches, with their salaried professionals, bureaucratic staffs and complex budgets, suggest themselves as the obvious 'site' of religiosity. But there are many people who are neither church members nor regular church-goers who nevertheless consider themselves religious, just as there are many people who can be 'at leisure' although they belong to no club and attend no sporting event. Like leisure, religion is very difficult to circumscribe; where does religious behavior end and political behavior begin? In religion, as in leisure, there are always those who want to alter its definition for the purposes of controlling the behavior of others. Thus groups dispute not only what a religion teaches but whether or not it is a religion at all and therefore entitled to protections accorded other religions. As we shall see, groups have fought over not only their right to enjoy a form of leisure but, more fundamentally, whether an activity should be regarded as leisure at all. The sociologist commits himself to one side or the other the moment he settles upon his definition of leisure.

The best way to proceed in the face of these definitional problems is to remember that 'leisure' is an abstract term. No concrete activity will necessarily exhibit all its defining characteristics in their purity. This should present no insurmountable obstacle. We study not leisure in general but leisure in particular. We focus on the specific and concrete. Observing changes in the programs people watch on television or accounting for the demise of the public house or saloon does not require that we decide in advance whether or not these are 'really' leisure issues.

I have defined leisure very broadly and consequently will treat most specific leisure activities very briefly and abstractly. I will devote considerable attention to sports. With the assistance of the mass media, they have become the most important component of the leisure-time industry. People want to be entertained in their leisure time, and those who run sports as a business have responded adroitly and zealously to this demand. But the reason that sports figure so prominently in a book on politics and leisure is not because they are so popular. Indeed, they rank fairly low in lists of leisure activities people prefer to engage in. Sports represent the most bureaucratized of leisure activities; they are most likely to brush up against political life. This is especially true when considering international affairs. Sports are vulnerable to the ministrations of the law; they stake a claim to scarce resources and a share of public goods (such as city spaces and airwaves); and they are erected on a complex scaffolding of economic agreements and contracts which almost inevitably brings them into contact with the state and renders them an object of attention from politicians and the state. Apart from the mass media, no other component of the leisure sphere has this corporate existence, no other component is so much a creature of past political decisions. Although I will be at pains to argue that all leisure is in some sense political, I will be able to demonstrate this most convincingly in the case of sports. In totalitarian regimes, where all activities are political, sports loom so large in the leisure world because they effectively administer free-time activities. Their promotion is testimony to the authorities' fears and suspicions of free, unorganized street play and private pastimes (e.g. hobbies).

Despite the fact that their relationship to politics is close. I shall allude only briefly to the arts, which are best treated as a topic in their own right. However, I shall have something to say about mass media such as radio and television, because people spend much of their leisure time attending to them and because they have an obvious 'public' or collective dimension which inevitably introduces political influence. The kind of casual, private and informal leisure that occupies a considerable amount of our free time rarely becomes part of the public world and impinges less upon politics even in totalitarian regimes. This part of the leisure world is politically important, however, precisely because it provides the 'room' for people to distance themselves from control and surveillance. I will therefore have something to say about it under the heading of 'resistance.'

## What Is Politics?

A study of politics and leisure must concern itself with states (as social institutions), with political processes (such as elections) and with the play of political ideas to the extent that they impinge upon people's free time. To take into consideration the 'political factor' in leisure is to acknowledge that people's use of their free time is not simply the result of social and economic forces but is the outcome also of political struggle. Leisure has seldom been a burning issue in election campaigns and is unlikely to topple a government or mobilize a social movement. However, leisure figures in many political debates indirectly; when groups contend over conditions of work, proper child care, censorship, adequate transportation, decent housing and a clean environment, they are also contending over leisure issues.

Leisure is also 'political' to the extent that 'the personal is political,' to the degree that the everyday lives of men and women, extending to control over their 'persons,' are shaped by relations of domination and submission. A common constraint experienced by large numbers of women who seek leisure satisfactions, for example, 'is that of male control, both on an individual basis (husbands or partners controlling where "their" women go) and through the fears generated in women by collective male control over female sexuality' (Deem, 1968a, p. 7). I shall have a great deal to say about collective, or public, control over women's leisure but not much to say about the more private forms. This is not to pretend that there is no 'micro-politics' of leisure; in a certain sense, all leisure activities take place within constraints imposed by other, more powerful groups. But such a broad definition of what is political threatens to undermine any discrimination the concept originally possessed. Not all relations can be reduced to struggles for power; not all struggles for power become institutionalized into political structures. Gender is an important issue for leisure at the micro-level, but it is equally important at the collective or macro-level, and it is with this level that the present book concerns itself.

## The Emergence of the State

Increasingly debates over the politics of leisure have focused on the state's role with respect to these issues. We should therefore begin with a discussion of the state and how its functioning can be explained. Badie and Birnbaum (1983, p. 105) define the state as a 'system of permanently institutionalized roles which has the exclusive right to the legitimate use of force, whereby it exerts sovereign power over a given territory.' Its component parts are the government (of the day), the executive, the military and other coercive forces, the judiciary, parliamentary assemblies and the various units of sub-central government. The formation of classes and the evolution of the state go hand in hand, although, as we see in the case of the political institutionalization of private property, it is often difficult to decide whether class formation is the cause or the effect of state formation.

The notion of a distinct political sphere separate from 'civil society' is peculiar to capitalism. The very individualism of capitalism, the fact that all subjects are formally free and equal to pursue their own ends, requires a separate structure, the state, to represent their 'common' interests. The result is the evolution of the state and its relative autonomy from other institutions like the family and the economy. However, this is not to say that the state is neutral. By and large, the state embodies and furthers the interests of the ruling class. For example, the state attaches to all individuals abstractly equal faculties for freely disposing of their own resources. This meets the capitalists' requirement that labor power be sold for wages through individual employment contracts. The state's guarantee of a relatively free market for goods and of the equality of individuals before the law serves the same purpose.

While the modern Western state is appropriately conceived as a capitalist state, it is by no means the case that political developments can be inferred directly from the configuration of class forces. We must therefore look upon the state as partially autonomous from economic conditions and class struggles. 'State power expresses at once the intentions and purposes of government and state personnel (they could have acted differently) and the parameters set by the institutionalized context of state–society relations' (Held and Krieger, 1984, p. 18). After all, it is only when the state is removed from a direct relationship with particular fractions of capital that it can provide the necessary conditions for general capitalist production.

> It follows from this, then, that the state cannot be conceived to be simply a servant of capital; although it has to cope with the general needs of the capitalist mode of production, the manner and direction in which it does this will be highly variable, depending on the conjuncture of a wide range of not only economic but also social and political forces as they operate within the context of specific national social formations.
>
> (Scase, 1980, p. 13)

The state, in other words, has needs of its own which will be pursued in part independently of the needs of capitalism. For example, state agencies will want to incorporate (and thus remove from the market) sections of society in order to make them easier to control. The state must also concern itself with foreign policy and military needs. Independent action on the part of state functionaries is also furthered by the tendency for state agencies to become isolated by virtue of their sheer size.

The state thus embodies general, not specific, interests. Yet it remains a capitalist state, and will choose policies which in general and in the long run serve to reproduce the capitalist system. This means assuming responsibility for functions and services beyond the scope and capability of capitalist interests (i.e. needs not met by the marketplace), sustaining and expanding the capitalist economy, regulating markets and labor relations, defending the national interest abroad and maintaining law and order. The criteria by which state agencies make decisions will naturally differ from those used by businessmen, being less obedient to the logic of the marketplace and less preoccupied with profit maximization. On the other hand, the state must react to problems which have been created by structurally imposed conditions of work and residence. As we shall see, there are no inherent 'leisure needs,' only needs created by conditions of work and residence. Helping to foster fitness and recreation when conditions of work threaten health, or satisfying the need for clean air and open spaces created by overcrowding and long-distance commuting, the state meets 'needs' which have been created by the economic system on which it, too, depends for support.

*Political Ideologies*
Politics in capitalist countries range from socialist, through reform and liberal, to conservative (Alford and Friedland, 1985). Extremes meet at either end of this spectrum in the anti-capitalist politics of communism and fascism. Conservative politics treats the operation of markets as self-regulating and attempts to limit the scope of state intervention in the belief that such interventions tend to undermine the efficiency of the market. Liberal politics assumes that the market can be made to work more democratically and hence more efficiently by limited state actions. Reform politics attempts to replace markets with state authority over corporate and labor elites; typical of reform politics is the fully realized welfare state. Socialist politics assumes that parliamentary representation alone cannot reshape either the state or capitalism in the interests of the people. Instead, mass movements must broaden the channels of political representation to create centers of popular power. As we shall see, leisure policy in capitalist states follows the contours of these differing political positions.

Since the Industrial Revolution, the dominant political philosophy in Western capitalist societies has been that of either conservatism or liberalism. In the nineteenth century, John Stuart Mill popularized the view that the specification of certain activities and practices that in principle are not harmful to others suffices to distinguish the private from the public. The private sphere thus demarcates that which is of no proper concern to others. The liberals and conservatives both locate leisure firmly within the private sphere, a region of life in which the individual can engage in those integral and significant social relationships that are the building blocks of personal identity. The private sphere connotes freedom and autonomy, while the public sphere means constraint and alienation. In the private sphere the individual is in control; in the public sphere the individual is under control. Today's conservatives believe in a negative relation between the individual and some wider public, including government, a relation of non-interference with thoughts and action. The private sphere is something we should 'keep politics out of.' Leisure is thus presented to us in many Western capitalist societies as essentially part of the private sphere and hence largely unrelated to the public functions of the state. Complaints about allowing politics to invade or interfere with sports preserve this distinction.

This is not to say that leisure attitudes can be neatly summarized on a continuum of political right to left. Frequently, political struggles over leisure issues fall outside the conventional left–right dimension, because, in general, such issues are seen as having little to do with equality or the redistribution of income. Thus we find, for example, middle-class groups advocating a kind of post-materialist politics which favors conservation, folk cultures and historical preservation, while a more materialist working class favors commercial entertainment, follows a strong work ethic and is not disturbed by the cultural homogeneity of the mass media. Environmentalism, movements to protect social communities or neighborhoods, and 'moral crusades' to defend a particular way of life and value system, all of which can have profound impacts on leisure, are difficult to force into a left–right polarity, As we shall see, leisure has also been closely tied to nationalist ideologies, which are likewise difficult to place on the conventional left–right continuum.

*The Expanding State*
The jurisdiction of the state in the West has expanded over time as more and more aspects of life are incorporated into its general welfare function. Although the reasons for this are many and complex, one important consideration is that the state is increasingly forced to underwrite the costs of capitalist production by direct involvement in renewing and maintaining the forces of production, intervening not only in the production process itself but also in the provision of health and social welfare facilities. Another reason is that, as family property becomes reduced to income from wages and salaries, the family loses its ability to look after itself in emergencies. The risks of unemployment and sickness must be covered by the state.

The expansion of the state means that the line between state and civil society is crossed with increasing frequency as the private sphere becomes more and more subject to state jurisdiction. But accompanying this is an extension of citizenship. There gradually emerges the idea that, in addition to civil and political rights, there should also be recognized social rights, a modicum of economic security and, in T. H. Marshall's words (1950, p. 8), 'the right to share to the full in the social heritage and life of a civilized being according to the standards prevailing in the society.' These social rights are distributed according to non-market criteria. The right to leisure is included among these expanded entitlements.

Not all capitalist countries have embraced with equal enthusiasm the idea of social rights. The dominant values and institutions of capitalism are on the whole quite inimical to the values underlying the provision of social services by the state. In politically conservative or liberal countries like the United States, social rights are recognized as an essential ingredient of citizenship only grudgingly. The state's proper role in the provision of leisure services and the regulation of leisure is intensely debated, the more left-wing forces generally favoring more intervention, the more right-wing forces favoring non-intervention by the state and greater reliance on individual initiative and private enterprise. Reform politics supports the idea of administered leisure, as if play, like any other welfare function, can be scientifically planned; while socialist politics seeks greater community and popular involvement.

Has the expansion of the state had a serious effect on leisure? It is impossible to ignore the many ways in which the state now encroaches upon leisure. These include laws pertaining directly to involvement in athletics such as those protecting (or denying) the rights of population categories (e.g. women, blacks and the handicapped) to sports participation, as well as laws regulating the use of open lands and water. State policies indirectly shape leisure through fiscal measures (e.g. tax laws affecting the profitability of professional sports), through labor legislation (e.g. hours-of-work rules, which affect the amount of free time and disposable income, and employment contracts in professional sports), through social legislation (e.g. obscenity statutes which affect the availability of books, magazines and films), defense policies (e.g. conscription laws affecting fitness requirements) and foreign policies (e.g. trade sanctions which prohibit the exchange of sports teams).

On the other hand, the capitalist state in a democratic society cannot totally determine leisure, simply because leisure has its own traditions, meanings and styles, including many oppositional features which make it very difficult for the state to regulate closely. Many of the most intensely fought battles within the sphere of leisure (e.g. amateurism versus professionalism) have taken place largely outside the state. As we shall see, matters are rather different in totalitarian regimes.

*Leisure in Totalitarian Regimes*
There are some major exceptions to the pattern of minimal state involvement in leisure and sports and these are, of course, the societies in which communist parties now rule and in the fascist societies of the 1920s and 1930s. These societies, with which I will deal separately, are witness to the fact that political ideology can have a profound impact on the relation between state and leisure. A political ideology, for example, assigns relative importance to work and play and structures and guides popular involvement in play accordingly. Where the state is totalitarian, the impact of political philosophy will be all the more pronounced. Both fascist and communist states have tried to incorporate the domestic or private lives of their subjects into their overall national and political framework to serve the interests of the party and of the state. Political participation is transformed 'by no longer recognizing the boundary between the public and private sectors or that between bureaucratic and political authority' (Alford and Friedland, 1985, p. 418). Both the state and the economy are brought under the direction of the national party. However, fascist and communist societies, although very similar with regard to social-control apparatuses, have gone about regulating the private sphere in very different ways and for different reasons, as we shall see.

# The Relationship between Politics and Leisure

We have defined leisure as activities undertaken voluntarily, without constraint or sense of obligation. Politics, on the other hand, denotes the struggle over scarce resources, the domination of one group by another and the exercise of surveillance and control in the interest of social order. The two would therefore seem to be completely different spheres. A little reflection on the fuller meaning of leisure reminds us, however, that it has never been completely free of politics. The etymology of the word reveals this. 'Leisure' derives from the Latin word *licere* meaning to be allowed or lawful. Now license can mean two things; it can mean liberty or lack of restraint or it can mean being permitted or authorized to do something, usually by some official body; we can get a license to drive a car but do so licentiously. This double meaning indicates the complex of associations the word 'leisure' has for us, suggesting both freedom and constraint. Regulation and control—in short, politics—is thus an inherent part of the meaning of leisure to us.

The political regulation of the use of space and time, usually legitimated on religious and moral grounds, has a long history, as we shall see. In fourteenth-century England soccer was forbidden by statute, and archery was made compulsory for all able-bodied men. In the sixteenth century Montaigne noted in his essay on the education of children that

> Wise administrators are careful to assemble the citizens and bring them together for exercises and sports no less than for the serious duties of religion; good fellowship and friendship are enhanced thereby. Moreover, there could not be found for them pastimes more orderly than those which are carried on in every one's presence and before the very eyes of the magistrate. And it would seem to be reasonable that the magistrate, and that the prince at his own expense, should sometimes gratify the common people in this way from a quasi-paternal affection and kindness; and that in the populous cities there should be places set apart and arranged for such spectacles: some diversion from worse and hidden doings.

At the heart of the political regulation of leisure has been 'public control over the ways that collectivities and individuals seek to obtain gratification' (Ingham and Hardy, 1984, p. 93). This is immediately obvious if we think of leisure in broad terms, to encompass not only play and sports but also drinking, the consumption of other stimulants such as marijuana, gambling and various forms of sexual behavior. Recent history records repeated attempts by state and local authorities to control these activities either on moral grounds or to keep the peace. What kinds of activity are thus controlled and why? Each instance reveals that certain classes of persons in any society are more susceptible to being charged with immoral leisure than other classes of persons. It seems that the behavior in which persons indulge (e.g. drinking, hunting, betting, or buying sex) is less important than the social category from which they come. Leisure is thus part of the struggle for the control of space and time in which social groups are continually engaged, a struggle in which the dominant group seeks to legitimate, through statute and administrative fiat, its understanding of the appropriate use of space and time, and the subordinate groups resist this control through individual rebellion and collective action. Increasingly, success in this struggle has depended on access to and control over the state.

During the nineteenth century, when the state in both the United

Kingdom and the United States was weak, local authorities fulfilled this role of regulator of space and time. 'Rational' recreation was part of a larger mission to provide adequate sanitation, housing, education, utilities and transportation. Various Acts of Parliament were passed in England increasing the powers of municipalities to regulate leisure time. In the United States, control over leisure was lodged even more firmly in the hands of states, counties and cities. During the nineteenth century, as local government units acquired ever greater power and increased in size and financial clout, wider responsibilities for the welfare and recreation of citizens were assumed. The trend was accelerated by competition between municipalities and boosted by the example set by capitalist philanthropists.

Leisure has felt the impact not only of conventional politics but of uninstitutionalized forms as well. Mass movements on both right and left have included play in their agendas for political reform. Campaigns to fight racism, sexism and other forms of discrimination, or those specifically aimed at reshaping the administration of athletics, have also sought to reform leisure. Leisure has been the object of political reform to the extent that its appropriate relation to work is seen as a social problem. Here efforts have been made to reshape the work–leisure connection to enhance opportunities for more 'uplifting' leisure and more 'meaningful' work. Other would-be reformers worry about the privatization of leisure as a result of the breakdown of traditional communities and neighborhoods and the commercialization of leisure. Privatization, they believe, destroys people's ability to conceive of social worlds other than their own and transforms them into objects to be manipulated by the market place or by the state. Such critics would reject the idea that improving people's leisure skills is the answer to this problem. The solution is not to shore up the private sphere but to break down the barrier between private and public worlds.

There is another aspect to the relation between politics and leisure. As leisure becomes one of several social services provided by the welfare state it takes on the character of all such services, combining an element of social control with that of provision. Welfare states operating in capitalist economies provide their social services in part to mitigate the effect of blind market forces. On the other hand, they must not consistently, or on a large scale, undercut the market. Thus, as we shall see, the provision of parks to mitigate the effects of overcrowded housing has been nested within powerful private property interests. These are, in turn, largely at the mercy of the blind forces of the market for land which helped create the overcrowding in the first place.

The politicizing effects of turning leisure into a social service do not stop there. The welfare state simultaneously embodies tendencies to develop the powers of individuals and to repress and control them in the interests of bureaucratic efficiency. For example, to help administer unemployment benefits welfare states develop legislation marking the boundaries between work and nonwork which makes it very difficult to see them as being integrated or overlapping. The reasons are administrative; a clear boundary between employment and unemployment, between being in the work force as opposed to being retired, makes the administration of this social service more efficient and, incidentally, more acceptable to a grudging electorate. There is also a tendency to stigmatize being out of work or leaving a job for the 'wrong' reasons. Unemployment benefits might be denied if the individual left a previous job without good cause, or was sacked for 'misconduct' or refused to accept an alternative job offer or was involved in a trade dispute. These regulations presuppose and encourage a particularly sharp distinction between work and non-work and reinforce negative stereotypes of those out of work for 'no good reason.'

## Leisure's Impact on Politics

The myriad ways in which politics affects leisure will occupy much of our attention in this book, but there is another side to the coin. Leisure is not merely the reflection of political forces and events. It is shaped not only by economic forces beyond the control of the state but also by its own internal political structures and ideas. The autonomy of leisure is evident in two major areas: professionalism and voluntarism.

*Professionalism*
It might seem odd to think of professionalism in association with leisure and even more peculiar to think of professionalism in political terms, but in truth much of our current thinking about leisure has been shaped by 'experts' in the use of leisure time, and these 'experts' owe their position to political action. For many years sociologists did not associate the professions with politics. They regarded the professions as occupations distinguished by the possession of a fixed set of traits such as altruism, career orientation, arduous training and strict licensing. More recently, however, the political aspects of professionalism have begun to attract attention. Professionals win their prestigious position by working against free-market competition in their speciality; the profession is an attempt to gain and secure

a monopoly over the provision of a given service. Professionalization is thus a political struggle to secure the right to be self-governing—setting up an autonomous organization, a code of conduct, a disciplinary procedure and a mechanism for screening applicants. The would-be profession fights for the right to have exclusive control over its 'turf' and rebuffs attempts by other, competing occupations to occupy it. The ultimate goal of the would-be profession is a political one: to obtain a license or mandate from the state to police itself and to regulate the flow of services in its particular field. Note that these are collective strategies. Professional status does not result from individual successes at discovering people's needs and satisfying them. Note also that the professionalizing project involves the would-be profession in helping define the very need it sets out to satisfy. Professionalism is, in short, a struggle for power, for control over the definition and provision of a service. In the ultimate case, this struggle involves the state as various groups fight for the mandate which would legitimate the monopoly each desires.

What we think of today as 'recreation' is largely the creation of leisure professionals; perhaps more accurately, the forces which produced one also produced the other. From its beginning in the late nineteenth century, the recreation movement maintained that play and leisure time in general should be of value to the individual and to society. The movement had three groups of advocates. Some were active in the playground movement (believing that play, although inborn, needs to be directed by society); some were physical educators, interested in making organized play part of the new, rationalized school curriculum; and some were active in parks management, interested in establishing the management of new urban parks on a more scientific footing. Each group viewed leisure as a potentially valuable aspect of personal growth, a significant social institution and an important community asset. Each regarded leisure as a social problem, created by the disappearance of meaningful work, by increasing free time and by overcrowding in the cities. Each believed that the government must play a role in the provision of leisure services (mediated and guided, of course, by suitably trained experts). Each group saw itself as a social mission to bring suitably structured leisure to the population at large on a non-profit basis.

The professionalization of leisure was, in part, a means of separating politics (or at least a centralized state) and leisure. The provision of leisure was to be left in the hands of scientifically trained experts rather than pork-barreling politicians. These sentiments were strengthened in the 1930s by the desire of many in the more democratic societies to maintain a distance from the tight control found in fascist and communist countries. It gained further momentum after the Second World War with the incorporation of leisure into a growing welfare state in which professionals in health, social work and other social services were already active. The results were mixed. The development of leisure provision was to some extent autonomous, independent of the fluctuations of political and economic fortunes. On the other hand, the leaders of the professions tended to be drawn from elite groups and shared many of the assumptions about proper recreation with other members of the elite.

*Voluntarism*

In most Western capitalist societies, leisure is administered largely through voluntary associations at the local, national and international level. In many cases, state participation is mediated through quasi-government organizations staffed by volunteers. This reliance on voluntary labor is only partly owing to the fact that it is cheaper. It also reflects the widespread opinion that the state should become no more intimately involved in the administration of leisure than it is, say, in the administration of the arts or religion. It is also a way in which governments can claim to provide leisure resources in an unbiased way, and to be seen as reacting to demands from the bottom rather than imposing leisure patterns from above.

The administration of leisure through voluntary associations has biased leisure services in the direction of the middle class: that is, those most likely to be involved in and leaders of voluntary organizations. In the United Kingdom, the government's role in the provision of leisure services was for many years steered by a voluntary organization, the Central Council for Recreative Physical Training, founded in 1935. Not only did this organization keep the state at arm's length, it was a powerful and influential lobby for a particular conception of the role of recreation in British life, a conception it fought to establish as government policy in the face of opposition from organizations of physical education teachers and from established youth organizations. Its policy-making committee was populated by 'establishment' figures, and the organization's hierarchical structure permitted little input from below. Similar battles between voluntary associations over control of leisure have taken place in the United States; the fight between the Amateur Athletic Union and the National Collegiate Athletic Association for control over the Olympic team is a case in point. Volunteers often find themselves at odds with the professionals, for whom the planned provision of rational recreation is a career.

The administration of leisure (principally amateur athletics and professional sports) now crosses national boundaries. International sports organizations have become political forces to be reckoned with. Each has its own mode of organization, its own set of codes and its own internal political struggles, some but not all of which reflect political struggles in the wider world. These international organizations are important for two principal reasons. First, they, as much as nation-states, will structure the development of leisure. We see this most clearly in the activities of largely private organizations such as the Marylebone Cricket Club (MCC) and its control over cricket and the Fédération International de Football Association (FIFA) and its control of soccer. The ties of Olympic organizations with nation-states are rather more complex, but there is sufficient autonomy for the committee in any given country to defy a ban on participation imposed by the central government. The second reason these international organizations are important is that their structure affects not only the development of the activity but also its distribution around the globe—the distribution of play resources and opportunities. Again, Olympic movement decisions to allow a given country to participate are an obvious example. Olympic politics (or FIFA politics) is not always the same as national politics.

*Play as Resistance*
It is not customary for us to think about play in the context of politics, for we regard the latter as very serious business. But this is because we have a very impoverished notion of what politics is. We are apt to dismiss the play element from politics altogether or relegate it to second place because we adopt a very materialistic and utilitarian perspective on political action; it is the sphere in which people struggle to dominate over others in order to further their material interests. Such a view not only blinds us to the amount of symbolic display and theatre which is involved in political action, it also lessens our appreciation of the play element in culture. As we shall see, politics, even in highly rationalized and bureaucratized modern societies, depends a great deal on what can only be considered play: the spectacular, the ceremonial, the dramatic. Much of this serves to legitimate the status quo. But we cannot overestimate the importance of play in movements seeking to bring about change. The Yippies are only one of the more obvious examples of recent years. The 1968 uprising in France also contained elements of the festival; spontaneity, gaiety, a reverence for the past and a playful irreverence for the future prevailed.

Play derives its critical thrust from its expressivity and creativity, the time out of structure and the open space it provides. 'Within this space and during this time, new social arrangements and relations previously precluded by conventional restraints are tested with virtual impunity' (Hearn, 1978, p. 217). Play helps the individual acquire an awareness of the self as the cause of an activity and as a participant in a cause. To lose the ability to play is to lose the sense that worldly conditions are plastic. This ability to play with social life depends on the existence of a dimension of society which stands apart, expressing intimate desire, need and identity. Play can thus function to legitimate the status quo by providing drama and spectacle to reify and mystify the workings of the political system, or it can have an emancipatory potential by providing room for experimentation and challenge. Either way we can no more keep play out of politics than we can keep politics out of play.

## Looking Ahead

In Chapter 2 I will describe how leisure has been politically controlled in capitalist societies since the early nineteenth century. The concern to impose controls over the use of leisure was particularly intense in the development of the modern city but it was also part of the organization of factories and offices and the modern school curriculum. The bitter class struggles during the second half of the nineteenth century provide the backdrop for upper-class efforts to impose morally uplifting leisure on the general population by the enactment of 'blue laws,' by controls on gambling and festivals and by reform efforts (such as the playground movement) intended to provide healthy alternatives to commercial amusements.

In Chapter 3 I will describe resistance to control over the use of leisure by those against whom laws and regulations have been aimed. I will also show how class, gender and regional groups have sought to defend indigenous forms of leisure against rationalization and standardization. We shall see that leisure has played a role, albeit limited, in movements of political liberation and reform.

In Chapters 4 and 5 I will describe the expansion of the state in the twentieth century and its consequences for leisure in the United States and the United Kingdom. Increasingly, the use of free time comes under the regulation and supervision of recreation planners, parks managers, physical education experts and government officials concerned with health and safety, law and order, environmental quality and conservation, equal opportunity and justice. Conversely, the population comes to look upon leisure as a right to which it is entitled and brings to this social service the kind of expectation it brings to other government services—of cheapness, efficiency, equity and responsiveness to demand. The period after the Second World War saw a considerable expansion in the government's role in the provision and supervision of leisure, especially in Western European societies. However, as we shall see, the government's role in leisure provision remains uncertain, erratic and often contradictory.

This could not be said for the state's role in totalitarian societies such as Nazi Germany and the Soviet Union, where the regulation of leisure was and is part of a general plan to administer the private sphere in the interests of party and nation. Chapter 6 will examine leisure in the fascist regimes of the 1930s, and in communist countries since 1918. We shall see that not all totalitarian regimes are alike. Fascist regimes exalted the sportive ideal. In the interest of promoting a virile forcefulness they attacked both the sloth of the proletariat and the effeteness of the bourgeoisie. Communist regimes also attack bourgeois ideas of athleticism but for their individualism, their appearance of disinterestedness and their commercialism. Communists use athletics in a more instrumental way to exalt political principles. However, they, more than fascists, experience a tension in their leisure world between the forces of nationalism and international socialism.

Communist countries openly use sport for purposes of political mobilization, but sport also serves this function in capitalist countries. In Chapter 7 I will examine the use of sport to promote community pride, national consciousness, national unity and international prestige. Since the nineteenth century, leisure facilities and sports success have been part of the boosterism of cities as they compete for business and population. The museums and parks of the Victorian era have simply been replaced as objects of municipal pride by the superstadiums of today. At the national level, sport is used to promote a sense of national unity in loosely associated federations (e.g. Canada and Australia), to foster a nascent sense of nationhood (e.g. Kenya and Cuba), to mark political boundaries (e.g. West and East Germany and the two Chinas) and, of course, to conduct war by other means (e.g. the USA and USSR). At the international level, athletic competition can foster changes in the game itself (e.g. forcing us to clarify the meaning of 'professional'), it can help in the international recognition of states (e.g. by receiving permission to participate in the Olympics), it can play a role in protecting human rights (e.g. by the imposition of boycotts on countries which violate them) and it can help ease diplomatic ventures. Leisure can also be used as a tool of imperial domination. The evolution of the system of international sports competition (e.g. track and field athletics, soccer, swimming and cricket) was largely the work of, and has been sustained by, Western capitalist countries. In many cases, imported pastimes, including the mass media, have replaced traditional forms of leisure.

In the final chapter I will look ahead and try to anticipate the future of the politics of leisure. Many of the projections of the 1950s about the coming of 'a leisure society' have missed their target by a rather wide margin. Political scientists have been no more accurate in their forecasts of the future of the welfare state. What does seem clear is that politics and leisure will become even more closely intertwined than they are now, both domestically and on the world stage. The state will reach further into the private sphere to inform and guide our free-time activities; leisure is likely to expand but much of it will be the 'forced' leisure of the unemployed, who will increasingly look to the state for the resources to occupy their non-work time. Political movements, which concern themselves more and more with consumption issues, will embrace leisure concerns more firmly and will choose as their target legislators and government bureaucrats rather than 'bosses' or 'big business.'

The focus of this book on politics and leisure should not be allowed to obscure the fact that there are many factors besides politics shaping leisure. How we spend our leisure time is most directly a family affair, governed in large part by our family responsibilities and our family's leisure habits. Leisure practices are also structured by our work schedules, the demands of our job and the people we meet at the workplace. Finally, leisure activities are guided by cultural forces such as religion; what we choose to do in our leisure time, and with whom, is determined in part by what we think is right and proper. None of these forces can be reduced to politics, although, of course, each is influenced by politics and in turn helps shape political life. My concern is to isolate the political dimension in leisure does not mean, however, that I regard politics as autonomous. Political life reflects, however indirectly, class, gender, racial, regional, national and other deep-seated social conflicts. As often as not, political institutions function only to mediate these conflicts or to mitigate their impact.

# 2
# *The Control of Leisure*

The word 'leisure' came into the English language through French from the Latin *licere*, meaning to be allowed. Leisure thus connotes permission, lawfulness and morality. But the word 'license,' meaning excessive or lawless liberty, comes from the same root. Leisure is at the same time that sphere in which the appetites run free and that sphere which is controlled or licensed. In this chapter I will describe how leisure has been politically controlled and manipulated to serve the interest of state and local authorities and those they serve. I will be looking both at the control of leisure and at leisure used as social control. In Chapter 3 I will describe how people have resisted these efforts to control their leisure time and, further, how leisure can be used as political protest.

Leisure relations are relations of permissible behavior. In other words, leisure activities are suffused with relations of domination and subordination. What is considered appropriate and inappropriate behavior in leisure time articulates prevailing power relations as succinctly as do the rules governing work. 'The rules of pleasure and unpleasure enable us to define leisure situations' (Rojek, 1985, p. 179). Leisure has been formed in the struggle between efforts at incorporation and suppression on the one hand and resistance and innovation on the other, a struggle over the use of time (e.g. Sundays) and the use of space (e.g. streets) and over such basic everyday activities as drinking, sex, play and sociality.

## The Politics of Time and Space

Before the Industrial Revolution, leisure times and places were not as distinct as they are today:

> a robust and ritualistic popular culture [was] rooted in the tightly

knit, inward-looking world of the country village, its calendar generously studded with festivals and holidays that derived their warrant and meaning from an intimate connection with the seasonal rhythms of the agricultural year and the working life of the community...there was no clear-cut division between labour and leisure and the daily round was seasoned with a good deal of complementary sociability. The material apparatus of recreation was rudimentary and for the most part freely available from the common resources of the community. With little discrimination between generation or sex the people made their own amusement...Popular leisure was public and gregarious, and both its great and small occasions were heavily bound by the prescriptive ties of communal custom reinforced by a powerful oral tradition.
(Bailey, 1978, p. 2)

Changes in this way of life began to occur in the middle of the eighteenth century. The Industrial Revolution and the advent of factory wage labor as the archetype of work organization demanded that a clear distinction between work and leisure be established and maintained, with work firmly established as a priority. The factory age did not therefore increase free time so much as it rearranged it. Furthermore, leisure activities themselves were to be regulated, and the bad pleasures subordinated to the useful recreations. The 'problem' of leisure was thus chiefly created by the restructuring of the work day with the advent of the factory system and wage labor. The new work discipline demanded a complementary play discipline.

Free time for factory workers was a threat to the middle class, however much they welcomed the relief from toil on humanitarian grounds. Most working men were seen as lacking the education and elementary accomplishments of 'social economy'—the proper management of time and money—which would qualify them for status as free agents in this new world of leisure. The new industrial working class was portrayed as sunk in bestiality, improvident, intemperate and sexually rampant. Their family lives seemed atomized, and their home life non-existent. They did not attend church and appeared to have few morals. They were the very negation of the bourgeoisie. While these negative attributes were certainly obtrusive in the world of work, it was during playtime that the working class seemed to display its savagery and bestiality to their fullest. Reformers sought to educate the masses in the rational use of their spare time—but not so much as to enhance the lure of the radical political movements which began to appear in the middle of the nineteenth century (Bailey, 1978, p. 37).

These early efforts to regulate leisure were by no means aimed exclusively at controlling the working class. The middle class, from which most of these efforts emanated, was also a new class, anxious to define itself as distinct from the aristocracy on the one hand and the working class on the other.

> From the turn of the mid-century the new and extensive bonus of leisure time threatened to subvert the internal disciplines of the middle class world by its invitation to indolence and prodigality. Unwilling or unable to deny the claims and attractions of leisure, yet anxious to maintain a sturdy and coherent code of values amid rapid innovation and social change, the Victorian middle classes sought a rationale which would relieve them of the need to apologize for their pleasures, yet still keep them within the bounds of moral fitness.
> (Bailey, 1978, p. 65)

The political regulation of leisure was thus as much an effort to keep the middle class true to its own principles (particularly its urban young adults) as it was an effort to incorporate the new working class. Gladstone set the tone by asserting that recreation was naught but change of employment. And the mainly middle-class Nonconformist churches were particularly vigilant in their supervision of leisure and their condemnation of amusements. Much the same message was sent to the middle class as to the working class, then, with the exception that the middle class was expected to be clever enough and well enough motivated to hear it, while the working class had to be preached to rather more insistently and, if necessary, have its leisure pastimes regulated by statute.

In the United States the appropriate political use of free time became a political issue with the Progressives, who saw holidays such as 4 July as potential tools in forging a new social and cultural order. They lobbied for 'safe and sure' municipally sponsored pageants and displays to replace what they saw as the disorder and danger of celebrations planned around streets and taverns. They wanted the government to assume a greater responsibility for both policing and entertaining its people on the 4th (Rosenzweig, 1983, p. 163).

The growth of cities in England intensified the struggle for control over leisure spaces. For the urban working class, the streets were the most accessible areas for play. But to the authorities assemblies of working people, large or small, indoors or outdoors, alehouses or soccer crowds, constituted a threat to authority. They squandered valuable urban space, dissipated spending power and encouraged gross immorality in public view. One of the principal uses of the 'new police' was to clear the streets for commercial traffic, thus not only depriving the working class of many of its sites of public assembly but also cutting off many of its diversions by 'moving on' street performers (Bailey, 1978, p. 21). So effective was this control that by the second quarter of the nineteenth century 'it was probably the police who were having the major impact on the leisure of the people' (Cunningham, 1980, p. 44).

The Industrial Revolution, the capitalization of farming and the growth of cities drastically rearranged social space. In rural areas, the enclosure movement toward the end of the eighteenth century closed off previously public spaces; land that had formerly been regarded as common and public, a center of communal activity, was rapidly privatized. The growing cities were seen as a repository and breeding ground of vice and immorality, as deleterious in their effect on the pastimes of the population as the worst of factories. Prostitution and drinking were regarded as especially urban vices, and their control occupied much of the attention of city fathers.

The pace of urbanization lagged in the United States, such that it was not until the turn of the century that life in New York's Lower East Side could be portrayed in the following terms:

> [its] streets, its stoops, and its corners presented the only opportunity for autonomous forms of recreation, play, and community. It was in these crevices of reality that people related to one another with their own style, in their own way, unrestricted by the factory or the family. For those who wanted privacy, the streets offered anonymity; for those who wanted community, that was there too. On the other hand, the streets were more than just social settings; they were the arena for spontaneous and organized political action involving everything from soapbox orations to the protest marches of the Socialist-led unions to enraged residents attacking upper-class bicyclists who sped through the Lower West Side on their way to work.
> (Goodman, 1979, p. 4)

Increasing population pressure on the cities, combined with intensified competition for valuable real estate and the needs of shopkeepers and other commercial interests for safe, efficient streets, turned playgrounds into thoroughfares. It did not help that the middle class saw the streets as dens of vice and places for the idle to loiter with impunity. 'All of the leading private and public recreation groups took as an article of faith the need to eliminate street play and games' (Goodman, 1979, p. 15). The parks and playground movement, which I will describe later, was the public antidote to the disorder and immorality of the streets.

Leisure spaces were also politically rearranged by means of licensing. Liquor licensing laws regulating the sale and consumption of alcohol not only furthered the commercialization of leisure, they also created a more standardized public institution—the public house or saloon—as a public leisure place clearly separated from both work and the home. In thus rearranging the ecology of leisure, the political authorities also sexually segregated leisure, since most public drinking places became male preserves.

To many middle-class people, the fluid and open territory outside the factory created such tension that the only answer seemed to be political repression. Political agitation to regulate the industrial worker's free space was

> not concerned with any simple repression of recognized pleasures, but with defining, regulating and locating them in their appropriate sites. Above all, perhaps, they were concerned to shift pleasures from the site of mass activity (fairs, football matches with unlimited players, carnivals verging on riot) to the site of private and individual activity.
> 
> (Mercer, 1983, p. 89)

This effort to privatize the use of space was, and continues to be, inevitably class biased, given the inequality of access to private space, much more available to the wealthy than the poor and hard to find for the young, who routinely have been forced to resort to public space for their leisure. The class bias in leisure space usage is clear in the 1906 Street Betting Act. This Act was promoted by those who saw betting as a threat to political stability, racial purity and civilized standards of conduct, but it was also supported by liberals who saw betting as simply another imposition on an already overburdened working class, a source of exploitation by rapacious bookmakers that even labor leaders sought to remove. But the Act prohibited off-course, cash, street betting only, while permitting betting in private clubs or at racecourses. This prohibition continued in force until 1960 when betting shops and working-class gambling activities like bingo were legalized in the UK's 1906 Street Betting Act (Dixon, 1980, p. 3).

The struggle for control over urban leisure spaces was only partly attenuated by the gutting of many inner cities during the suburbanization which followed the Second World War in both the United States and the United Kingdom. Parliamentary debates in Britain continued to harp upon the theme that cities were dangerous places for the breeding of immoral and harmful pastimes. Viscount Kilmuir, speaking as Lord Chancellor in 1961, affirmed 'the importance of sport as a background for dealing with delinquency and the positive help it can give in the maintenance of moral standards' (McIntosh and Charlton, 1985, p. 7). A 1975 White Paper on *Sport and Recreation* expressed the hope that 'by reducing boredom and urban frustration, participation in active recreation contributes to the reduction of hooliganism and delinquency among young people' (McIntosh and Charlton, 1985, p. 15).

The policing of public space in Britain's inner cities remained an explosive 'leisure' issue in the 1980s: 'stop-and-search powers produced recurrent confrontation between the police and working class (particularly black) youth on the streets' (Clarke and Critcher, 1985, p. 126). The authorities recognized that a certain element of 'play' was inevitable and indeed desirable. But they were convinced that, if this disposition for play were not properly controlled and confined, it would lead to political disturbance. Official apprehension over the use of free time by the lower orders today is heightened by widespread unemployment among working-class and minority-group youths and by the insidious temptations of commercial and illicit pleasures. The Brixton 'riots' in England in 1981 prompted the inevitable Commission of Inquiry. Its chairman, Lord Scarman wrote:

> It is clear that the exuberance of youth requires in Brixton (and in similar inner-city areas) imaginative and socially acceptable opportunities for release if it is not to be diverted to criminal ends. It is clear that such opportunities do not at present exist in Brixton to the extent that they ought, particularly given the enforced idleness of many youths through unemployment. The amusement arcades, the unlawful drinking clubs, and, I believe, the criminal classes gain as a result.
> (Quoted in Clark and Critcher, 1985, p. 4)

The Scarman Report, like many official reactions to the inner-city 'riots' in the United States in the 1960s, despite being more sensitive to the structural causes of civil disturbance, thus firmly located the 'leisure problem' within the context of law and order and facilitated its politicization. In this process, leisure is given both too much and too little emphasis. Too little because civil disturbances *do* frequently originate in leisure-time activities. The Omaha riot of 1966 broke out after police stopped a fireworks display on a 4 July weekend; the Chicago riots of 1966 started after the police turned off fire hydrants being used by children for bathing on a hot summer evening; the

Detroit riots of 1967 erupted after the police raided an after-hours drinking spot. The poor, unlike the rich, must conduct their leisure in public. Leisure is given too much emphasis, however, when its misuse is singled out as one of the more important causes of disorder. As Fogelson (1971, p. 51) points out, the leisure activities and the police actions directed against them were fairly routine events, part of an ongoing struggle for control of the streets in the cities, and cannot by themselves account for the severity of the disturbances which followed. And while it is significant that the events which precipitate riots usually occur in public, when people are on the streets, this too is a routine aspect of inner-city life and cannot be singled out as a cause of a disturbance. Compared to structural inequalities in jobs, education and housing which give grounds for the grievances articulated in the protest, precipitating events are trivial and symptomatic.

## From Repression to Cooptation

Political repression has been only one strategy for dealing with deviant pleasures. Incorporation has been another. Cooptation was the only strategy available to voluntary associations like the YMCA. Led mostly by middle-class people, they lacked the authority and force of the state. They used a mixture of education, propaganda and entertainment to make their sanitized leisure popular among the masses. The bulk of the nineteenth-century campaign to incorporate working-class leisure into the bourgeois mainstream did not therefore involve the state or local government directly and relied instead on voluntarism. This reflected the typical Victorian chariness about the use of the state and a strong tendency to eschew its use whenever private efforts could suffice. It also reflected the prevailing view that a person's conduct, especially leisure conduct, was a measure of that person's character and could be changed not by statute but by individual effort.

It is not surprising that the clergy were prominent in efforts to provide a kind of 'social police' for the working class at play (Donajgrodzki, 1977, p. 16). Often under their guidance and sponsorship, friendly societies and working men's clubs became approved and licensed leisure locales for laborers. The Club and Institute Union was founded in England in 1862 by a Unitarian minister, Henry Solly, to combat intemperance, illiteracy and improvidence among the working class. He cleverly pried money from middle-class donors by pointing out the growing political clout of the working class and the importance of having a sober and thrifty workforce.

Other pastimes functioned to reduce class tensions and political antagonisms. Choral societies and brass bands mixed working-class and lower-middle-class people. Bandsmen, for example, saw their bands as in large part politically neutral (Russell, 1983, p. 105). Music provided some compensation for deprivation, especially for those lacking material possessions and social status, and perhaps turned people away from seeking political solutions to their problems. 'In an important sense, leisure and politics were always fighting for the time, money, and commitment of the working population' (Russell, 1983, p. 111). The working class, and particularly the labor aristocracy, did not always actively resist these efforts at incorporation. The more skilled occupations were divided on whether the traditional forms of working-class recreation were worth defending: 'many political activists saw these traditional pastimes as positively "counterproductive", in the formation of a working class capable of fighting this struggle for control over work' (Stedman-Jones, 1983, p. 49).

In the United States, the strategy of coopting leisure was not favored until the more repressive measures against illicit pleasures came under attack by the Progressives in the first quarter of the twentieth century. Progressives came to realize that 'the most promising long-range strategy of urban moral control was not repression but a more subtle and complex process of influencing behavior and molding character through a transformed, consciously planned urban environment' (Boyer, 1978, p. 221). The idea was to create an environment in which objectionable patterns of behavior, finding no nurture, would gradually wither away.

English middle-class sentiment in favor of using the state apparatus in this strategy of incorporation began to grow by the 1870s, when occasional voices could be heard calling for political subsidies for approved popular pastimes.

> To the mid-Victorian middle class, leisure was too important to be left to the entrepreneurs and the free play of market forces. By their leisure they would be judged. Hence leisure's emergence as a favorite subject of charity, hence the growing insistence on government provision.
>
> (Cunningham, 1980, p. 185)

The Museums Act of 1845 and the Libraries Act of 1850 had already authorized municipal boroughs to finance museums, art galleries and libraries out of the rates and to charge nominal admission prices in order to encourage public attendance: 'the belief was strong that, because of middle class exclusiveness as much as working class immorality, the working class had no pleasures other than those of drink and sex—both of these enjoyed in private, both dangerous to morality, neither in any way conducive to self-improvement or to the creation of a sense of community' (Cunningham, 1980, p. 106). The movement to provide open spaces in towns was given strong legislative support when the Recreation Grounds Act of 1852 facilitated bequests of recreational land (Myerscough, 1974, p. 11).

By the end of the century, cities on both sides of the Atlantic had begun to include 'harmless public amusements' along with good drains and street lighting as amenities for their citizens. Local authorities took the lead in abridging popular recreations and substituting more suitable pastimes.

> The cultural dimension of the 'Civic Gospel' . . . aimed to utilize leisure to promote the pursuit of personal fulfilment and social control, with the energies and aspirations of the working class directed into approved channels which would result in civilization, uplift and improvement...Rational recreation was provided by means of libraries and art galleries, parks and sports fields, public baths and lecture courses.
> (Richards, 1983, p. 38)

The provision of parks meant shifting leisure activities from terrain controlled and defined by the working class to terrain regulated according to middle-class values. In the United States,

> Some activities were widely popular but excluded from park life; these exclusions further describe the ideal of enjoyment and reveal its class bias. Gambling stimulated the emotions and acknowledged the importance of fate rather than rational control, so it had to be driven away from the park. Folk entertainment like horseshoe pitching, tomahawk twirling, and bullet throwing were not refined enough for city parks despite their popularity, and vaudeville filled the newspapers but not the park programs.
> (Cranz, 1982, p. 19)

City parks were intended to transcend political divisions, not reflect them, hence the ban on political and religious meetings and proselytization.

Rarely were these public leisure amenities provided on the grounds of leisure as such. Leisure was usually seen as a means to a further and more worthy end. The public health movement made people uneasy about the loss of urban open spaces and the effect this would have on the spread of diseases. By the 1880s and 1890s, most larger municipalities in the United Kingdom were, for this reason, willing to foot the bill for providing a park (Meller, 1976, p. 112). Swimming-baths were justified for much the same reason. At first baths were provided to encourage middle-class standards of hygiene among working-class people but gradually, as the municipalities grew in tax base and political clout, they were looked upon as a public amenity, much like street lighting, which would partly compensate in a collective way for housing deficiencies and partly ensure some distributive justice. Cities like Birmingham, Manchester and Liverpool came to believe that 'caring for the health of the community meant caring for the physical health of the individual' (Meller, 1976, p. 115).

American initiatives to bring parks and organized play under the umbrella of civic amenities were undertaken by the many humanitarian and progressive reform groups which emerged in the final quarter of the nineteenth century. Organized play for youth, in particular, was considered to be 'an important surrogate for a rural upbringing, the disappearance of the household economy, the absence of early work experience, the weakened authority of religion, and the breakdown of the small geographic community' (Rader, 1983, p. 147). These advocates of organized play believed that modern life had become too soft and effeminate now that frontiers, battlefields or the rigors of rural life had ceased to harden the nation's youth.

In the United States, there can be little doubt that Americanization of the immigrant "hordes" was also a goal of associations like the Public Schools Athletic League. The zeal of the playground movement advocates is exemplified in the conviction of sociologist Clarence Rainwater that the long-range objective of the movement should be to shift from the supervision of children to the 'control of the remaining 80 percent of the population during the sixty-four hours per week in which even the laboring element is at leisure' (Boyer, 1978, p. 251).

Ironically, parks advocates discovered what had already been found by museum and gallery advocates before them, that playgrounds appeal more to the middle class than the working class.

> The children of the slums tended to admire physical prowess—particularly as expressed in streetfighting—spontaneity, and defiance of authority rather than the values of self-restraint and cooperation so dear to the playground leaders. Conflicts between recreation supervision and ghetto youths were inevitable. To

attract such youths, the leaders had to make compromises with the values of the slum subculture and remove heavy-handedly detailed supervision. Yet the absence of direction not only ran counter to prevailing playground theory, it could result in the transformation of the playground into an asphalt jungle in which the strongest and most vicious boys ruled the grounds by intimidation.

(Rader, 1983, p. 160)

The parks people thus largely failed to transcend class divisions to the extent they wished. Working-class people either stayed away from the parks or turned them into an arena for conflict to replicate the conflict in the workplace and on the streets. In large part this failure was a consequence of the fact that most of these leisure reforms were imposed on people who did not necessarily agree that they had a problem to be solved. 'One of the curious factors about the municipal provisions for leisure and pleasure was how little their development owed, in most instances, to popular demand' (Meller, 1976, p. 97).

The strategy of cooptation through the public provision of suitable leisure has altered in direction and form from the time of its inception, usually following the eddies and currents of political opinion, at least in the United States. The first parks were seen as recreating rural space, albeit sanitized of their less pleasant rural pastimes. As the frontier receded and as class conflict intensified, leisure policy came under the influence of the Progressive movement. Parks were created and run with a reforming zeal, and at times their advocates spoke of them as if they were municipally run settlement houses. 'The keynote of reform parks was to organize activity, since urban park planners considered the masses incapable of undertaking their own recreation' (Cranz, 1982, p. 61). Activities in parks were supposed to be conducive to good citizenship rather than ends in themselves. It is significant that the first professionals employed by parks departments were social workers, a profession incubated in settlement houses and, later, park field houses.

The political philosophy of the parks and playground movement accurately reflected the thinking of the Progressives, situated somewhere between the increasingly popular socialism being fostered by the new immigrants and the *laissez-faire* policies of the Social Darwinist businessman.

> Playground social training...was designed to create a new and viable middle ground or equilibrium between individualism and collectivism. Play organizers stressed social order over individual freedom, cooperation between groups instead of competition

between individuals, and peer-approved goals rather than individual aspirations. They did not, however, want to destroy the individual's freedom, his economic initiative, or his quest for advancement; they wanted to foster a new balance between these values and their counterparts, a balance that could harness individual drives to communal ends.

(Cavallo, 1981, p. 8)

During this struggle for control over urban space, reformers and developers were often in a position to give each other support. The economic advantages of boosterism were a recurrent appeal in park literature—parks would make the city more attractive for real-estate investors, provide inducements to keep the rich in the city, attract tourists and improve the morale of the workforce (Hardy, 1982, p. 72). And when businessmen's associations promoted the economic, political and moral welfare of the city as a whole, their actions had a philanthropic cast. Most aspects of progressive urban environmental reform, especially as expressed in the city beautification vogue, the civic pageant enthusiasm and the city planning movement, were initiated, guided and promoted by organized elements of a business elite interested above all in urban social stability and orderly growth (Boyer, 1978, p. 282).

Whereas the earliest parks, recreating and romanticizing the frontier, attracted mainly middle-class people (carriage-borne visitors were favored over those who walked), the reform parks were deliberately situated in or near working-class neighborhoods. The only problem was that this location frightened off middle-class visitors. To make matters worse, reform park commissioners tended to prohibit the kind of athletics and popular entertainment that would have attracted the working-class people in the vicinity. 'It never occurred to these experts that the people know best' (Cranz, 1982, p. 236). Parks administration eventually became a bureaucratic role in its own right, with the attendant bureaucratic tendencies of self-promotion and aggrandizement, rationalization and urge to quantify. 'Like all bureaucracies, the parks department took on a life of its own and came to be committed first of all to its own maintenance and enhancement' (Cranz, 1982, p. 109). The 'somewhat ominously named' American Institute of Park Executives was founded in 1898 to give expression to 'the activist conception of the urban park administration' (Boyer, 1978, p. 240).

By the 1930s parks administrators had largely abandoned the idea that parks could be a mechanism of social reform and were content to lay claim to the acceptance of recreation as an essential part of life, like health, education, work and religion. The rapid social changes, individual mobility and diversity of the 1920s had brought about a liberalization of parks policy—now parks administrators believed that the most pressing danger for the cities was not disorder and degeneracy but a sterile conformity (Boyer, 1978, p. 292). The urban masses were now treated more as consumers whose spontaneous demands it was the task of the city to meet. The norm of public service was ignored, the sense of reforming mission dissipated, and the task of parks was to relieve boredom and provide amusement. The park was now seen as an important arena for the preservation of democracy and social order because in it people from different walks of life could rub shoulders and share amusements. Despite much talk of parks being essential for the morale of a Depression-ridden population, however, park expenditures and income evaporated during this period.

After the Second World War, and especially after the affluent 1950s, the emphasis again shifted, to that of providing open, uncluttered space. Parks were intended to be 'adventurous, colorful, seductive, chic, hip, hot, and cool' (Cranz, 1982, p. 138). Parks were now places where 'anything goes,' where 'happenings' occurred. During this period, park administration recaptured some of the reforming zeal it had displayed during the Progressive era.

Throughout all these changes, park administrators never seriously questioned the social system which made the form of leisure they advocated and supervised necessary. 'No modern park planner has advocated abandoning efforts to create parks until everyone has clean, well-ventilated, spacious housing' (Cranz, 1982, p. 235). This was in large part because parks planners, as city officials, were not in a position to question the sanctity of the free market which governed the provision of housing in the United States. But it was also a result of the fact that many early parks and playgrounds advocates were also members of the early professional recreationist movement. Other members of this movement were drawn from departments or schools of public health and physical education, while others were former social workers.

## Leisure Professionals

The idea that, if people no longer have work to fill substantial portions of their time, the other outlets they might find would be harmful to society, that increasing leisure was a 'challenge,' led to the growth of a professional group whose special expertise was in the rational supervision of leisure. Thus a new hierarchy of leisure was created. This trend was abetted by the growth of general social welfare programs and by wider acceptance of specifically designed programs for special populations. Recreationists took it upon themselves to help retarded children, disadvantaged youth, the handicapped and the aged 'find meaningful roles in society' (Kraus, 1978, p. 7). At first, 'play theory' emphasized the benefits of team games in fighting the delinquency of street children; character-training value lay in the teamwork and collectivism of games. Later, psychological theories were used to develop an understanding of 'proper play' that would prepare children for 'the flexible management of the information culture in which they live.' The emphasis on play as an essentially group activity was replaced by an emphasis on what the individual could achieve through play, even solitary activity in which the individual could master basic anxieties (Sutton-Smith, 1986, p. 90).

Professional orientations toward leisure became both more secular and more disposed toward state action by the turn of the century. The earlier voluntaristic movements had concentrated on influencing individuals or families, whereas those of the Progressive era were based on the conviction that the moral destiny of the city would be most decisively influenced through broad programs using a full panoply of government power. Theories of leisure became largely secular and science-based. For example, the goal shifted from 'social purity' to 'social hygiene' as correct leisure became a matter of public health. The Playground Association, founded in 1906, was a private organization, but it had Roosevelt's strong support. Its leaders hoped to make control of play a state responsibility, chiefly by getting cities to operate playgrounds and by making physical education a required part of the curriculum of public schools. As an additional effort to promote professional training in recreation, the Playground Association sought to provide a more explicit science base to the role of recreator and thereby give it the connotation of disinterested public service. It developed *The Normal Course in Play*, a curriculum plan of courses on play leadership on several levels. The Association became the Playground and Recreation Association of America in 1911 and, in 1926, was renamed the National Recreation Association. Further professional consolidation occurred in 1965 with the formation of the National Recreation and Park Association.

Professional recreationists assumed that rural life was better than urban life, that the family could no longer be depended upon to regulate the use of leisure time, that it had become necessary to teach people how to play properly and that recreational facilities were a 'public good' to be provided by the people at large, either through charitable efforts or, better, through government action. The recreationists sought to modernize leisure without, however, permitting it to become totally commercialized.

The recreation professionals, like all other would-be professionals, claimed that they catered to a vital social need. Play could and should be of value to the individual and society. Play should not therefore be purposeless but should aim at achieving desirable and constructive results. Indeed, this idea is built into the very definition of recreation. 'Recreation is socially organized for social ends' (Kelly, 1982, p. 26). Recreation is play structured by experts, it is the routinization of enjoyment on a scientific basis. Play that has been subjected to the reorganization of a recreation specialist thus becomes a means to some other end. 'When youth...participate in recreation programs, it becomes possible for adults to develop relationships with them, to assist them directly or refer them to other agencies or services, to help them enlarge their life perspectives and ultimately to become contributing and valuable members of society' (Kraus, 1978, p. 336). Undeterred by the lack of empirical evidence to support their arguments, recreation professionals listed the 'functions' of community recreation as providing therapy (for the mentally ill), social support (for the aged), rehabilitation (for prisoners), integration (for divided racial groups), solidarity (for communities), enrichment (for cultural life), release (for pent-up hostilities) and concern (for the environment).

The modern recreation profession has changed little in its basic orientations and assumptions since its foundation. The profession has always believed firmly that organized recreation programs are intended primarily for those with free time, mainly children and the aged; that recreation is activity (primarily sports); and that recreation professionals meet a public need and provide a service to 'clients' by responding to implied demand. To better meet these demands, the profession experiments with ever more sophisticated methods for quantifying specific supply and demand variables and relating them to the public's collective decision to engage in activities. Its focus has been almost entirely upon leisure itself. Concerned with the 'quality of life' of its clients, it has nevertheless assumed that the life with which it should deal exists outside of work, although it should relate to work (re-creation). The profession has been slow to develop policies and practices appropriate for a more holistic recreationist policy that takes into account all twenty-four hours in the day, including the hours spent at work. Leisure professionals have thus placed themselves in an adjunct, politically subordinate role by assuming the task of educating individuals up to the level of leisure expertise that would enable them to compensate for alienated work.

Recreation professionals, then, like physicians and lawyers, have endeavored to create a monopoly over the provision of a public service on the grounds of a claim to superior training, expertise and supervision. They have been especially active in the United States. By 1975, 345 colleges in the USA and Canada offered curricula in recreation (Kraus, 1978, p. 284). However, the advocates of recreational professionalism have by and large failed to secure professional status for this occupation and thus have not obtained political control over play in the form of state licensing or accreditation. The supervision of play is still not considered by the general public to be something for which special preparation or long-term training is required, despite the fact that a self-administered system of department accreditation has been established. Voluntary agencies still continue to hire professional group leaders from a wide variety of backgrounds.

## The Mass Media

Publicly provided leisure opportunities were never the most popular in either Britain or the United States. Gatherings for amusement and social entertainment most often occurred in saloons, public houses and music halls. By the 1920s, however, the mass media had begun to compete with these attractions, principally in the form of radio and the cinema. In the fight over Sunday opening of cinemas, sabbatarians seeking to maintain state control over Sunday activities found themselves fighting not only the obvious desire of working people to attend cinemas on Sundays but also the film industry eager to make profits from this demand.

Cinema-going was indisputably the most popular form of entertainment in Britain by the 1930s, with weekly admissions reaching as high as 23 million. The bulk of the cinema-goers were young, urban working-class women (Richards, 1984, p. 15). But cinema-going was closely regulated by state and local authorities. Cinemas were not allowed to open on Sunday until the passing of the Sunday Entertainment Bill in 1932, which gave local authorities the mandate to control Sunday opening. Not all forces of law and order were against going to cinemas on Sundays. The police believed it might reduce juvenile delinquency in cities by keeping youngsters off the streets. Concern was also displayed at this time about the *contents* of the films being shown, but the power of commercial interests (not the working class) was demonstrated vividly by their ability to head off a move to institute state licensing of films by proposing a self-imposed rating system.

The content of films had been closely regulated in the early days of the British cinema. Foreign films were limited in the interest of promoting British life and ideals. 'The control exercised over the content of films was far tighter than that exercised over stage productions by the Lord Chamberlain, precisely because the cinema was *the* mass medium, regularly patronized by the working class and the working class were deemed to be all too easily influenced' (Richards, 1984, p. 89). Formal censorship was supervised by the British Board of Film Censors, set up in 1912 because the 1909 Cinematography Act, while not *explicitly* doing so, had implicitly given local authorities the power to prevent objectionable films being shown. The industry thus set up its own censoring machinery; and despite frequent calls from moral entrepreneurs during the 1930s for the government to censor films, this was always resisted. The Board of Censors occupied a position somewhat equivalent to that of the Board of Governors of the BBC. The president was appointed only after consultation with the Home Secretary, and the Board would frequently ban films or impose cuts in films which it considered 'too controversial'—that is, containing politically oppositional material. For example, no criticisms of the monarchy were permitted, and references to industrial disputes had to be oblique and generally optimistic. The Board 'positively welcomed films which preached class harmony and the cheerful, uncomplaining acceptance of the status quo' (Richards, 1984, p. 121).

In the United States political influence on and through film has always been very indirect. Films lost a measure of constitutional protection early in their life when, in 1915, the Supreme Court declared films to be entertainment rather than vehicles for ideas and denied them the protection of the First Amendment. The film industry thus felt exposed to charges of political bias and manipulation, and in 1934 the Motion Picture Producers and Distributors of America adopted their own Production Code to ensure that 'no picture shall be produced which will lower the moral standard of those who see it.' The Code was enforced by the Production Code Administration, headed by Will Hays, who operated in conjunction with local censorship boards. The Production Code Administration declared that 'Nothing subversive of the fundamental law of the land, and of the duly constituted authority, can be shown' (Maltby, 1983, p. 107). But it was film's commercialism rather than its political circumspection that led to it being 'apolitical.' Producers' need to appeal to a mass audience meant offering inoffensive films. 'Since the righteous were more vocal, if not more numerous than the prurient or permissive, once the industry had begun to seek respectability in the early 1920s, it expressed a more or less consistent willingness to cooperate with the most morally conservative elements of society' (Maltby, 1983, p. 56). Films like *The Grapes of Wrath* and *How Green Was My Valley* were stripped of their economic and industrial-relations content, and the family as the stabilizing influence was pushed to foreground.

Local censorship, at the county and city level, has had a greater influence on America's film-going opportunities than either federal or industry efforts. Local censors in the South frequently barred films for seeming to promote miscegenation and threatening the 'good order' of the community. However, during the 1960s this kind of censorship waned, as did that enforced by the film industry itself. In 1968 the Production Code was abandoned, and the Production Code Administration was replaced by the more permissive Coding and Rating Administration.

The shift in leisure habits toward movies, radio and television means the massification of leisure practices, an experience of leisure culture through media which homogenize and standardize the leisure world. This shift has had profound political consequences. The mass media, by bringing the culture of leisure into everyday life, wrench it from the tradition which had guaranteed its distinctivness and authenticity, just as techniques of mass reproduction such as photography deprive a work of art of the uniqueness upon which its 'aura' rests.

The mass mediation of culture is of political importance because it makes it more difficult for distinct class cultures other than that of the dominant class to survive. The most popular medium, television, is the most insidious. Television portrays the conventional as good and conformity as normal. In most television series, the regular characters are good, intruders are evil, and violation of social norms is routinely and swiftly punished. Situation comedies 'offer opportunities to experience solutions to everyday problems that take the form of rites of submission to one's lot and resignation or rites of problem-solving through correct activity and change or adjustment' (Kellner, 1982, p. 397). Television in particular has assumed tremendous power to 'signify' events as real and important, to establish collective understandings of events, becoming part of the 'production of consent.' The mass media, whether public or private, are also clearly linked to elites in terms of recruitment, ownership, legal regulation and control.

People's leisure lives have become increasingly solitary with the development of the radio, the movie and television. A survey of the leisure activities and desires of 5,000 people in major urban areas in the early 1930s showed the most popular activities were going to movies, reading newspapers and magazines and listening to the radio. One of the chief reasons given for pursuing these leisure activities was that they could be done alone (Goldman and Dickens, 1984). The emptiness of work, the emergence of mass production and a deeply rooted ideology of individualism make the identification of a private life of consumption as the avenue for liberation and fulfillment readily acceptable, given the absence of cultural alternatives. Freedom thus becomes not simply privatized but also situated in the practices of commodity consumption.

In the television age, the public sphere is witnessed almost exclusively through the lens of the camera. The network news is our window on the world. The private networks directly and the public networks indirectly must 'sell' their images in order to be competitive. Political events are packaged so that they will be 'entertaining'—and it does not take long for those events to be staged in order that the networks can sell them. These 'pseudo-events' create a system of pseudo-gratifications so that the mass media can function 'as a sort of social regulator, attempting to absorb tensions arising out of everyday life and to deflect frustrations which might otherwise actualize themselves in opposition to the system into channels which serve the system' (Aronowitz, 1973, p. 111). The mass media thus restructure the public sphere, transforming the 'public' into a 'mass,' shifting the ratio of givers of opinion to the receivers in favor of small groups of elites who control, or have access to, the mass media. Furthermore, the mass media engage in one-way communication that does not allow feedback, thus obliterating another feature of the democratic public sphere. 'Mass art is a one-way communication and thus takes on the character of domination' (Aronowitz, 1973, p. 100).

Western democracies have, for both political and economic reasons, adopted the view that the mass media should be, by and large, free of political control. The mass media, for their part, are ostensibly apolitical and 'objective.' Ironically, this claim to 'impartiality' the media must make to secure their public acceptance requires the intervention of the state in some kind of regulatory role; the media's messages must therefore become sufficiently generalized, sufficiently uncritical and unexceptional, to secure the stamp of legitimacy.

> Probably the most crucial of all the relationships which bind any media organization to its society is that between the organization and the government...From time to time all broadcasting organizations undergo review by the state in order to obtain re-licensing or re-chartering. These periods of scrutiny have profound effects on all internal decision-making over programmes, since the

organizations tend to construct their programme schedules in ways designed to gain the political support of various sections of the community. Since the BBC was established fifty years ago, it has been subjected to at least twelve major reviews which have affected its internal interests.

(Gallagher, 1982, p. 162)

The mass media, especially radio and television, have been politically defined as somewhat akin to a public utility or public service. As such, they are subject to political regulation the closeness of which varies from one country to another. In France, for example, at least until very recently, the Ministry of Information has played a large part in deciding which themes would or would not be spoken of during the news broadcasts. Until the Mitterand government gave television greater freedom, the French people could count on hearing only those broadcast journalists sympathetic to the administration's political beliefs. As in the case of the BBC, early French television and radio adopted the role of educators, providing the public with access to great works of art in the form of drama and stories. In both countries, the commercial competition provided by alternative channels has replaced a predominantly political logic with a predominantly economic logic. Even the 'public' channels have become privatized, by agreeing to display spot commercials and endorsements.

In the United States, the mass media have enjoyed the greatest freedom from state control. The Federal Communications Commission has followed the example set by the Interstate Commerce Commission, founded in 1887, in being ostensibly independent of the executive, legislative and judicial divisions, offering an alternative to business regulation, fused with the public interest, staffed by experts and free of direct political control. Big business has usually welcomed this kind of political machinery because it regulates competition and reduces paperwork. The Radio Act of 1927 defined the airwaves as a limited *national* resource, akin to public land, and set up a Federal Radio Commission to allocated frequencies for three-year intervals. The Commission was given no censorship powers, except that of dealing with gross abuses on a case-by-case basis. The Federal Communications Commission succeeded it in 1934, but its already minimal powers waned with the passing of the New Deal era. Ironically, the Commission has not been free of political influence, since its policies are influenced greatly by Presidential appointments. However, the Commission, in the opinion of one historian, has been 'a small, toothless dog kept on a very short leash' (Baughman, 1985, p. 169).

## Sports

Organized games and sport have, throughout their history, been subject to political control. This control had reflected the interests of the ruling class directly and indirectly. Nineteenth-century reformers suppressed 'domesticated animal pit' sports but showed a remarkable tolerance toward 'wild-animal-run-for-life' sports. The latter were, in turn, strictly reserved for the landowning class. 'During the early part of the nineteenth century, offences under the game laws accounted for a third of all crimes' (Whannel, 1983, p. 39).

'Disorder' was common at horse-racing events in mid-Victorian England and, later, at soccer matches. The disorder created considerable alarm in Parliament, and it is tempting to attribute its subsequent decline to better police work. However, more peaceable sports crowds were not the result of direct political action but reflected instead the rise of commercial interest in professional sports. 'Sports promoters...had a lot to lose if disorderly crowds got out of hand and destroyed valuable property...there was also the threat to gate receipts if spectator violence dissuaded people from attending or if it led the sports authorities to close the ground or revoke the license of the race course' (Vamplew, 1983, p. 22). Soccer clubs took measures to make sure games started on time, to segregate rival fans, to control drinking and gambling in the stadium and to exclude obvious troublemakers. These measures, taken in the interest of profit, were more effective than any legislation in controlling crowd violence.

In the 1960s the 'social problem' of crowd violence erupted once more in Britain, beginning with invasions of soccer and cricket pitches in the early years of the decade and escalating to vandalism to trains, buses, shops and public houses and gang assaults on black and Asian minorities. The mass media contributed in no small way to the 'moral panic' associated with these outbursts, and the reactions of the authorities doubtless amplified the violence. The very Act used to punish those arrested in sports crowd troubles, the 1936 Public Order Act, although drafted to cope specifically with problems of political crowds, was used most severely against football 'hooligans.' Walvin (1968, p. 66) underlines the irony in this—that the state came to see a much greater threat in sporting crowds than in 'real' political crowds: 'the "football hooligans" have established themselves as a unique and distinctive social (and political) problem in need of special treatment.'

Pointing out the amplification effects of the media and the police should not obscure the fact, however, that the threat of injury to the traditional working-class supporters of the game was real: 'the holding of a soccer match was close to becoming an occasion of fear and anxiety throughout significant sections of local working-class populations' (Taylor, 1982, p. 159). The fact that other working-class people were the chief victims of crowd violence is perhaps the reason that the first official inquiry into 'football hooliganism' was not begun until 1969. The report resulting from this inquiry emphasized the need to expand the amount of seated accommodation available in football grounds and for better cooperation between clubs and the police, thus presenting the problem rather narrowly as one of crowd control. Later 'reforms' included the introduction of specially trained squads of police to infiltrate crowds, the segregation of fans, the installation of surveillance cameras, restrictions on the sale of alcohol and increasingly severe sentences for soccer-related offenses.

Taylor (1982, p. 158) notes that this essentially 'law-and-order' response to crowd violence, largely ignoring the wider social context of unemployment and displacement fostering the violence, but possessing the virtue of immediacy and directness, resonated well with the generalized unease among working-class people themselves, many of whom responded to Prime Minister Thatcher's law-and-order campaign by electing her into office. The state, in this sense, portrayed itself not only as the protector of the middle-class shopkeeper but also as the guardian of the working class against itself. What was not made explicit, however, was the contribution made by the state to the decomposition of the working class which made this protective role necessary. The response of the police and other state agencies was very often called for by members of the working class, who had been rendered vulnerable to attack by the weakening of traditional family and community support resulting from rehousing policies and widespread unemployment. The state thus was endowed with legitimacy for a political response to a problem that was above all else social and economic in origin.

Sports like soccer have their origins in and are popularly associated with the working class. The question thus arises as to the impact of its commercialization on the political consciousness of the working class. To a certain extent, soccer (or baseball in the United States) built upon existing class and community pastimes and thus strengthened class solidarity. On the other hand, the commercialization of sports had a number of consequences which weakened the political strength of the working class. Association football did become identified with the 'cloth cap' and other marks of working-class life, and many teams were originally works clubs, but ownership and control over professional football soon passed into the hands of the capitalist class. Players were forced to consider unionism as early as 1898, and their union struggled without much success until the 1960s to achieve a more equitable distribution of the wage fund (Walvin, 1975, p. 83). The state was not a totally passive actor in the rise of professional soccer. The emphasis placed by state schools on physical education and on soccer in particular 'was undoubtedly a determining factor making soccer the national game' (Walvin, 1975, p. 59).

The commercialization of soccer also legitimated the distinction between the elite amateur and the proletarian professional. The ideology of amateurism, which first appeared in sport in mid-nineteenth-century rowing, firmly relegated play for pay to an inferior status and, by implication, relegated the whole world of professional sport to the working class.

> Playing for fun expressed the individualisation and relative independence of the public school elite, the fact that they could use their leisure principally for themselves...In the North, however, a different sort of social configuration and different values were coming to prevail. There, the majority of players were not so individualised or independent. They played as members of a close-knit community with which they identified strongly. At the same time, the community identified strongly with them with the consequence that communal pressure was put on players to train and play seriously in order that victory might be ensured.
> (Dunning and Sheard, 1979, p. 149)

Cricket and golf developed two classes of players to replicate these wider social divisions; rugby split into two quite different games; football retained the same game but developed different league systems; while tennis, swimming, rowing and athletics banned professionalism.

Many middle-class people in Britain associated the working-class commercialized sports with corruption, vice and disorder. In the more democratic and less class-ridden United States, mass spectator sports were more likely to be tolerated as a safety valve, capable of absorbing the urban discontent that followed from the closing of the frontier (Paxson, 1917), although even there Progressives condemned 'spectatorism.'

Amateur sports gradually lost much of their aura of exclusivism and elitism (in some part due to the Olympic Games), but in neither country did their political control become more democratic. Indeed, control gradually shifted more and more into the hands of bureaucratically organized professionals. In the United States, the

Amateur Athletic Union, founded in 1879, gradually assumed the role of gatekeeper to participation in the Olympics. The National Collegiate Athletic Association (NCAA) was not founded until 1906 but eventually came to dominate amateur sport and thus limit participation by those not in college. The NCAA had the advantage over the AAU in that, as part of the educational establishment, sport was a full-time and often lucrative business for the NCAA—professional in all but name—while for the officials of the AAU sport remained an avocation. The AAU had volunteer coaches, but the NCAA had full-time professionals aided by their loose affiliation with science-based physical education departments. The politics of amateur sports thus came to be structured by the interests of big-time college athletics and their businessman boosters.

Mass spectator sports also had political effects in separating the producers from the consumers of leisure, a separation widened by the advent of the mass media. They tended to fragment first the community and then the family by encouraging the privatization of leisure. And by fostering the idea that free time was properly occupied with the consumption of leisure goods and services, they helped legitimate the bourgeois ethos of individualistic consumerism.

## Sexuality

There are few areas of leisure in which so much dispute has taken place over the rules of pleasure and displeasure as erotic conduct. Sexuality is simultaneously a domain of restriction, repression and danger as well as a domain of exploration, pleasure and agency. Sexual matters carry enormous symbolic weight, disputes over sexual behavior often becoming the vehicle for displaced social anxieties. The realm of sexuality also has its own internal politics and modes of domination. It is organized into systems of power which reward and encourage some individuals and activities while punishing and suppressing others. The sexes have traditionally been divided in an unequal power struggle, in which men have defined a woman's identity and controlled the nature of her sexual expression. Women's powerlessness is expressed and reconstituted daily as sexuality, discoverable and verifiable through women's intimate experience of sexual objectification. In short, sexuality is as much a human product as is any other form of leisure. Like these other forms, sex is both pleasure and danger, both creative and destructive.

The boundaries and forms of erotic life, like all other leisure domains, are continually being renegotiated. The political struggle is over who is going to make sex and in what form. What rights do sexual minorities have? What aspects of sex can and should be debated? What erotic experiences should children be encouraged to have? What constraints, if any, should there be on sexual expression? What is the proper role of the state in regulating sexuality? Can sex ever be a purely private matter? What should be the relation of sexuality and procreation? In the interest of regulating erotic conduct, a steady stream of morality crusaders have attacked literature, film, drama and dancing as obscene and have also sought to regulate sexual practices to make them conform to Judaeo-Christian images of proper erotic conduct. Indeed, much of the sex law currently on the books dates from nineteenth-century morality crusades. It remains a crime in the United States to make, sell, mail or import material which has no purpose other than sexual arousal.

Nineteenth-century attitudes toward sexual behavior conformed to an overwhelmingly male and heterosexual set of assumptions in which sexuality was seen as an independent force or energy disciplined by personal or social constraints. The 'spending' of semen meant a loss of energy in other areas of life; masturbation, the willful loss of semen, was therefore especially condemned. The explicit political discourse on sexuality thus concerned the proper controls to be placed on the expression of sexuality, a preoccupation with normal and deviant practices, defining areas of acceptable erotic conduct for females and males, young and old, white and black.

Official Victorian attitudes toward dangerous sex are revealed in the reports of the great Parliamentary Commissions which, in the 1830s and 1840s, investigated working conditions in factories and mines. According to Weeks (1981, p. 20), they 'were saturated with an obsessive concern with the sexuality of the working class, the social other, displacing in the end the actual social crisis from the area of exploitation and class conflict, where it could not be coped with, into the framework of a more amenable and discussible area of "morality".'

Typical of the role of the state in the regulation of sexual practice in the nineteenth century were the Contagious Diseases Acts of 1864, 1866 and 1869. Instituting police and medical inspection of prostitutes (but not of their customers), these Acts were ostensibly designed to control the spread of venereal disease among the military in garrison and dock towns, but they served two other purposes. Local civilian officials warmly endorsed the Acts as a means of curtailing street disorders and disciplining the unrespectable civilian poor in their community. The Acts also legalized the double standard of erotic conduct which sanctioned sexual license for men while enjoining extramarital chastity for women.

> Through the control of sexuality, the acts reinforced existing patterns of class and gender domination...Under the acts, extramarital sex became a question of state policy, a matter of vital national importance...Thus medical and police supervision in turn created an outcast class of 'sexually deviant' females, forcing prostitutes to acknowledge their status as 'public' women and destroying their private associations with the general community of the labouring poor.
>
> (Walkowitz, 1980, p. 4)

In effect, the Acts helped 'decasualize' extramarital sex by setting up a category of 'professional' prostitutes.

Although the Acts were repealed in 1886, they indicated a newfound enthusiasm for state intervention into the leisure lives of the poor on medical and sanitary grounds. We have already seen this motive at work in the parks movement. Here, as with drinking, gambling, dancing and other forms of working-class diversion, the medical and the moral were interwoven: 'literally and figuratively, the prostitute was the conduit of infection to respectable society' (Walkowitz, 1980, p. 4).

In the United States, the federal government did not become especially active in controlling erotic conduct until the end of the nineteenth century. Feminists decried the double standard of morality for men and women and joined with the social purity movement to attack prostitution and the 'white slave' traffic. At the federal level, this pressure resulted in the Mann Act, while many states and municipalities passed laws against soliciting.

In neither country, however, has erotic conduct proved to be easy to control by political means. As often as not, the net effect of heightened state surveillance, far from wiping out vice, has been to change its form. The English had absorbed this lesson on prostitution and homosexuality by the time the Wolfenden Committee wrote its report in 1957. It recommended more severe restrictions on streetwalking and soliciting by prostitutes, in the full knowledge that this would lead to an increase in the call-girl system and in touting.

Besides altering the form and occasion of erotic conduct, social purity legislation encouraged the emergence of a subculture of sexuality. 'By the end of the nineteenth century there was a widespread and often international homosexual argot suggesting a widely dispersed and organized subculture' (Weeks, 1981, p. 111). Sex laws thus did little to alter the direction of erotic liberation that had begun toward the end of the nineteenth century.

New erotic communities formed. It became possible to be a male homosexual or lesbian in a way it had not been previously. Mass produced erotica became available, and the possibilities of sexual commerce expanded. The first homosexual rights organisations were formed, and the first analyses of sexual oppression were articulated.

(Rubin, 1984, p. 310)

By 1920 heterosexual eroticism and female heterosexual eroticism in particular had gained much wider public acceptance, but only as long as sexual expression was contained within, or firmly tied to, the family.

While a concept of female sexuality independent of men's finally became thinkable, homosexuals continued to be subject to particularly vigorous repression. Crackdowns on gay individuals, bars and social areas continued in a routine manner. The severe repression of the 1950s was in part a backlash against the expansion of sexual communities and possibilities during the Second World War. Homosexuals had always been considered a threat to national security. Homosexuality was considered incompatible with military service. To repress homosexual conduct the police used not only laws specifically aimed at sodomy but also the usual variety of laws employed to repress deviant leisure.

> Police invoked laws against disorderly conduct, vagrancy, public lewdness, assault and solicitation in order to haul in their victims. Gay men who made assignations in public places, lesbians and homosexuals who patronized gay bars, and occasionally even guests at gay parties in private homes risked arrest. Vice squad officers, confident that their targets did not dare challenge their authority, were free to engage in entrapment. Anxious to avoid additional notoriety, gay women and men often pleaded guilty even when the police lacked sufficient evidence to secure convictions.

(D'Emilio, 1983, p. 15)

In addition to the formal legal repression of erotic behavior, there have always been indirect forms of sexual political conflict in which erotic minorities are portrayed as dangerous and perverted, either brainwashed or the victims of drug addiction. This official propaganda pictures the minority's world as bleak and insecure and tries to prevent information about its boundaries and location from spreading.

Heterosexual as well as homosexual erotic conduct continues to be subject to state control. Although the 1940s and 1950s saw the generalization across class lines of the ideal of mutual sexual pleasure, this was still very much confined to a stable marital relationship. In Britain, the new welfare state assumed the role of guardian and provider for the traditional monogamous marriage. The idea that erotic pleasure should properly be found only in marriage runs through 'a series of major commissions and reports, including those of Beveridge in 1942, the Curtis Committee on children in care in 1946, the Population Commission of 1949, the Morton Commission on Divorce, 1955, the Ingleby Committee on Children and Young Persons in 1960, up to the Finer Report on one parent families in 1975' (Weeks, 1981, p. 237). The most important of these was the Beveridge Report, not so much because of what it had to say about erotic behavior but because of its assumption that proper sexuality was linked to marriage. Ostensibly concerned with Britain's falling birth rate, Beveridge nevertheless believed that 'the interest of the state is not in getting children born, but in getting them born in conditions which secure to them the proper domestic environment' —and he accordingly recommended that no maternity grants be made to unwed mothers (quoted in Bland, McCabe and Mort, 1979, p. 100).

The more permissive English legislation of the 1960s (the Obscene Publications Act of 1959 and the Sexual Offences Act of 1967) was partly a response to new affluence, partly an effort to reform archaic laws humanely, partly an adjustment to the new social and economic position of youth and partly a reflection of the changing role of women. Many of these reforms eased restraints on erotic behavior in private places while at the same time increasing policing of public sexuality. The unifying element in the Wolfenden Report was the belief that, by ceasing to be the guardian of *private* morality, the law could more effectively become the protector of *public* decency and order. Fines and sentences for public sexual solicitation were increased. The Wolfenden Committee thus refrained from making any moral judgments (which would have forced a comparison of the morals of the male client with the female prostitute) and argued, instead, that the visibility of the prostitute offended public decency more than the more furtive behavior of the client. Wolfenden did represent some liberalization of official attitudes toward female sexuality. Unlike the discussions of the Victorian period, which viewed women (especially those in the middle class) as basically asexual and thus legitimized the 'sexually frustrated' husband's resort to prostitution, the Wolfenden Committee had to acknowledge the basis of modern marriage in mutual sexual pleasure. Hence the emphasis on the prostitute's affront to public decency.

The Wolfenden Committee decriminalized private homosexual

acts between consenting adults, although it had nothing to say about lesbianism. This, too, reflected the Committee's desire to limit public eroticism. However, this part of the Committee's recommendations created much more opposition than that devoted to prostitution. It was opposed not only on the grounds of its affront to the family but also in view of its threat to the 'moral fiber' of the nation. The recommendation on prostitution was legislated as soon as 1959, while the homosexual reforms had to wait until the passage of the Sexual Offences Act in 1967.

Political controls over public sexuality are more direct, explicit and harsh than controls over private sexuality. This can be seen with regard to pornography as well as prostitution and homosexuality. Pornography is a major leisure industry in both the United Kingdom and the United States. It is officially tolerated as long as the production, distribution and consumption are relatively secluded. Overt pornography, in the mass media or on the streets, is officially condemned as an offense to public decency. Illicit leisure practices are thus allowed provided they are secreted from public gaze.

In both countries the liberalization of controls over erotic conduct was reversed again in the late 1970s as enforcement of existing laws against prostitution, homosexuality and pornography was intensified. The social agenda of the 'new right', first in the United States and then in Britain, called for the intervention of the state in sexual behavior on a scale that would not be tolerated in other areas of social life. However, the fact that the enforcement of sex laws is left up to local authorities means wide variation in the laws that are applied in any given locale. Sex laws are easy to pass because legislators do not want to appear to be soft on vice; they are usually very harsh, carrying penalties for violation out of all proportion to the social or individual harm done; and they are very difficult to remove.

The political regulation of erotic conduct has created considerable tension within the new right, between the 'big government' aspects of the political control of morality on the one hand and the ideology of individual freedom and belief in the sufficiency of market forces for determining social outcomes on the other. Many on the new right itself hold the view that, in their leisure as much as in their business activities, individuals should have the freedom to choose what kind of activity they spend their time and money on. Others, however, adopt the view that, just because an individual freely chooses to engage in an activity, this does not thereby sanction it. The hegemony of this latter view is expressed in the laws defining the age of consent and the protections afforded innocent children against being exposed to 'adult' material. Some forms of sex are considered so intrinsically vile that no one should be allowed to participate in them, even by their own choice.

We can see from this discussion of sexuality that leisure relations are structured not only by political control exercised by one class over another but also by political control exercised by one gender over another. Patriarchy, the pattern of dominance of men over women, has been very influential in shaping the political control not just of erotic conduct but of women's leisure in general. Women's leisure practices are shaped by class relations and their political organization in much the same way as are those of men. Nineteenth-century reformers (many of them middle-class women) were especially keen to control many aspects of the leisure lives of working-class women. But in the case of women, to class oppression must be added gender domination. Thus women's leisure is structured by the kind of work they do but it is also structured by their changing relationship to men. Girls' leisure is influenced less by the move from school to waged work than it is by their relationship to men. Their leisure is structured by the move from best (female) friends, to boyfriend, to 'steady', to husband and father. The construction of femininity on behalf of men occupies a considerable amount of girls' time. Leisure activities must be chosen with care to avoid endangering girls' 'reputation.' Steady dating demands of girls (but not of boys) a transformation in leisure activities to focus around the needs of the boy, as an adjunct to his leisure, so that the girl can be admitted to male-dominated leisure spheres on male terms.

This pattern of patriarchal control of leisure is obscured by commonsense 'wisdom' and much policy-oriented writing on leisure, which reflects all too faithfully patriarchal ideologies of leisure. The 'conventional' approach to leisure is 'gender' biased in a number of ways. First, it assumes that most of the work (against which leisure is contrasted) is *paid* work. Full-time employment is the category of activity from which we rest or recuperate in leisure. The problem with this view is that many women 'work' but are not in full-time employment and cannot, for this reason, have 'leisure time.' Second, the conventional view of leisure separates work and leisure locales, whereas for many housewives in particular their workplace and their 'leisure' place are the same. Thus women are especially likely to be doing several things at once, only one of which might be leisure. Third, much of what men regard as leisure (e.g. eating or sex) represents work for women, while the opposite is rarely the case. Women's work allows men to have leisure time. Fourth, the tendency to think of leisure as 'free time' reduces the amount of 'leisure' available to women. Not only is their range of choices about the use of time limited by their subordination to men (who typically impose constraints on their public freedom), but even their 'free time' (e.g. dancing or drinking) is defined and controlled by men. Women are constructed as leisure by men; men's leisure often depends on female participation. Fifth, to the extent that leisure is seen as a reward for work, as something to which work leads, then the more rewarding the work, the more rewarding leisure should be. This 'moral economy' of leisure disadvantages women, whose (house)work typically goes unrecognized or is devalued. They are not allowed leisure because they have not earned it. Most men believe that because they work they are 'entitled' to leisure; fewer women believe they too have a similar entitlement (Deem, 1986b, p. 69). Sixth, the idea of individual freedom, which constitutes our understanding of 'real' leisure, is more meaningful to men than women. Many public leisure places (e.g. pubs and saloons) can be used only by men *as individuals*. It is only males who casually frequent such establishments. Women do so at their own risk. This is particularly true of working-class women, who, as opposed to middle-class women, are less used to organizing their daily existence as independent and self-sufficient individuals. There is, then, in the very meaning of leisure a powerful measure of political control by men over women; the politics of women's leisure extends to much more than public policies or the intentions of politicians.

## Politics and the Market

The formal controls over leisure invested in political institutions, from the national down to the local level, are only one way in which politics affects leisure. In the mixed economies of capitalist democracies, people's leisure is shaped most directly by what the 'leisure industry' is offering, and only to the extent that the state sees itself as regulating or subsidizing this industry do they feel the impress of political actions. The dominant ideology of leisure in these societies, which portrays leisure as essentially a private, individual choice, legitimates this relationship. Leisure is something to be 'consumed,' selected from an array of offerings produced and distributed by a highly competitive and enterprising leisure industry. This ideology, and the dynamism and volatility of the leisure market, helps perpetuate the notion that 'having fun' and 'being entertained' are entirely free of political consequences.

While it is easy to overlook the political effects of the operation of the leisure market, they can be just as pronounced as are the more direct forms of political control. Entrepreneurs, in their search for more predictable and dependable leisure consumers, restructure leisure experiences as powerfully as do social reformers and government officials. Rosenzweig (1983, p. 217) describes how the coming of the movies to Worcester, Massachusetts, in the 1920s broke down much of the informality and communality of the ethnic working-class saloon and the nickelodeon. 'The lavish settings, the militarily attired and drilled ushers, the fixed starting times, the disinfected air, the lighted clocks, and the "finely appointed toilet rooms" had all made moviegoing a more controlled, structured, and anonymous experience.' The coming of the talkies only accelerated the trend toward privatism set in motion by the silent movies.

The ideology of 'consumer sovereignty' encourages us to regard leisure choice as an exercise in individual freedom; and it lends support to the notion that politics, which connote domination and control, should be kept out of leisure. So powerful is this ideology that it permeates even publicly provided leisure. We express disquiet at allowing politics to enter leisure but seem to be less alarmed at the tendency to allow market criteria to determine the public provision of leisure. A market or consumer model of leisure planning dominates the recreation profession as well as government bureaucrats; leisure services (including radio and television) must be developed to meet 'preferences.' The market model competes vigorously with the much more feeble idea that leisure services must compensate for deprivations or disadvantages, and the equally unpopular idea that leisure services should uplift or educate. Of the United States, Kaplan (1975, p. 264) writes: 'The leisure dimension... inasmuch as a portion of it is dominated by goods and services provided for financial profit, is efficiently served instead of purposefully elevated.'

The ideology of 'consumer sovereignty' disguises the extent to which capital controls leisure. 'Modern leisure corporations may follow consumer demand, but they can also create it, and their ability to do so increases with their growing domination of leisure production' (Clarke and Critcher, 1985, p. 200). The extent of this domination is in no way affected by the high turnover rate experienced among leisure enterprises. Specific markets may be difficult to control, but there is no question of capital's collective control over the production and distribution of leisure.

Consumer sovereignty in the sphere of leisure is a fairly recent development. In the nineteenth century, the chief concern of the capitalist was to mold a new industrial labor force, and leisure was something to be structured and paced for the purpose of encouraging sobriety and punctuality; the watchword was deferred gratification. As early as 1907 the economist Simon Patten (1912) noted a shift from a 'pain economy' to a 'pleasure economy' as the capitalist system moved from a condition of scarcity toward one of potential abundance. Now the need was not for asceticism and hard work but for consumption and play. Corporate liberal businessmen encouraged the rise of consumerism because they believed the future of American business lay in the development of mass markets. The modern industry of advertising, much of it devoted to the hawking of leisure goods, was born at this time. Organised labor did not fight these developments. Indeed, it used them to argue the case for a shorter working week, on the grounds that this would give workers more free time to go out and spend their money.

In mixed economies, the state's role with respect to leisure has been chiefly to limit the excesses of commercialization (e.g. censorship, zoning, hygiene and safety laws) and, in part, to remedy the deficiencies in the provision of leisure services that the search for profit creates. Ironically, those middle-class social reformers seeking to use government power to regulate the manner in which the working class spends its leisure time have encountered resistance not only from the working class itself but also from businessmen seeking to earn a living by providing diversions and entertainment. The interests of government are best served by law and order. Often, however, businessmen demand and encourage just the opposite; brewery customers get drunk, betting-shop patrons lose all their money, sports spectators get out of hand, television viewers become vegetable-like, vacationers vandalize property, dance patrons disturb the peace, street performers offend public decency. The state seeks to place limits on the results of the play of market forces by systems of licensing and regulation; but in a mixed economy, the health of the leisure industry will be its paramount concern, and it will stop short of impeding the search for profit. It is no accident that during the Progressive era recreational services for children were much more acceptable to politicians and businessmen than public leisure facilities intended for adults. The children had no money and were thus not potential customers. Adult services, however, competed with business for the discretionary dollar. It is also noteworthy that the government has traditionally concerned itself chiefly with outdoor leisure facilities (with the exceptions of museums), which act as a kind of backdrop and are not accessible on a daily basis to working adults and do not compete with commercial facilities that are.

The uneasy relation between the state and the market is well illustrated in the case of gambling. Despite a long history of moral disapproval of gambling and an equally long history of its association with the 'criminal element,' the state has only loosely regulated gambling. Regulations have eased in recent years as part of a general trend toward the decriminalization of victimless crimes and the conviction on the part of many governments that they, too, can make money from gambling. The state's attitude toward gambling has been a tacit acknowledgement that people will gamble, that it has mass appeal and that the task of eliminating it is beyond the reach of a democratic government. It has also been impossible for the state to ignore the potential gambling has for raising revenues; it can tax private gambling enterprises or become directly involved in the running of gambling operations. The job of keeping gambling within socially acceptable bounds has thus been left largely to the self-imposed controls of the gambling (and sports) industry itself, with the state becoming involved only to try to exclude organized crime and to ensure public order. This limited amount of intervention is precisely what private enterprise welcomes most enthusiastically. The 'evils' of gambling are largely ignored by state officials, who are content to leave control over individual gambling habits to private agencies like the church. In the United States, for example, the federal government has nothing to do with gambling and has no gambling policy—except to prohibit interstate wagering. States vary enormously in their policy toward gambling, and few devote many resources to its control. Rather, each state retains the option of imposing further regulations on the gambling industry if excesses seem to be occurring (Frey, 1985).

Working-class leisure has thus been molded in the long run by the joint effect of capital and the state. In the United States, this is nicely illustrated by the gambling case. In the United Kingdom, it is illustrated by the case of the music hall. At the turn of the century, municipalities and local capital did not always see eye to eye on what to do with public houses and singing saloons. Political authorities were anxious to suppress them, while private enterprise saw them as an opportunity for profit. Each achieved its objective, in part: 'The reinforcing interaction of the government's concern to create orderly places of popular entertainment and the proprietor's need to protect the investment of capital led to the selection of types of institutions and entertainment which were not so much conducive to, as actually part of, the development of capitalist social relations' (Summerfield, 1981, p. 237). Local authorities clamped down on the soliciting, hawking, general milling about and drunkenness associated with saloons—a policy which suited very nicely the music-hall 'chains' which began to appear at this time. Saloons gradually lost their class character as licensing laws were passed to eliminate their smaller, more class-specific forms. By the time the music hall had reached the pinnacle of its popularity it had largely abandoned its roots in the working-class community. 'Management had succeeded in impressing something of a more compliant manner upon the members of this robust institution' (Bailey, 1978, p. 168). Capital and the state together had thus succeeded where political reformers alone had failed.

In view of the 'rising entitlements' to leisure mentioned in the introduction, there is a certain irony in the fact that capital has succeeded in resisting the claim for democratic leisure forms better than the state. Many of the nineteenth-century pastimes of the working class, especially those associated with the chapels, were quite democratic; the congregation or club organized and ran its own affairs. As commercial music halls and, later, cinemas became more popular, the working class lost control over its leisure forms. These were now presented on the basis of the aspirations of the entrepreneur to make a profit, with very little feedback from the audience except for approval and disapproval voiced through the box-office. The rise in popularity of the mass media—radio and television—has done little to arrest this movement away from popular control. The extent to which it is possible to offer political opposition to this form of control over leisure time is the subject of Chapter 3.

# 3
# Resistance

The popular amusements which were so often the target of social control—the fairs, festivals, pantomimes, music halls—were in fact very resilient and resisted attempts to regulate them. As fast as old forms were suppressed (e.g. bear-baiting), new forms developed (e.g. running) or became popular (e.g. soccer). Most working people's orientation to leisure was shaped by harsh and dehumanizing working conditions. They resisted efforts to control their free time that focused on leisure alone and ignored conditions of work or housing. Resistance was particularly strong where occupational communities had formed and where the lodge or tavern was a focus not only for play but also for work culture. These communities and neighborhoods were spaces 'won' from the dominant culture and were not to be surrendered easily.

The emergence of mass leisure is, then, the story of a continual struggle over the use of time and space, a struggle elites did not always win. For example, the works choral societies and brass bands that became so popular in the working-class regions of Britain in the nineteenth century no doubt coopted some workers and their families into a paternalistic relation with factory and mine owners. But they clearly intensified solidarity among many others: 'popular musical life reflected or extended class tensions in local society,' and bands were often engaged to lead strike processions (Russell, 1983, p. 108).

Working-class communities, especially those marked by militancy in industrial conflict, were structured around free-time activities just as much as they were structured around the workplace. Still today British miners

> spend much of their free time with members of the same industry. This is the result of the pit village social structure and is not so much the case in large cities. Their entertainment has been for

generations centered on the Miners' Institute—a social meeting place combining the functions of the pub, music hall and, often, political hall.
(Watson, 1983, p. 13)

Outside the tightly knit working-class communities, Victorian moral reformers, in tacit alliance with brewers, licensed victuallers and entertainment entrepreneurs, promoted a commodified but 'licensed' leisure in the form of public houses and music halls. But working men's clubs more than held their own in the competition for free time and discretionary money. The paternalistic institutes and clubs set up by English landowners and capitalists (often in the person of their 'ladies') reached their high water mark as early as the 1860s and 1870s. By the 1880s the working-class members themselves had largely taken over the running of these clubs, rejecting the patronage of the rich, reducing the emphasis on 'education' in favor of entertainment, aligning themselves more closely with socialist causes, distancing themselves from the church and cooperating more regularly among themselves (Taylor, 1972). It was only at the turn of the century that such clubs began to lose their overt political functions and to operate as purely social venues.

Saloons and clubs were also important sites of resistance to class control of leisure in the United States. 'The most popular forms of workingmen's recreation...were the saloon, lodge, and club, places in which male camaraderie resonated with working-class economic and social concerns' (Peiss, 1986, p. 17). Saloons were particularly important to newly arrived immigrants in search of jobs and a place to stay. Fraternal lodges and clubs frequently used the back rooms of saloons for meetings and entertainments, as did trade unions. Until the coming of Prohibition, moral reformers made little impact on these working-class leisure habits, especially in the larger cities of the North.

Drinking continues to be largely segregated by class, especially in the United Kingdom, where 'public houses' have 'saloons' and 'lounges' to separate working-class from middle-class drinkers and are solidly identified with one class or another by their location. The public house held a central position in the local articulation of working-class culture as a sort of colonized institution which, though not formally owned by that class, had been internally molded by the class's customs. In working-class culture, the pub had been a 'local,' 'a term signifying its patronage by an established local clientele who shaped the internal dynamics, relationships and patterns of socializing' (Clarke, 1979, p. 245). Only since the 1960s has the hold of the working class on their leisure-time activity become precarious. The rationalization of brewery organization and pub design has transformed its clientele from 'member' into 'consumer,' the enterprise itself shifting from its status as a 'local' to that of a franchise.

Some of the decline of the English pub as a source of resistance to leisure control can be attributed to changing housing patterns. The disintegration of many urban neighborhoods and the transformation of many villages into bedroom communities means that the working class has lost some of its spatial identity. Nevertheless, even in the new towns and the homogenized commuter settlements, leisure subcultures distinctive to that class survive. They

> focus around key occasions of social interaction: the weekend, the disco, the bank holiday trips, the night out in the 'centre', the 'standing-about-doing-nothing' of the weekday evening, the Saturday match. They cluster around particular locations. They develop specific rhythms of interchange, structural relations between members: younger to older, experienced to novice, stylish to square. They explore 'focal concerns' central to the inner life of the group: things always 'done' or 'never done', a set of social rituals which underpin their collective identity and define them as a 'group' instead of a mere collection of individuals. They adopt and adapt material objects—goods and possessions— and categorise them into distinctive 'styles' which express the collectivity of their being as a group...Sometimes, the world is masked out, linguistically, by names and an *argot* which classifies the social world external to them in terms meaningful only within their group perspective, and maintains its boundaries.
> (Clarke, 1981, p. 64)

In this more amorphous and free floating form, less attached to specific locales or regions, the working class has continued to resist the political regulation of its leisure despite the privatizing influence of the mass media. Street and neighborhood dances and festivities continue to provide opportunities to transgress middle-class norms of propriety through drinking, making love, communal singing, dancing and playing instruments. The Notting Hill Carnival, which originated in 1966 as a conscious effort to revive the nineteenth-century Notting Hill Annual Fayre, is a conspicuous example. Its organizers intended it to promote the integration of the immigrant population into British society and culture—race riots had occurred in Notting Hill in 1958. But the festival quickly took on other layers of meaning. During the period of preparation for the Carnival organizers were in effect mobilizing the local working-class population, both white and black, for a campaign against local landlords and the local authorities on behalf of better housing and more playgrounds. By the 1970s a further item had been added to this informal agenda as the Carnival became an almost exclusively Afro-Caribbean affair protesting white racism. A split occurred in the ranks of the organizers as white opposition, aided by the police and Borough Council, intensified. The Afro-Caribbeans thus adapted a carnival which in Trinidad ritually expresses nationhood and solidarity to articulate protest, resistance and confrontation in their adopted home (Cohen, 1982).

Despite their efforts to control street life directly, city fathers have never succeeded in eliminating the use of streets as leisure spaces. Efforts to provide supervised leisure had always run up against the 'unclubbables,' those who simply refuse to conform to the regimen of leisure activities run and supervised by middle-class adults. Contrary to middle-class opinion, city streets have been considered crime-free, comfortable places by those who actually live on them, chiefly because they are almost always thickly populated, and the street games, which could attract hundreds of spectators, offered a framework for fun and relaxation and contributed to a sense of community. Only since the Second World War with the gutting of inner-city areas has this pattern changed.

The rapid expansion of the commercialized sports in the 1870s and 1880s also reflected considerable resistance to middle-class regulation. As soccer became more commercialized it became more closely associated with working-class communities while at the same time providing the working class with a national interest and language. 'The initial transformation of football under the control and patronage of the earlier Victorian Bourgeoisie...and its later transformation under the auspices of the bourgeoisie, who made football a business, did not prevent working-class people colonizing football and in a restricted sense making it their own' (Hargreaves, 1982, p. 52). Ironically, commercialized sports also reproduced class conflict internally, as labor and management fought for control over shares of the profit and control over decision-making. Today, the spectator sports popular among the working class—soccer, auto and motorcycle racing, speedway, horse and dog racing—are 'part mass therapy, part resistance, part mirror image of the dominant political economy' (Robins, 1982, p. 145). While there is undoubtedly an apolitical escapism in these sports, and while they thoroughly immerse many of their devotees in the world of mass consumption, they are also distinctively part of the proletarian public realm, part of 'prole culture.'

The crowd 'disorders' associated with professional sporting events can be seen as 'rituals of rebellion.' Much of the behavior of the 'hooligans' at soccer matches is quite literally a fight over space or 'spots' on the terraces. This aggression is directed not so much at the police as it is at rival fans, but the violence does have its own 'rules of disorder,' dictating when attacks on rival fans are appropriate, what course fights should take and when and how fights should be terminated (Marsh, Rosser and Harre, 1978, p. 110). The territories that are won are 'free' from conventional systems of social control, a space (much like street corners) where working-class children can impose their own hierarchies of command and pursue their own, often deviant, careers. Taylor (1982) sees another political dimension to soccer hooliganism. Much of the violence, he believes, is a reaction to the decomposition of the soccer club as a neighborhood institution of the working class. This detachment began to take place as soccer became a mass-mediated, national entertainment sport aimed at paying spectators. Fans lost their sense of natural identification with the club, which became increasingly an aspect of 'local civic power.' As a consequence, they have sought, through the means of demonstrations directed at reimposing their control over the game, to recolonize the sport.

When non-elites resist the control of their leisure time by elites they are making a political statement about how their time and space should be defined and used. This is largely a reactive role as the subordinate group seeks to resist the colonization of its leisure. However, leisure can also be used as an expression of rebellion against the social order. People's theatre, festivals, blues, jazz, folk music, dress styles, dime novels, nickelodeons, popular magazines and even films have all served to unite the oppressed in an oppositional culture. Popular entertainments, through the collective festivity they offer, the fabulous sets, glittering costumes, exciting music, lively action and enthusiastic performers, especially those working through satire or parody of the great, satisfy the taste for and sense of revelry, the plain speaking and hearty laughter which liberate by setting the social world head over heels, overturning conventions and properties.

It is natural that leisure should figure in political rebellion. People always need a material base on which to organize their autonomy against the surveillance of the political apparatus. The workers' homes and friends long provided a retreat from the world of authority and domination. 'Only in the secrecy of their homes, in the communication of taverns, in the joy of street gatherings may they find values, ideas, projects and, finally, demands that do not conform to the dominant social interests' (Castells, 1983, p. 70). Union organizing and radical socialization have usually taken place in lodges, taverns, public houses and other venues for entertainment and amusement. There, leisure time and space provide the interstices in the social fabric necessary to escape its routine and its oppressiveness.

Each of the three fracture points of modern capitalist societies—class, gender and race—have created controversies over the use of leisure as subordinated groups incorporate demands for their own kind of leisure in their protest against oppression.

## Class

It is now customary during May Day and other labor rituals associated with socialist and communist parties in capitalist countries to combine public and private merry-making and good cheer with the assertion of loyalty to the movement. But left-wing movements and organized labor were initially reluctant to use sports politically, partly out of a certain intellectual bias. Many radicals were suspicious of sports because they were a pastime of the bourgeoisie; others associated organized sports with dissipating vices like drinking, while others relegated non-work interests to second place in the hierarchy of demands, behind the need to earn a living.

Nevertheless, the association of physical culture and left-wing movements has a long history. Socialist workers' sport clubs were formed as early as the 1890s, with Germany taking the lead. By 1913 the Belgian, Gaston Bridoux, had succeeded in bringing together representatives of the Belgian, English, French, German and Italian labor sports federations to form the Socialist International of Physical Education (Wheeler, 1978, p. 196). Workers' sports differed from bourgeois sports in being open to all, women as well as men, and in placing less emphasis on competition. Activities like gymnastics, cycling, hiking and swimming were favored over rugby, soccer, cricket, boxing and the like. In 1925 the Socialist International, which collapsed during the First World War, was refounded as the International Union for Physical Education and Workers' Sport; five years later it was renamed the Socialist Workers' Sports International. 'These name changes symbolised the increasing importance of organised sport, and correspondingly competition, as opposed to simple physical activity,' a shift in response to 'grassroots pressure from working people' (Wheeler, 1978, p. 197). By the late 1920s workers' sport federations were active in Germany, Austria, Czechoslovakia, Belgium, Britain, France, Italy and the United States. At its peak, the workers' sport movement united well over four million people, making it by far the largest working-class cultural organization (Riordan, 1984a, p. 98).

Those capitalist countries with the strongest tradition of socialist politics developed the most active workers' sport organizations. The British Workers' Sports Federation, for example, battled for rights of access to the landscape, often coming into conflict not only with landowners but also with the more middle-class Youth Hostels Association. Their activities included 'mass trespasses' on land they believed should be open to the public. But even in the United States left-wing groups used sports to mobilize support for the cause. From the late 1920s to the mid-1940s communist youth, fraternal and trade union organizations sponsored independent sports leagues in cities throughout the country, participated in anti-fascist Olympic boycott movements in 1932 and 1936, sponsored numerous track meets and benefit games for political prisoners and waged a thoroughgoing effort to end the exclusion of blacks from major league baseball (Naison, 1985, p. 129). A Labor Sports Union was founded in 1927. During the height of labor militancy in the 1930s trade unions developed a wide range of recreational activities for their members to draw them out of their employer-sponsored programs.

The most visible of workers' sport federation activities were the national and international meets organized to cement worker solidarity in capitalist countries and to raise socialist consciousness. The most popular of these were the Workers' Olympiads, begun unofficially in 1921 and formally inaugurated in 1925. The workers' sport federations made a point of including the 'losing' nations in the recent war, in sharp contrast to the 'bourgeois' Olympics of 1920 and 1924 when they were excluded.

> The accent was on mass participation and socialist fellowship: every athlete took part in the opening and closing artistic display; the atmosphere was festive and unashamedly political. The opening ceremonies and victory rituals dispensed with national flags and anthems, featuring instead red flags and revolutionary hymns like the 'Internationale'. The centre-piece was a mass artistic display accompanied by mass choirs, and featuring multi-purpose pyramids and tableaux, symbolising working class solidarity and power in the class struggle.
> 
> (Riordan, 1984a, p. 104).

The second Workers' Olympiad in 1931 was in many ways the high point of the workers' sport movement. One hundred thousand athletes from twenty-six nations took part. Soon thereafter, a division between socialists and communists split the workers' sport movement, a split not healed until the third (and final) Olympiad held in 1937, by which time Italian, German and Austrian groups had been suppressed by fascist governments, and attendance had fallen to 27,000.

It is hard to say what effect the workers' sport movement had on the political consciousness of the working class between the two world wars. No other organization incorporated so many working-class people from so many different countries. On the other hand, the movement suffered from the unwillingness of the Soviet Union to participate on an equal basis and from splits between socialist and communist sports organizations. In the United States the workers' sport movement was bedeviled by ethnic divisions. Most communists were Finns, Jews and Southern Slavs who favored their own immigrant sports (e.g. soccer). These had little appeal to native Americans or second-generation immigrants who had passed through the American educational system with its heavy emphasis on football and basketball. The movement also suffered from its early opposition to spectatorism. The movement did not therefore solidify the working class on the left. And on the right, in both the United States and Europe, the sports clubs of the middle class proved more than a match for workers' organizations in attracting popular support. At no time did workers' sports membership outnumber that in bourgeois sport clubs. The latter were well established by the time the socialists got into the act; and they were often run democratically. They also tended to be much better funded and, unlike the socialist clubs, did not bore their members with tedious political indoctrination. 'What many workers' sports leaders seemed to have failed to comprehend was that a sports organization might be *more* politically effective by being *less* explicitly political' (Riordan, 1984a, p. 110).

After the Second World War the workers' sport movement abandoned its strategy of separatism in sport, partly as a result of the Soviet Union's decision to participate in the Olympic Games and partly as a result of the increasing involvement of Third World countries in bourgeois sports. Leftists turned their attention more to reforming bourgeois sports rather than using their own sport organization for purposes of consciousness raising and mobilization. The surviving worker sport movements (as part of the International Workers' Sport Committee) seem to be more interested in promoting equality of opportunity in sport than in using sport to raise revolutionary consciousness or pointing out the evils of capitalism (Riordan, 1984a, p. 109).

As the mass media have come to dominate the leisure time of the working class, the notion of leisure providing an opportunity for class rebellion seems less and less plausible. And yet there are ways in which the mass media have been turned to the advantage of non-elites, even if they do not control them. The messages of the medium are not uniformly hegemonic but a complex of 'hopes and fears, dreams and nightmares, ideological celebration of the status quo and utopian transcendence, moments of rebellion and its attempted containment' (Kellner, 1984, p. 204). Individual viewers are not passive receivers of encoded messages, but rather tend to process television images according to their life situations and cultural experiences. The same can be said of film, which now comprises such a large proportion of television fare. Far from being passive, the viewer or spectator is assigned a task which must be performed if he or she is to elicit meaning from a film. 'The audience, then, have to work at their entertainment; they have, in fact, to entertain themselves from the material at hand' (Maltby, 1983, p. 22).

The images and messages of television are contradictory in their content and their effects. Programs like *All in the Family* were explicitly emancipatory in the sense of awakening and enlightening people to sources and forms of oppression against class, ethnic and gender groups. Furthermore, while the mass media could efficiently reproduce images, they could not produce them, and for this relied on creative artists. They therefore contain a contradiction between the need for stability, equilibrium and reproducibility on the one hand and the need for creativity and innovation on the other. Of course, we must not exaggerate the emancipatory potential of the mass media. Despite the possibilities for cooptation and resistance, such is the structure of the mass media industries that there is little likelihood of their being taken over and used for purposes of political rebellion.

Working-class resistance in mass society is also possible through the struggle over the use and interpretation of cultural artefacts and significant symbols. Societies exhibit clear hierarchies of culture and circulate cultural rewards in the same way that more tangible rewards are distributed. Much of the conflict over leisure reflects patterns of domination and subordination in the cultural hierarchy 'just as different groups and classes are unequally ranked in relation to one another, in terms of their productive relations, wealth and power, so *cultures* are differently ranked, and stand in opposition to one another, in relations of domination and subordination, along the scale of "cultural power"' (Clarke, 1981, p. 54).

Resistance thus becomes a matter of rejecting mainstream cultural hierarchies and replacing them with others. This takes place, essentially, in the free time we call leisure. It is a question of 'style.'

Style is usually a predominant feature of youthful subculture. The

> precious gains of working life, money and leisure, become invested in dramaturgical statements about self-image, which attempt to define an identity outside that ascribed to class, education, and occupational role, particularly when the latter is of low status.
>
> (Brake, 1980, p. 13)

The shock value of many subcultural styles imparts to them a seemingly 'radical' character. But subculture is not a direct attack on work hierarchies. Hebdige (1979, p. 95) reports a youth as saying, 'I wouldn't wear my punk outfit for work—there's a time and place for everything.' Nor is their message overtly political. Subcultures arise when people are facing problems for which no social solutions presently exist. They 'solve,' but in an imaginary way, problems which at the concrete level cannot be dealt with. 'Thus, in the expropriation and fetishization of consumption and style itself, the "Mods" cover the gap between the never-ending-weekend and Monday's resumption of boring, dead-end work' (Clarke, 1981, p. 65). Punk style served the same purpose. Punks 'wore clothes which were the sartorial equivalent of swear words, and they swore as they dressed—with calculated effect, lacing obscenities into record notes and publicity releases, interviews and love songs' (Hebdige, 1979, p. 114).

Ironically, the style rebellions of the working class have tended to be less overtly political than their middle-class equivalents. Working-class youth subcultures are more part-time, temporary episodes of short duration, neighborhood-based, with local peer-group affiliations. Unlike middle-class youth, working-class teenagers do not have the luxury of being able to 'drop out' so easily or for such extended periods of time. Middle-class subcultures tend to demand more full-time and longer commitment, to transcend rather than oppose work authority and to articulate broader political opposition to the mainstream culture (Brake, 1985, p. 83). Many of the more middle-class hippies rather easily made the transition to the Yippies and readily associated themselves with peace and conservation movements, thus making more explicit their opposition to dominant political values and institutions, whereas working-class rockers or punks did not clearly articulate political opposition. Even when working-class groups have been overtly political, elites have discounted this political dimension in favor of treating them as delinquents. Middle-class drop-outs, on the other hand, have been seen more readily as 'disaffiliated' from mainstream politics (Clarke, 1981, p. 73).

Unfortunately, the creation and diffusion of new styles are bound up with the whole process of production, publicity and packaging, which inevitably leads to the defusion of the subculture's subversive power: 'both mod and punk innovations fed back directly into high fashion and mainstream fashion' (Hebdige, 1979, p. 95), as did hippie styles of the 1960s. Ironically, this cooptation is partly the result of the fact that subcultures take objects from the mass culture (such as automobiles) and provide them with their own second-order meanings. There exists a two-way street. The culture industries can take the symbols of subcultures, divorce them from their everyday codes, trivialize them with less radical meanings and make them marketable to the mainstream culture. 'For example, the signifier "punk rock" was sanitized by the Top 40 radio industry and changed to "New Wave"' (Gottdiener, 1985, p. 996). Subcultures are vulnerable to this kind of cooptation because, while rebellious, they seldom reach the state of articulated opposition to the existing order. It is also due to the fact that subcultures are heavily populated with youth, who are temporarily outside the confines of work or marriage but soon exit from that status.

Cooptation also helped dissipate the cultural rebellion in France associated with the student uprisings of May 1968. The students rejected not only the bureaucracy of the mass university, the factory and the office but also the bureaucracy and rigidity of historical revolutionary parties. Instead, they emphasized spontaneity and immediacy, impermanence and expressivity. The fundamental belief in the virtue of what was called 'festivity' re-emerged, in which everyone rediscovers a sort of *joie de vivre* that has been lost in both individual and communal life.

The students thus revived a very old political tradition of using 'play' to create space for political protest. One political function of play is to offer a dramatic commentary on reality, a heightened re-enactment of communal traditions. This runs counter to the approach to play which sees it as an escape from reality. Indeed, the latter is to a large degree an ideological production of the commodification of leisure. But play can have a critical thrust. 'The social order experienced in play often proves more satisfying than the prevailing social arrangments; it enables the individual to acquire an awareness of the self as a cause of activity and as a participant in a cause and, in turn, it invites transgressions of conventional restraints' (Hearn, 1976, p. 150). In play the past can be imaginatively reconstructed, portrayed not as it actually was, but as it should have been. Play thus creates an open space and a time out of structure within which new social arrangements and relations previously precluded by conventional constraints can be experimented with.

It did not take the mainstream culture, fascinated with the

spectacle of the student protest played out on the television screen, very long to absorb and dilute the more potent of the rebellion's images, much to the chagrin of the students. As one student protestor complained:

> A distinction must be made between, on the one hand, what we think and do, and on the other, *what the bourgeoisie does with what we think*, the way in which the bourgeoisie has an interest in presenting our ethic and acts of contestation. The bourgeoisie wants to turn our action into merchandise in order to kill it, to turn us into mere reflections. We are reduced to the state of *images* so that we can be observed more easily.
> (Willener, 1970, p. 141, original emphasis)

The students found that their expressivity, if not their politics, could be coopted and redefined by the capitalist system. They discovered 'That contestation of culture must be done in such a way that culture cannot absorb the contestation and use it in a new form for its lies' (Willener, 1970, p. 142).

Political resistance to certain forms of leisure began directly to affect the world of sports in the 1960s in the aftermath of the 'new Left' activism of that decade. Leftist critics saw in modern sports many of the symptoms of the malaise they believed had affected all capitalist institutions. They were yet another instance of obsession with individual performance and competitiveness, more in tune with the ideology of meritocracy than that of democracy. Professional and collegiate sports were attacked as exploitative and dehumanizing, for players and spectators alike.

Leaders of the movements to reform sports sought to rescue play in the name of democracy and freedom. Play, they believed, had lost its innocence, its capacity to help individuals act 'as if,' its power to envision alternative futures. In the hands of physical education instructors and college coaches play had become thoroughly bureaucratized, thus merely replicating the work world, and in the hands of promoters had become thoroughly commercialized, an escape from reality rather than a novel confrontation with it. The reformers endowed play with the potential to emancipate because it was 'the one human activity within capitalist society that is non-instrumental' (Aronowitz, 1973, p. 61). Reform efforts focused on making sport less hierarchical and competitive, more democratic and spontaneous. Each individual was encouraged to become involved and participate fully, regardless of skill and experience. The goal of the reformers was to distribute the basic benefits of participation (e.g. health, self-respect and affiliation) more equitably.

Many of the social movements of the 1960s explicitly aligned themselves with the working class (or in the United States, 'the poor'). Their manifestos called for the more equitable distribution of leisure resources. Other movements are more difficult to categorize in class terms. Environmentalists cleverly couched their demands for conservation not only in terms of protecting the ecosystem from destruction but also in terms of preserving scarce recreation resources, realizing that the government itself had always linked its call for public funding for recreation to conservation and preservation themes. However, environmentalists were chiefly middle class, and environmentalism in the form of better parks and recreation facilities usually favored middle-class interests.

Other movements, equally difficult to categorize in class terms, rebelled against the system of capitalist exploitation and consumerism by separating themselves from it entirely and establishing communes in which new forms of work and play could be devised. In these societies life became 'a never ending search for health and well-being through exercise, dieting, drugs, spiritual regimens of various kinds, psychic self-help, and psychiatry' (Lasch, 1977, p. 140). Alienation was reinterpreted to mean a loss of self or of control over self. The proposed solution was to become once again one's true self by turning inward for renewal through a more holistic lifestyle. Many communalists approached work as a game and sought to overcome the division between work and play characteristic of the 'straight' world. Those imbued with socialist ideals sought ways of achieving leisure that did not depend on the exploitation of others. Many communalists also rejected 'straight' norms about sexual behavior, ideologically disavowing exclusive sexual access and, in some cases, practicing group marriages.

The counter-culture also spawned efforts to invent new ways of playing sports. The New Games Foundation, founded in 1974 in California, was a non-profit organization which had as its goal bringing play back into people's lives. Its founders believed that there was a need for games that everybody could play, regardless of ability, age, sex, weight, or height. In the games (often variations on sports like baseball, or revivals of old children's games, or imports from other countries) rules were fluid and constantly changing to fit each situation. Earthball, for example, a game in which the object is to push a six-foot ball across the opposing team's goal-line, can be played by two people or by two hundred. Players can wander in and out of the game at the end of each segment of play. In New Games activities, a conscious attempt was made to define everyone as a winner by having winning redefined as the maximization of participation and pleasure. Few New Games were structured to eliminate players. Most often tagged or 'out' players simply shifted to other teams rather than going to the sidelines.

## Gender

The leisure pursuits of women have been determined in large part by the nature of their relationship to men. Resistance to control over their leisure has taken the form of efforts to achieve independence from men in the leisure sphere as well as in the world of work. Women have not only enjoyed less leisure time but they have also traditionally been denied a public leisure. Until women began to enter the labor force in large numbers, the constraints on married women's leisure were in large part shaped by the work rhythms of the home and by the husband's control over the purse-strings. This homework included the provision of leisure for others—erotic pleasure for men and outings and play for children. Wives and mothers could find leisure only close to home, snatched between household chores.

The pattern began to change only with the spread of commercialized leisure in the early twentieth century. 'Loosening the ties between leisure, mutual aid, and male culture, commercialized recreation fostered a youth-oriented, mixed-sex world of pleasure, where female participation was profitable and encouraged' (Peiss, 1986, p. 6). The dance hall was a particular favorite of young unmarried women. 'The commercial halls were public spaces they could attend without escorts, choose companions for the evening, and express a range of personal desires' (Peiss, 1986, p. 106). Women flocked to dance halls in the winter (and beach resorts in the summer) to experience the freedom the new commercialized leisure provided. The cost of this freedom was a more thorough immersion in the consumer culture of dress, cosmetics and the like, and much of the liberty was used to establish relations with men which were just as exploitative as before. But women had, by the First World War, secured for themselves a public sphere of leisure and broken down much of the homosocial world of amusements.

Dance halls, particularly those frequented mainly by the working class, were acknowledged to be places of relative sexual freedom. Patrons typically did not attend the dances as heterosexual couples but used the occasion to meet members of the other sex. The most popular dances were those which permitted the expression of sexual desire. 'Balconies...were accepted zones of free behavior, and women could be observed on men's laps, hugging and kissing in the dark corners of the hall' (Peiss, 1986, p. 105). The new movie houses, too, offered convenient and cheap places for meeting men and 'spooning.' The entertainment industry was thus providing many opportunities for women to shake off the traditional constraints on many of their leisure-time pursuits.

Women had already been busy in the political arena fighting for more sexual rights. As early as the 1880s women had banded together across class lines in organizations like the Ladies' National Association to protect mainly working-class girls from predatory upper-class men. Victorian feminists were particularly opposed to the Contagious Diseases Acts because, in forcing women alleged to be prostitutes to submit to vaginal examinations and licensing, they functioned simply to allow men to have sex with prostitutes without the risk of venereal disease and thus perpetuated the double standard. Victorian feminists were, however, overwhelmingly middle class, and their resistance to gender oppression was couched in terms congenial to middle-class women. Having won battles against the medical regulation of prostitutes in both Britain and the United States, middle-class reformers went on to sponsor legislation to abolish prostitution altogether, thus forcing working-class women to see themselves as victims and emphasizing the dangerous aspects of sexual pleasure. Middle-class reformers also sought to raise the age of consent and thus deny traffickers their 'victims.' but in so doing fostered hostility to girls' sexual activity. 'These moralistic reformers, some of them feminists, allowed the criminal justice system to take over the task of disciplining teenage girls to conform to respectable morality' (Dubois and Gordon, 1984, p. 35). Throughout the second half of the nineteenth century a small minority of feminists insisted that increased sexual activity was not inconsistent with women's dignity, and this same stream of political activism fed the support for birth control at the turn of the century, women arguing that sexual abstinence was an unnecessary price for women to pay for reproductive self-determination and that sexual indulgence in the pursuit of pleasure was good for women. This same argument was to be heard over half a century later in the debate over abortion. The fight to legalize abortion was, in part, born of the conviction that women had the right to be sexual without enduring the punitive consequences of pregnancy. They, too, could have pleasure without danger.

By and large, this emancipatory struggle has been conducted outside the conventional political conflicts. Progressive politics and sexual radicalism have always coexisted uneasily. The official left wing in the United States from 1930 to the 1960s largely ignored or repudiated any association with sexual rebellion. However, the generation of radicals that came of age in the 1960s tried to divest itself of the old Left's sexual restraint. Multiple and varied sexual relationships came to be associated with cultural liberation. The revolt against political and sexual conformity thus became more closely aligned. However, as many feminists were quick to point out, this did not result in sexual liberation for women, as the socialist groups of the 1960s perpetuated gender assumptions taken from the 1950s.

The 1960s saw a revolution in sexual mores as various erotic subcultures took advantage of the political shift to the left. An urban gay and lesbian subculture had begun to emerge after the Second World War. It was nurtured by the freedom and movement of the war years and by the single-sex bonding encouraged in the military. The Kinsey Report's findings on the prevalence of male homosexual encounters overcame many men's feelings of isolation and guilt. The 1950s, during which the homosexual menace to national security was a constant theme of an American politics dominated by McCarthyism, also 'hastened the articulation of a homosexual identity and spread the knowledge that they existed in large numbers' (D'Emilio, 1983, p. 52). Until the 1960s, however, a largely defensive and secretive subculture had been divorced from the tiny militant gay rights movement which had originated in left-wing circles in the early 1940s. In the 1960s, largely through the encouragement of more radicalized gays, the two converged, and the modern gay rights movement was born.

Rather belatedly, feminists turned their attention to play in the 1960s, attacking the patriarchial power structure of the sporting world. In the United States, one of the major weapons in the fight against gender discrimination in sports was civil rights legislation. Title IX of the Education Amendments (to the Civil Rights Act of 1964), passed in 1972, barred sex bias in any education program or activity receiving federal financial assistance, and feminists used this piece of legislation to attack discrimination against women athletes. Title IX altered the whole structure of intercollegiate athletics. Before its passage, the mostly male National Collegiate Athletic Association (NCAA) seemed uninterested in assuming any major leadership role in women's athletics. That role had been assumed by women themselves in 1971 with the formation of the Association for Intercollegiate Athletics for Women (AIAW). Beginning as an informal Commission on Intercollegiate Sports for Women in 1966, it had grown from a membership of 278 institutions in its charter year of 1971 to a peak of 970 in 1979 (Carpenter, 1985, p. 63). The AIAW had been formed because its organizers believed that they could provide a model for American intercollegiate athletics quite different from that of men. Since the nineteenth century female physical educators had fiercely resisted the professionalization seen in men's college athletics: 'educators wanted female students to learn the good sportsmanship, cooperation and other values supposed to accrue from team play, without the evils they considered inherent in high level competition and its attendant commercialism' (Chandler, 1985, p. 11). The credo was 'sport for all.' Skilled women athletes were not given special attention or encouraged to compete with each other but were used instead as a model of performance or as instructors. So divorced was women's collegiate athletics from the men's athletic world that preparation for participation in the male-dominated Olympic Games, limited as it was before the Second World War, was placed in the hands of the Women's Division of the AAU. Nevertheless, even though recruiting was severely restricted and scholarships were limited, the AIAW seemed to many women to represent a departure from the amateur ideal. The most talented female college athletes were now to be encouraged to excel through top-flight competition.

It is ironic that Title IX brought about the demise of the AIAW. Men were not about to subsidize athletic activities they did not control. The NCAA initially adopted the position that Title IX did not apply to athletic programs and (when it became obvious that the government thought otherwise) it launched a strong and successful campaign to exclude revenue sports, such as football and basketball, from the jurisdiction of Title IX. At the same time, however, the NCAA sought to increase its control over women's athletics. 'Soon the AIAW lost both [membership and television revenue] to an attractive NCAA strategy that included such things as offering to pay travel expenses for championship participants and encouraging buyers of broadcast rights to the popular men's basketball games to purchase also the broadcast rights to women's events through the NCAA' (Carpenter, 1985, p. 65). The AIAW could not withstand this offensive from such a powerful and well-financed organization and dissolved itself in 1984.

One reason for the rapid demise of the AIAW was that sport, or indeed leisure in general, had not been an important item on the agenda of feminists during the 1960s and 1970s. Although the cry of 'the personal is political' became a rallying point for feminism, few feminist writers paid much attention to the denial of equal rights to leisure opportunities for women outside the highly publicized worlds of professional and (in the United States) intercollegiate sports. Feminists were well aware that female sexuality and physicality (vulnerability, passivity, softness, impracticality, emotionality and domesticity) were defined by men but they paid much more attention to the function of advertising, pornography and the mass media in propagating these definitions than the role of the leisure industry (e.g. fitness clubs) or sport. Feminists were also aware of the inequities in the distribution of free time created by domestic labor and the structure of work, but few used these insights to analyze leisure itself. They tended to overlook the fact that women's leisure does not fall into the usual categories identified by people studying men's leisure; it does not usually take place at a time and place separate from work, for example. The few feminist writers who concerned themselves with leisure focused their resistance to gender control of women's free time on efforts to provide better child-care facilities, a more equitable division within the home of child-rearing tasks, the abolition of sex-segregated physical education in schools and the improvement of the infrastructure of transportation, social services and housing to make possible the more equal usage of public and commercial leisure opportunities (Deem, 1986b, p. 78).

## Race

The exclusion of racial minorities from places of power and from the richest rewards in sport is well documented, especially for the United States. The civil rights movement of the 1960s saw the first concerted effort to combat racial discrimination at all levels of organized play. Chief among these was the Olympic Project for Human Rights (OPHR) organized in 1966. Its aim was to politicize the black athlete and muster American support for the African-led proposed boycott of the 1968 Mexico City Olympics. The boycott fizzled because South Africa was eventually excluded from the games, but some members of the OPHR nevertheless went ahead with their protest against racism in American sports. During the Mexico Olympics, Tommie Smith and John Carlos, after placing in the 200 meter sprint, raised their gloved hands and lowered their heads when giving the Black Power salute during the playing of the United States national anthem. A wave of 'rebellions' and boycotts occurred on high-school and college campuses, reaching a peak of 180 in 1969. Typical was the demonstration organized by fourteen black football players at the University of Wyoming, who wore black armbands for the game against Brigham Young University to protest the beliefs of the Mormon Church about the racial inferiority of blacks and the absence of blacks on the Brigham Young team. The players were dismissed from the team and lost a court suit to be reinstated. Brigham Young was also the target of protests by the

University of Texas at El Paso track team. Blacks organized protests against their own athletic programs at Ohio State, Michigan State, the University of California at Berkeley, San Francisco State, the University of Kansas, the University of Washington, Iowa State University and many other campuses. At the 1972 Munich Olympics, Wayne Collett and Vince Matthews, after running second and first in the 400 meters, stood casually, chatted, joked and turned away from the American flag during the victory ceremony. The organized effort within sport itself to improve the conditions of black athletes in sports did not last more than three or four years. The Olympic Project for Human Rights was little more than 'one-man show' (Spivey, 1985, p. 248), and black athletes themselves were sharply divided as to the wisdom of political militancy in sport. As important as these direct efforts at improving black athletes' conditions have been, the enforcement of civil rights legislation in high school and college and profit-driven competition between colleges and professional franchises for the best athletes, regardless of their color, have been much more effective in desegregating sports in the United States.

On the international sporting stage, the most important racial issue has been South Africa's policy of apartheid. When the Nationalist Party came to power in 1948 it had little need to impose apartheid on sport because it was already segregated. Nevertheless, a certain number of general and specific laws were passed which, without imposing an explicit ban, effectively rendered the playing of multiracial sport illegal. However, this 'hands-off' policy by the state was sufficient to legitimate dealings with South African sport authorities by sporting organizations from other societies. Both parties could maintain that they were keeping politics out of sport, and the South African sporting bodies could claim that they were not responsible for the absence of black athletes.

In the 1950s, however, black sport federations began to seek ties to the international sporting world as a means of bringing pressure to bear on the South African government. This was no easy matter, for most international sporting federations had long-standing links with Britain and the white Commonwealth. South Africa had often been one of the founding members of these federations, and their voting distribution was often weighted to favor European and British Commonwealth countries. Nevertheless, the South African government did feel obliged in 1956 to enunciate a formal policy on sport which made more explicit the ban on mixed-race competition. The initial result of this foray into international politics was thus to polarize the sporting worlds and to further embroil the South African government in sport itself. No longer could sport be painted as a world free of politics. By 1966 a Minister of Sport and Recreation had been appointed.

The South African Non-Racial Olympic Committee was formed in 1962 and, from its exile in London, organized the campaign that culminated in South Africa's expulsion from the Olympics. Racial discrimination in South Africa was first brought to attention of the International Olympic Committee (IOC) in 1955 by the International Boxing Federation. The issue was tabled at that time, but brought up again, in a more general way, by the Soviet delegate in 1959. Again, no action was taken, the reason being that the IOC chose to apply its nondiscrimination rule only in terms of whether athletes of Olympic caliber were being allowed to participate in the games, and chose not to ask the question of whether racial discrimination had led to there being no black Olympic-caliber athletes.

More explicit South African strictures against mixed teams in international competition and intensified pressure from Third World countries caused the IOC to warn South Africa in 1962 that, if its policies had not changed by 1963, South Africa would be expelled. South Africa did not comply and was excluded from the 1964 Tokyo Olympics. The IOC initially voted to allow a mixed-race team from South Africa to compete in the Mexico games in 1968 but, after many threats of withdrawal from Third World countries, it withdrew the invitation.

More concerted opposition to apartheid had been facilitated by the founding, in 1966, of the Supreme Council for Sport in Africa (SCSA), with a membership of thirty-two African states. This was a semi-autonomous subsidiary of the Organization for Africa Unity, whose members were not only governments but also national Olympic committees. The motives of the SCSA were obviously political and thus ran counter to the principles of the IOC. Nevertheless, the IOC could not ignore the weight of international pressure against it on the apartheid issue and, having suspended South Africa in 1964, finally expelled that country in 1970, the first to be so treated.

While South Africa's expulsion from the Olympic movement was a severe blow to that country, the government was as seriously affected by recurrent 'rugby crises' during the 1970s (Archer and Bouillon, 1982, p. 74). In some ways these crises caused more upheaval within South Africa, owing to the enormous popularity of the sport and the South Africans' prowess at it. Demonstrations at international rugby matches began in the 1960s in New Zealand: 'South Africa's next tour with the All-Blacks, planned for 1967, was cancelled; huge demonstrations ruined the Springboks' tour to Britain in 1969—70, and to Australia in 1971' (Archer and Bouillon,

1982, p. 61). During the 1970s South Africa's rugby isolation was such that the Springboks could rarely tour abroad.

The movement against South African rugby also affected other sports. South Africa was expelled from sporting federations throughout the 1970s: boxing in 1968, wrestling and cycling in 1970, weightlifting in 1972, swimming in 1973, soccer and athletics in 1976 and basketball in 1978. Anger at the refusal of the South African government to admit Basil D'Oliveira (a black expatriate South African) as a member of the 1968 England cricket team led to a 1970 ban on international cricket tournaments with South Africa. The extent of South Africa's isolation was signaled by the signing of the Gleneagles Agreement in 1977, in which all the Commonwealth countries agreed not to sanction international sporting competition involving South Africa.

International pressure forced the South African government to make some minor changes in the political control of sports. In 1970 the government announced that blacks would be allowed to participate in a few sporting events, which would be termed 'multinational' or 'open international' events because they would involve blacks from the newly created 'homelands.' In essence, this policy allowed the different racial groups in South Africa to compete against each other as four separate nations; but only at the 'international' level would mixed sport be tolerated. No mixed-sport or multiracial sport was to be allowed at the club or provincial level. The government has also been careful to facilitate (by the granting of visas) and encourage (by offering tax concessions) the promotion of commercial sport. At this level, a certain amount of racial mixing has been permitted, particularly in golf and tennis.

## Cooptation

We have seen in this chapter that leisure time and space, the target of political control by dominant groups in society, are also the site of resistance to control. Subordinate groups not only resist the colonization of their leisure but just as skillfully use leisure to achieve broader political aims. Chapter 2 indicated that social control of leisure must necessarily stumble over the essential spontaneity of play; it cannot be totally administered without becoming something else and triggering a reaction or a withdrawal by the population against whom it is directed. But the same is true of the resistance to leisure. Leisure rebellions can be coopted for the very same reason they are initially effective—they trade on familiar and everyday artefacts and symbols which are all too likely to be reabsorbed into the mainstream culture. We have also seen that leisure is no more central to political rebels than it is to the authorities and has therefore, with a few exceptions, been relegated to a minor role in political protest. Political rebels, speaking for materially dispossessed groups, are often just as disposed to interpret life and liberation as a matter of material gain as the authorities against whom they struggle. As often as not, the subordinate groups succeed merely in achieving more equal opportunity to compete for the privatized and commercialized leisure the capitalist state encourages.

# 4
# Leisure in the Liberal State: the United States

All democracies assume that there is some private area of human life which should be beyond the scope of legal government regulation. Leisure is firmly placed in this sphere, protected from political influence. Politics, on the other hand, is considered too serious a business to concern itself overmuch with how people entertain themselves. In these societies, as opposed to those governed by totalitarian regimes, there is perennial debate about whether or not leisure is an appropriate issue with which the state should concern itself. The answer to this question will depend to some extent on how the state itself is conceived (it is regarded as more interventionist in some democratic societies than in others), to some extent on how citizenship in general is conceived (some democratic societies have more firmly established ideas about 'entitlements' than others) and partly on how leisure is conceived (the more businesslike and conflict-ridden it becomes, the more likely is the state to be involved).

According to the philosophy of liberalism, the state is the institution that is charged with protecting persons and property and, simultaneously with guaranteeing maximum freedom from interference to each individual. Whether autonomy or self-fulfillment is the primary emphasis, liberalism's belief in the ultimate worth of the individual is expressed in political egalitarianism; if all individuals have intrinsic and ultimate value, then their dignity must be reflected in political institutions that do not subordinate any individual to the will or judgment of another. Freedom thus amounts to non-interference in the life of the individual.

The dominant view in liberal democracies is that leisure is an element of mass culture produced specifically for the market by a specialized 'culture industry.' It is not the role of the state to determine what leisure needs are—although it can protect citizens' rights to leisure by securing them against private monopolies (e.g. in the mass media or landownership): by supplying the infrastructure necessary to maximize individual leisure choices (e.g. roads, parks and lakes); by upholding minimal standards of public health and security; and by ensuring a measure of distributive justice in access to leisure facilities. The state typically limits itself to plugging gaps in the market for leisure services left by private enterprise and to stimulating interest in leisure pursuits. Indeed, the market and its agencies will be jealous of state-supported leisure activities in otherwise profitable fields (as illustrated by the resistance of commercial television to public television) unless the state promises to become an important purchaser or the state functions to fuel demand for commercial leisure.

A philosophy of politics is not the only reason for the minimal involvement of the liberal state in leisure. Not only does liberal philosophy have implications for how we think about the proper role of government. It also has something to say about the meaning of leisure. Political intervention in leisure has generally been more cautious, less conspicuous and less pervasive than in other areas of social life (such as health and welfare) because leisure and privacy are so closely linked. There is great reluctance to see leisure as a legitimate area of social concern for governments. Where the state does intervene, reasons other than those intrinsic to leisure are invoked. Leisure policy will thus be justified in terms of the need to increase worker productivity, to reduce antisocial behavior, to promote economic development, encourage conservation, or prepare for national defense.

Recall the federalist principles upon which the American political system is based, combine this with popular support for individualist values and take into consideration the strength of the private sector, and it should come as no surprise that the state is probably less associated with leisure in the United States than in any other democracy. Americans are left by the government to choose their leisure much as they please and they do not customarily look to their government to meet their leisure needs. Of course, the leisure of Americans is not entirely a private matter. The state has long been active in securing, protecting and managing recreational areas and in providing the infrastructure (chiefly roads) necessary for the enjoyment of those facilities. That these facilities have often been legitimated on grounds other than leisure—conservation, protection of mineral resources, or national defense—does not diminish the impact of the government on active leisure pursuits.

In the United States a federated system is strengthened by a general antipathy to 'big government.' Combined with a powerful patronage system at the municipal level, judicial activism and firm subscription to the philosophy of possessive individualism, this federalism results in a 'hands-off' policy by the government when it comes to leisure. To this should be added the fact that government bureaucrats in the United States lack the prestige and authority of their European counterparts and are not so well protected from private interest groups and powerful lobbies. The result is that government planning for leisure has less legitimacy in the United States than in Europe.

## The Entitlement to Free Time

The bias of liberalism has always been in the direction of liberty rather than equality, even if liberty creates inequality. Politics in the liberal state will be unconducive to the idea that its citizens are entitled to any form of equality except equal treatment before the law. We will not therefore find the 'revolution of rising entitlements' far advanced in the United States with respect to leisure or any other kind of need. However, there has been some acknowledgement that Americans are entitled to some free time, although that acknowledgement has usually been made indirectly, through appeals to greater productivity or safety in the workplace.

Before the Civil War, those seeking to reduce working hours focused on the need for good citizenship. New industrial workers needed time to 'improve themselves' in order to exercise their citizenship rights effectively. The second half of the nineteenth century saw shorter hours being promoted in the interests of health and safety and, ultimately, greater productivity and lower labor costs. Early twentieth-century reformers were joined by those who realized the need to stimulate demand for consumer goods in a mass-production age and who saw increased leisure time as a means of meeting this demand.

Trade unions in their most militant period—from the 1880s to the 1930s—generally included a call for shorter working weeks in their demands. These demands were second only to higher wages in labor's struggle and were seen by most labor leaders as a necessary and integral part of higher wages. On the other hand, union leaders' motives were usually those of work-sharing and reducing unemployment rather than creating leisure, and such demands were usually dropped before the hard bargaining over wage rates and pensions began (Levitan and Belous, 1977, p. 35). American businessmen consistently opposed shorter working hours on 'share the work' grounds, believing that this would result in lower productivity and higher costs. Even Roosevelt initially opposed calls for a thirty-hour week at the beginning of the Depression (Hunnicutt, 1980, p. 208). It should also be remembered that a quarter of the US population still lived and worked on farms in 1930, and no efforts were being made to regulate their working hours.

Legislation to limit the industrial working day was slower in coming to the United States than Britain. Union pressure was largely responsible for the passage of the Adamson Act in 1916, which established the eight-hour day in jobs with federal contracts. The most important piece of working-hours legislation was passed in 1938. The Fair Labor Standards Act mandated overtime pay for work in excess of forty hours a week. This legislation was largely a result of the Depression, when unions had to concern themselves more than ever before about spreading jobs, whatever the wage, and employers had to worry about underconsumption caused by unemployment. It was also part of a more general assumption of responsibility by the New Deal state for stabilizing the economy and promoting its growth.

The development of social security systems and tax-subsidized private pension plans in the United States has provided more leisure time for older Americans. The existing system encourages retirement at 65 by providing income maintenance and by making receipt of benefits conditional on having no wage income (Owen, 1986, p. 78). This is a truly public arrangement for the provision of leisure in that funds are transferred from younger cohorts to provide retirement leisure for the elderly.

## Leisure Services in a Liberal State

The role the liberal state plays in leisure is disguised by the fact that it is usually related to leisure indirectly. A good example is the part played by federal, state and local government in organized play. Athletics in the United States is tied to educational institutions to a degree unknown in other democracies. Although the municipal provision of leisure services might be meager, the local high school or college will boast the most modern and most commodious of facilities. Until recently, the importance attached to sports in American educational institutions rivalled that attached to academics. In this sense, local governments and states have been intimately involved in the provision of leisure services, much more involved than would appear to be the case at first glance. This has important repercussions for the structure of leisure. It means, for example, that leisure pursuits which are regarded as unfit for the school environment are grossly underfunded or ignored. It also means that once an individual has graduated from high school or college it will be difficult to get access to leisure facilities.

The idea that government should assume some responsibility for recreation programs and services became widely accepted in the 1910–20 period. At first, school buildings were used, and not only for reasons of expediency. The teachings of educationists like John Dewey encouraged the view that recreation should be an essential part of children's development. Efforts to combat the rise of commercialized amusements such as pool rooms, bowling alleys, cinemas and dance halls intensified the effort in the 1920s to provide more wholesome leisure facilities. 'More and more states passed laws enabling local governments to operate recreation programs, and between 1925 and 1935, the number of municipal recreation buildings quadrupled' (Kraus, 1978, p. 173). Educators and law-enforcement officials endorsed the view that the bulk of crime, especially among juveniles, resulted from 'wrong' play or simple idleness, so that the local authorities entered not only into the business of providing facilities but also into the regulation of competition from the private sector. 'In city after city, permits were required for operating dance halls, pool parlors, bowling alleys, and places for the sale of liquor' (Kraus, 1978, p. 181). The timing of this state expansion into leisure is significant. The 1920s marked the period of the growth of mass consumption and the emergence of an economic philosophy which no longer looked upon leisure as an impediment to capital accumulation but as a boost to it. This is not to deny that there was within the recreation profession at this time considerable debate as to the value of consumer-oriented leisure. The Progressives who helped form the playground movement and designed physical education curricula for schools were hostile to many 'amusements' as simply being 'entertainment,' not suitably rational or preparatory for work.

This close association between leisure and education (especially the team sports of football, basketball and baseball) has changed its character in recent years. High-school and college athletics now function as a feeder system for the professional game. The earlier concerns for public control over the recreational use of time and space have given way to a concern for the productive control over children's athletic labor. School sports have become spectacles put on by pre-professional athletes. In this sense, they are thoroughly commercialized. On the other hand, the remaining ties to education mean that, to the extent that education is subjected to federal or state regulation (e.g. equal opportunity laws), sport will also be affected.

The impact of government on American sport is, then, mediated by educational institutions. The same could be said for many other areas of leisure. The federal government finds itself caught up in leisure-related issues without necessarily having a clear 'leisure policy.' Protection of the environment, land management (e.g. flood control), provision and maintenance of roads, airports and canals, regulation of mass communications and programs to aid adult education criss-cross and have often contradictory impacts on people's free time. Federal provisions for leisure are thus not an integrated package.

The establishment of the Outdoor Recreation Resources Review Commission in 1958 did represent a beginning in the coordination of outdoor activities. The Commission garnered considerable support from the environmental movement and, in 1962, became a permanent Bureau of the Department of the Interior. Nevertheless, over ninety federal agencies are still involved 'in some aspect of outdoor recreation' alone (US Congress, Senate Committee on the Interior, 1974, pp. 154, 169). The activities undertaken by these agencies tend to be incidental to other missions such as health, education, welfare, land management and historical preservation. Only the National Park Service has recreation as its primary purpose. The ambivalence and uncertainty felt by state officials with regard to government involvement in leisure surfaces when agencies like the US Forest Service (which has multiple functions and objectives) request funds. The recreation part of that request competes with what many in Congress believe is the Forest Service's more fundamental function—the supervision of timber cutting, mineral development and range management. Budget requests for 'timber resource management' are rarely challenged in committee, while recreation requests are almost always reduced. Only about 5 percent of all the money spent in the United States on recreation each year comes from the budgets of government agencies and philanthropic organizations combined, the rest coming from individuals and private corporations. This indicates the strong preference for highly privatized leisure, such as that found in country clubs, sports leagues, gambling and drinking (Kraus, 1978, p. 13).

The economic boom of the 1950s intensified calls for better government planning for leisure as more and more people competed for scarce public goods and exerted mounting pressure on the environment. The states were slow to respond to these calls and were especially reluctant to enter the market for leisure services. Only land that nobody wanted or land deeded to the states by Congress for educational use was set aside for recreational purposes (US Congress, Senate Committee on the Interior, 1974, p. 174). Often, those who had the greatest need for public leisure services and open spaces were precisely those who had the most limited access to them. Local governments were somewhat more willing to spend tax revenues on leisure personnel. A 1977 study revealed that over 2,000 municipal agencies, 1,211 counties and 345 special districts were employing at least one full-time recreation officer. In over 80 percent of the cases the political unit had set up a separate agency for recreation and leisure (Kelly, 1982, p. 386).

Calls for federal action became more urgent as the effects of the urban sprawl of the 1950s became more evident. 'In the suburbs, where more and more people choose to live, man finds himself amid unchecked sprawl and waste, because political entities too often lack the requisite legal and organizational muscle and sometimes the commitment to guide growth' (US Congress, Senate Committee on Interior, 1974, p. 6). However the federal government, like the states, made only limited efforts to improve leisure services. The Land and Water Conservation Act of 1965 had clear recreational goals and provided for the grant of financial aid to states and cities for the acquisition of land and water suitable for recreation. But most of the money was used for non-urban projects and had to be annually requested. It was not until 1968, after major urban riots had occurred, that a $200 million annual appropriation was made to support the conservation effort and the funds targeted on the cities.

The social turmoil of the 1960s resulted in tremendous increases in government spending on all kinds of social programs, including those having to do with leisure. Between 1960 and 1978 federal government spending for recreation in inflation-adjusted dollars rose from $85 million to $718 million. During the stagflation of the 1970s and then as a result of the political shift toward less 'big government' during the Reagan years, federal recreation efforts were drastically reduced. The Bureau of Outdoor Recreation was abolished, and the Land and Water Conservation Fund was all but eliminated. Recreation spending fell from $718 million in 1978 to $538 million in 1983. The policy of the Reagan administration has been to stop the growth of federal park and recreation holdings; to reduce the dollars expended for federal recreational landholdings and recreation programs; and to eliminate financial support to non-federal public recreation agencies (McLellan, 1986, p. 48). Although this policy was certainly designed to help cut government expenditures and lower taxes, it was also intended to reassert the long-standing American principle that the provision and control of leisure services are the responsibility of local rather than the federal government.

## Politics and Amateur Sports

Government policy toward amateur sport has also been fragmented and often contradictory, with myriad congressional committees deliberating sport policy, several administrative agencies seeking to control the conduct of sporting competition at home and abroad, and chronic disagreements between legislative, executive and judicial branches of government. There have also been frequent clashes of opinion and interest between federal and local authorities with respect to sport policy. The President's Council on Physical Fitness and Sport, a purely advisory body, is the only ongoing government agency solely concerned with physical fitness and sport.

The United States amateur sports community is made up of sports organizations which have sprung up over the years to serve varying purposes and to meet different needs. Colleges, high schools, clubs and other amateur athletic organizations frequently conduct programs and competitions in the same sport. Because no real structure exists which serves to define the jurisdictional limits of the various organizations, disputes have occurred with great frequency. In their struggle for power and control over a sport, organizations have frequently told their athletes that if they choose to compete in a rival organization's program they will be declared ineligible for future competition. As the chairman of the President's Commission on Olympic Sports pointed out:

> No clear policy or direction in amateur sports, physical education or physical fitness can be or has been maintained. Incessant organizational squabbles waste time and talent and threaten the fundamental rights of athletes to take part in the most challenging competition for which they are qualified.
> (US Congress, Senate Committee on Commerce, 1977, p. 40)

The two most powerful contending parties for ultimate control over amateur sports in the United States have been the National Collegiate Athletic Association (NCAA) and the Amateur Athletic Union (AAU). The latter has been most firmly linked to international sporting organizations. Indeed, it has in many ways been a 'franchise' of international sporting federations. These two organizations have fought long and hard for control over the United States Olympic Committee (USOC). The USOC, for its part, has been 'drawn into the vacuum created by the unmet needs in US amateur sports' (President's Commission, 1977, p. 17). With the schism between the NCAA and the AAU, the USOC has been forced to function *de facto* as the centralized directorate of amateur sports.

The political conflict at the heart of amateur sports in the United States has weakened the country in international competition and has frequently led to the denial of athletes' rights. The President's Commission on Olympic Sports heard of many instances of athletes being prevented from competing in Olympic trials because of franchise disputes between rival sport organizations. Individual athletes found themselves torn between the desire to compete internationally and the threat that doing so might jeopardize their eligibility for interscholastic athletics when they returned. These disputes became more acrimonious because there existed no central sports directorate to which the contending parties could appeal. By the rules of the international sporting order, a dispute between two organizations as to which should be the national governing body for that sport would normally be appealed to the international federation for that sport. But international federations have been very reluctant to become involved in 'domestic squabbles.' The United States Olympic Committee for its part has been too weak to function as a dispute resolution agency—'despite the fact that many international sports federations look to the National Olympic Committee to certify the best contenders for National Governing Body status' (President's Commission, 1977, p. 17). The rancorous disputes that led, in part, to the formation of the President's Commission typically involved the AAU as the incumbent national governing body and, as the challenging group, an NCAA-backed single-sport federation composed of individuals disenchanted with the AAU's leadership. The sports of gymnastics and basketball did indeed break away from the AAU, aided and abetted by the NCAA, but wrestling and track and field have been less successful in their bid for independence.

The need to centralize amateur sport policy-making and organization in the United States was underlined by some signal failures in international competition. The United States was particularly embarrassed by administrative problems experienced at the 1972 Munich Olympics which diminished its medal total. Blaming the AAU, the NCAA withdrew from the USOC in 1972 in protest over this mismanagement, and returned only in 1978, when the power of the AAU had been much reduced. In 1975 the President's Commission on Olympic Sports was set up with the mandate to determine how best to correct the existing disorganization of amateur sports and improve the country's international performance. Two years later its chairman reported that amateur sports policy in the United States was indeed inadequate and misguided.

In contrast to other successful systems, the US has little in the way of early identification and encouragement of talent in a range of sports. Coaching is often haphazard and unscientific...We have little tradition for selecting national teams or national coaches, except those named a short time before the Olympics or other international competitions.

(US Congress, Senate Committee on Commerce, 1977, p. 42)

Despite this strong criticism, the Presidential Commission concluded that, apart from minor actions such as issuing special Olympic coins and stamps, direct federal intervention in amateur sports was inadvisable—although it did call for the establishment of some kind of central sports authority to settle jurisdictional disputes and better coordinate on a permanent basis the preparation of the United States for international athletic competition.

The Commission's report inspired what eventually became the Amateur Sports Act of 1978. This piece of legislation backed off even further from involving the federal government by rejecting the idea of a central sports authority and, instead, affirmed the role of the USOC as the coordinating body for amateur sports. It reconfirmed the status of the USOC as a nongovernmental, private corporation with a 'charter,' issued by Congress in 1950 under the Title (36) of the United States Code which deals with 'patriotic societies.' However, a more assertive role for the USOC was sketched out in the Act. The USOC was asked to establish national goals and foster 'productive working relationships among sports-related organizations so that those goals can be met.' One of the most important of these goals was a much broader-based advocacy of physical fitness and public participation in sports than hitherto. The USOC was further required to assist in providing and coordinating technical information used in coaching and training athletes and was given a one-time grant of $12 million to develop two Olympic training centers. The USOC was also given the important 'accrediting' power to recognize as representative a national governing body in an Olympic sport.

Certain conditions were placed upon this empowerment of the USOC, the thrust of which was to make administration of sport more democratic. Among the criteria for the recognition of a national governing body were that it be autonomous (that is, not under the control of the AAU, the organization that had hitherto dominated the Olympic Committee), that it equitably represent females and that it have at least 20 percent active, or recently active, athletes on its governing board. The Act in this way sought to democratize and open up the administration of amateur sports.

If the AAU lost power through the Act, so too did the NCAA.

National governing bodies were given the exclusive right to sanction international events. The message was clear that the NCAA could not use its authority to bar a college athlete from interscholastic competition simply because he or she had participated in an event sanctioned by a national governing body. The role of the USOC was thus considerably enhanced vis-a-vis the AAU and the NCAA. However, the Act by no means federalized the USOC. Its status as a self-perpetuating private corporation was reaffirmed, and the resolution of franchise disputes was to be put in the hands of a private agency, the American Arbitration Association. In return for this freedom, the USOC was required to post in the Federal Register advance notice of constitutional changes and to submit annual reports to Congress. It thus functions rather like the Sports Council in the United Kingdom but with considerably more freedom—and with a much greater reliance on philanthropic support and revenues from its constituent organizations.

Besides failing to give statutory authority to the administration of sports, the Amateur Athletic Act also perpetuated the elitism in the existing policy. The USOC was authorized to appoint governing bodies for sports, but only for those sports included in the program of the Olympic or Pan-American games. The intent seemed to be not so much to encourage broad-based participation in non-Olympic sports as to develop world-class athletes for international competition. The failure to budget regular funding was perhaps an even clearer indication of lack of real reform. To provide some money for the Lake Placid Winter Olympics funds were allocated from a program administered by the Economic Development Administration, an agency of the Department of Commerce, on the grounds that Lake Placid is located in an economically depressed area (Nafziger, 1983, p. 92). The 1984 Los Angeles Olympic Games epitomized the American approach to amateur sports in that federal, state and municipal governments were almost totally uninvolved. The USOC relied exclusively on corporate support and private donations in putting on the games.

## Government and the Sports Business

The state has become involved in *professional* sports because they are big business, and to the extent that the government regulates business it will be called upon to regulate professional sports. Sport is regarded as a public trust which must be protected from the ravages of the marketplace, to guarantee the public equal access to it, to help eliminate discrimination, promote fair competition and impose law and order. On the other hand, many people, including many sports business operators and not a few politicians, believe that sports are not strictly a business and should not be regulated in the same way. Sports business owners thrive in an unregulated environment because, under the exclusive contract system that dominated sports for many years, professional athletes could be denied the right to choose which team to play for. Not surprisingly, then, many in the sports business have sought diligently to keep politics out of sport; others adopt the opposite strategy of trying to use the state to protect sport's privileged status.

Congress rarely recognized sport as a substantive legislative issue before 1950. Since then, however, sport has seldom been absent from its deliberations. Congressional concern for sports reached its peak in 1976 when the House of Representatives set up a Select Committee on Professional Sports to hold public hearings on a wide range of public policy issues having to do with sport. While most congressional debate has focused on the monopolistic behavior of professional sports promoters, Congressmen have rarely even considered action that would undermine the privileges of franchise owners or upset the balance of power between owners and players.

No sport issue has been so often deliberated at the federal level as that of the proper application of anti-trust laws to professional team sports. It has been the subject of debate since a New York state court declared in 1914 (in *American League Baseball Club* v. *Chase*) that baseball was not subject to the Sherman Act because 'Baseball is an amusement, a sport, a game that comes clearly within the civil and criminal law of the state, and is not a commodity or an article of merchandise subject to regulation of Congress.' Six years later, Justice Holmes, speaking for the Supreme Court of the United States, affirmed the *Chase* dictum in the landmark *Federal Baseball* v. *National League* case. Although it has been challenged often in the ensuing years, the courts have upheld the 1922 decision, despite the fact that the federal government greatly expanded its powers relating to commerce during the New Deal, and despite the fact that sports such as baseball have become progressively more involved in interstate broadcasting and telecasting.

Why should professional sports leagues be considered cartels in the first place? The reason is that several of the practices in which a professional sports league must engage in order to fulfill its purpose would in almost any other line of business be considered collusion for the purposes of restraint of trade and therefore subject to criminal prosecution. Members of a league do not allow unrestricted competition for employees. Not only do they 'allocate' new employees to respective franchises (the draft) but they also restrict the freedom of existing employees to move to a new franchise (the reserve system). Second, leagues place restrictions on the freedom of new 'firms' to enter the 'industry.' Third, leagues operate on the principle of exclusive marketing territories, restricting the rights of league members to move from one location to another when this would financially disadvantage existing league members. Finally, leagues pool the sale of national broadcasting rights and otherwise restrict broadcasters' rights to games (blackout rules) in order to negotiate more profitable contracts with television networks and more evenly distribute revenues.

Sports team owners and their representatives have consistently argued that their's *is* a unique industry. Baseball commissioner Bowie Kuhn pointed out that

> when you are in a team sport you can't compete the way you can if you are in the steel industry or the bread business or something else where you can put your competitor out of business and if he is gone that is the system and the system will work without him, whereas if you put your competitor out of business by outcompeting him in professional sports you destroy your league and when you destroy your league you destroy the business you operate in. (US Congress, House Select Committee on Professional Sports, 1976, p. 30)

The 'product' that professional sports sells *does* necessitate cooperative rather than independent action between firms. The production of a season of events and a championship requires even closer collaboration. The quality of the product is not independently determined by individual clubs. The commercial success of one team is thus dependent to some extent on the success of the others. Competitive balance is therefore in every team's interest—although each individual club would like to win each year. A league could not be viable without restrictions on entry into it, unlike other industries where it might merely be in the interest of owners for there to be these restrictions. Sports teams do not compete with each other for customers but rather compete with other ways of spending the leisure dollar.

Not surprisingly, the state has been uncertain and inconsistent in its application of anti-trust policy toward professional team sports. The posture of successive administrations is that baseball is an 'anomaly' and that other professional sports *should* be subject to the anti-trust law. Football was explicitly denied the immunity granted baseball in a Supreme Court decision handed down in 1953. Baseball has thus been 'immunized,' an immunity successive Departments of

Justice have questioned and asked Congress to act upon. The courts recognize that there is likely to be more interaction between 'firms' in the sports industry than is perhaps normal (e.g. scheduling, officials, methods of scoring), but have generally adopted the position that the anti-trust laws can be applied on the 'rule of reason' basis. Under this standard, the anti-competitive agreement is identified, its competitive effects are measured and quantified as well as possible, and these are compared against its alleged benefits or justifications. Some of the agreements will therefore be reasonable and some will be unreasonable. Needless to say this results in almost continuous litigation. In professional football, the courts have found restrictions on player mobility to be 'unreasonable' on this count (in 1974 in the Joe Kapp case and in 1975 in the John Mackey case). Such practices, unlike scheduling, were found to be not absolutely necessary to the financial survival of the league. Another kind of 'unreasonable' arrangement is the 1983 National Basketball Association stipulation that a franchise owner cannot 'trade away' first-round draft choices in two consecutive years. This amounts to protecting franchise owners from their own mismanagement, going far beyond the kind of cooperation needed for scheduling and playing-rules changes.

The state has thus chosen to move against professional sports on anti-trust grounds in some cases. On the other hand, it has occasionally seen fit to 'exempt' even non-baseball sports from anti-trust laws. Congressional exemption was granted to permit the merger of the American Football League and the National Football League (NFL) in 1966. Public Law 87-33 (1961) permitted professional sports teams to pool their broadcasting rights to sell them to the highest bidder. This resulted in a fivefold increase in revenues for baseball and an eightfold increase for football in the ensuing eight years. The leagues have jealously guarded this privilege. When cable television began to expand in the late 1970s, existing Federal Communications Commission regulations permitted cable television companies to import distant signals of competing sports contests into major league markets. The major leagues argued that such uncontested cable carriage would have an adverse effect on gate attendance and on the value of the rights negotiation with the major networks and sought to block the growth of cable.

The groups bringing the most pressure on the state to apply anti-trust laws against sports leagues have been the players' associations. Ed Garvey, then executive direction of the National Football League Players' Association, reminded legislators that 'Congress has favored the owners of professional team sports with special privileges over the years without exacting a price for that privilege' (US Congress,

House Select Committee on Professional Sports, 1976, p. 214). His case was typical of players' associations in all the team sports: that the reserve system had been designed to hold salaries down and to maintain control over the professional lives of the players rather than (as the owners alleged) a necessary means of achieving competitive balance between clubs.

The players' associations testified against legislation to immunize professional sports for the purposes of limiting franchise movements (discussed below) on the grounds that any immunization from anti-trust laws would make more likely unreasonable restrictions on player movements through the draft and the reserve system. The players' associations also took this occasion to point out that revenue sharing reduces competition among owners for players and thus depresses wages, because each owner, regardless of his win–loss record, can be assured of about the same revenues.

Another force seeking to clarify the status of professional sports with respect to the anti-trust laws has been municipalities, especially those threatened with the loss of a professional franchise and those desirous of obtaining a franchise in their city but balked by the league's refusal to expand in the interests of maximizing profits. City officials appear to be convinced that major league sports franchises are a valuable asset to the city, not only economically, but also as a boost to morale and as a means of integrating the city. San Francisco city mayor Diane Feinstein observed that the victory parade held when the 'Forty-Niners' won the national football championship represented 'every age group, every racial background, every economic and social value on Earth' (US Congress, Senate Committee on the Judiciary, 1983, p. 135).

Two 1980s cases illustrate how the government can find itself involved in territorial battles in professional sports. When, in 1979, the Oakland Raiders of the National Football League sought to relocate from Oakland to Los Angeles, the NFL owners voted to prohibit the move. The owner of the Raiders and the owners of the Los Angeles Coliseum (the prospective new home of the Raiders) sued the NFL for violation of Section 1 of the Sherman Act. The Raiders alleged that the real reason the NFL opposed the move was that a 'new' franchise in Los Angeles was worth a great deal more to existing owners than moving an existing franchise there and situating a new one in Oakland.

The Raiders' claim was upheld in the district court. The NFL's claim that it was a single firm because some 90 percent of revenues were shared among the league's members was not accepted by the jury. Nor was its argument that, in order to maintain a competitive balance in the league, there had to be much more cooperation than would be warranted among an association of normal business firms. The jury did not see much resemblance between the NFL and a corporation or partnership with several different branches in different cities.

On appeal, the Ninth Circuit Court sided with the jury and the Raiders. It said that the separate franchises in the NFL have individual and conflicting policies and goals regarding investments, personnel recruitment, concessions, profitable playing locations and so on. They maintain separate entity structures and separate books and records—and they do not share liabilities. Furthermore, the court said, the NFL had developed no clear guidelines for deciding when a move was injurious to itself, the fans, or the community. It added that not only had the NFL failed to prove its case on technical grounds, but it had acted through 'whim, malice and caprice' against the Raiders' controversial and outspoken owner.

In making its judgment, the appeals court did 'grant' the NFL considerable powers in the restriction of mobility in the league; it affirmed the league's right to deny transfer of ownership of franchises, to decline to add new clubs, to assess compensation when one club is allowed to invade another's territory, to share gate receipts and broadcast revenues and to pool resources in order to bolster ailing franchises. The court even granted the league the right to prevent franchise movements, but asserted that the league's rule that 21 out of 28 owners approve such movements was unconstitutional. A simple majority vote would have been legal.

This typically mixed message was repeated when the city of Oakland asked the courts to allow it condemn and purchase the Raiders under its power of eminent domain and to operate the team itself or resell it to private parties who would keep the club in Oakland. The city's Chamber of Commerce calculated the value of the Raiders to the city at $36 million in extra business each year. In addition, the city argued that the Coliseum in which the Raiders played had been built for the purpose of housing a football team (in 1966) and that a service debt of over $1.5 million faced the city beyond the year 2000. The Raiders denied this claim in court, arguing instead that the Oakland Coliseum was not purpose-built and could make a profit without a football team. The courts eventually denied the city's claim of eminent domain, saying that Oakland had not convincingly demonstrated that the football franchise was essential to the city's economy. But it did not deny that the claim of eminent domain over a sports franchise was appropriate.

The 1984 relocation of the Baltimore Colts to Indianapolis did not provoke a law suit by the NFL because the owners, chastened by their defeat in the Oakland Raiders case (not to mention nearly $50 million in punitive damages), chose not to prohibit the move. And the city of Baltimore's claim of eminent domain over the franchise was quickly denied. The mayor of Baltimore had complained that, when a major sports team leaves a city, 'It is the equivalent of us losing a major industry' (US Congress, House Committee on Energy and Commerce, 1985, p. 33). One of the Senators from Maryland argued before the same House committee that sports is not 'simply another business,' while the other pointed out that 'the sports industry enjoys...a very preferred status under the antitrust laws...this preferred status is...responsible for the artificial scarcity of sports teams' and that, in return, individual franchises should not be granted the same freedom to move as businesses, which do not enjoy this preferred status.

The NFL did not join in the eminent domain suits brought by Oakland or Baltimore, fearful that success might be a precedent for communities to block any franchise moves approved by the league, nor did it support legislation introduced in 1984 that would have made franchise moves more difficult. The NFL testified against the Professional Sports Team Community Protection Bill, seeing it as an invasion of the right of partnerships to conduct their own business affairs and arguing that it should be free to regulate franchise movements itself (and thereby asking that Congress consider legislation that would prevent further rulings such as those in the Oakland case). The Bill, which was never enacted, would have banned all franchise moves unless they were considered necessary by the league and proposed an arbitration procedure in case of disputes between the league and an individual owner. It also stipulated criteria (such as stadium adequacy, fan support, financial support from public agencies and net operating losses) to be used in judging a franchise's right to move.

Franchise location issues have not been confined to football. In 1985 a case was finally settled in which the Ralston-Purina Company, owners of the National Hockey League (NHL) St Louis Blues, filed suit against the NHL when the league prohibited the sale of the franchise to a Canadian group of businessmen who wanted to move the club to Saskatoon. The case was dropped when the franchise was sold to a California businessman who agreed to keep the club in St Louis.

The problem Congress and the courts encounter in trying to regulate commercial sports is that professional sports leagues fall somewhere between a wholly private enterprise existing in a fully competitive market and a public utility. The 'free market,' keep-politics-out-of-sport argument would run as follows. The anti-trust laws exist to prevent private groups from taking over the regulation of commerce, a power the Constitution gives to Congress. The American tradition is that if regulation is required in the public interest, it must be done by a politically responsible agency and not by a private group biased by a powerful self-interest. With respect to professional sports, if there were a genuine need to protect the public interest by limiting competition between firms one would expect that the authority to regulate would be entrusted to a federal sports commission (much like the Federal Trade Commission or the Federal Communications Commission) whose members would include representatives of the cities and the fans, not just the teams' owners. Moreover, and consistent with the Constitution, one would expect the authorizing legislation to lay down criteria for the exercise of power and to provide to affected parties an opportunity for a hearing. One would normally expect that the decisions of the agency would be subject to judicial review. One would also normally expect that the profits of the firms protected from competition for public policy reasons would be subject to control by the agency.

We can see how far removed from this position sport policy in the United States has been. The courts and Congress have, by and large, allowed the leagues to function as cartels, while also allowing each individual operation to consider itself an independent business for accounting and tax purposes. Thus Congressmen find themselves arguing *for* legislation to leave sports alone—a seemingly contradictory position. The co-sponsor of the Major League Sports Community Protection Bill, Howell Heflin, argued that 'the best way to solve this problem [of franchise moving against a city's will] is within the league: give the NFL the authority, give them a chance to solve their own problems, allow them an opportunity to clean their own dirty linen' (US Congress, Senate Committee on the Judiciary, 1983, p. 3). This is an argument to immunize the NFL from anti-trust prosecution in the name of keeping politics out of sports! The Bill's sponsors, in seeking to clarify the intent of Congress with respect to the applicability of anti-trust laws to sports, were arguing that the public interest in preventing monopoly and price fixing was superseded by the public interest in franchise stability. The owners and their representatives have bitterly opposed federal intervention; baseball commissioner Ueberroth testified that 'It is not the task of the federal government to intervene in decisions by sports leagues; and football commissioner Rozelle argued that 'there is little or nothing in recent sports league history to warrant governmental control or direction of sports league operations' (US Congress, Senate Committee on Commerce, 1985, pp. 57, 64). But they have not hesitated to seek legislative action to protect their unique position.

At the federal level, franchise location poses anti-trust problems. At the local government level, sports teams pose special problems having to do with their peculiar status midway between public utilities on the one hand and economically important corporations on the other. Those who see sports franchises as public utilities point not only to the impact of a sports team on a city's national image and on its citizens' morale but also to the amount of public funds that are used to subsidize the franchise. The semi-public status of sports franchises is well illustrated in a case which occurred in 1983 when the New York Yankees, because of delays in renovations at their stadium, proposed to play their opening games in Denver. The stadium sought to prohibit this in court, and the State Supreme Court went along with this, arguing thus:

> The Yankee pinstripes belong to New York like Central Park, like the Statue of Liberty, like the Metropolitan Museum of Art, like the Metropolitan Opera, like the Stock Exchange, like the lights of Broadway...Any loss represents a diminution of the quality of life here, a blow to the city's standing at the top, however narcissistic that perception might be.
> (*New York Times*, January 11, 1983, Section 2, p. 6)

In return for locating and remaining in the city, sports teams have been able to extract sizable financial concessions from municipal governments persuaded of their public utility. Between 1960 and 1983 twenty-five NFL clubs have managed to secure improvements in the stadiums in which they play either by extensive renovations to the existing structure or by moving to a new stadium altogether, in each case public funds or public guarantees of financing playing a major role in the construction (US Congress, Senate Committee on the Judiciary, 1983, p. 58). In effect, cities bid against each other for major league teams. The owner of the Baltimore Colts managed to get the 'blue laws' against Sunday morning trading changed so that games could begin at 1.00 p.m. on Sundays (to suit television) rather than 2.00 p.m. The city also negotiated with the franchise continual improvements in the stadium in order to try to keep the team. It even offered to float a $22 million bond issue to build a new stadium in return for a fifteen-year lease and, when that commitment was refused, spent $7.5 million on renovations in return for a six-year lease. City officials had calculated that the departure of the team would cost the city $35 million. When the NFL Eagles threatened to leave Philadelphia the city council agreed to add fifty luxury boxes to Veterans' Stadium and to defer $600,000 annual rent for an (undisclosed) number of years. It also undertook to improve practice facilities, aid promotions and provide free game security. In return the club signed a lease extending to the year 2011. The threat of the departure of the St Louis Cardinals baseball team prompted the city government to promise to build a new $100 million stadium. As part of the agreement to construct the Hubert H. Humphrey Metrodome in downtown Minneapolis, the NFL itself guaranteed the stadium a professional football tenant for at least the next thirty-five years. The city of Oakland offered the Raiders reduced rent and expenses, a share of the concessions revenue, the construction of private stadium boxes and the expansion of the stadium's seating capacity in return for an extended lease, but the Raiders' owner would not sign. Johnson (1982, p. 210) estimates that between 1980 and 1982, 13 of the 42 American communities hosting major league sports franchises were confronted with demands for increased sport subsidies. 'Almost without exception, removal of the franchise from the host community was an implied, if not explicit, threat underlying negotiations.'

The demand by communities for sports franchises far outstrips their supply because of the refusal of the leagues to expand. The owners' joint control over the number and location of franchises has thus given each individual owner tremendous leverage over cities desirous of attracting or keeping a franchise. This leverage is especially powerful given the social problems already caused by industrial decline and regional migration. A Congressman whose district includes Oakland argued that 'To lose a team implies that the community is in trouble or is in a deteriorating market, and this, of course, becomes a self-fulfilling prophecy' (US Congress, Senate Committee on the Judiciary, 1983, p. 21). The possession of a famous sports franchise is, once again, attached to municipal pride and becomes a weapon in the competition between cities in different regions of the country for jobs and investments. Congress, by its inaction in regulating the siting of sports franchises, is willing to see cities act as public entrepreneurs, competing for sports businesses on much the same terms as they compete for any other kind of business. In the long run, despite almost continuous congressional discussion of these issues, the state has seen fit to leave professional sports alone and leave it to the parties concerned to settle by litigation, and on an almost *ad hoc* basis, the myriad anti-trust issues that have arisen over the past fifty years.

## The Market and the State

The tension between privatized and public forms of leisure in the United States is evident from this brief survey of current developments. Americans, at least in so far as this is reflected in public policy, remain largely committed to the idea of privatized leisure. The marketplace means flexibility and adaptability in the provision of leisure services; it is an efficient and politically 'neutral' method of rationing scarce leisure opportunities; it seems to be the only way leisure activities high in capital investment but low in volume of use (e.g. sailing) can be provided; it strongly reinforces ideals of personal freedom and individual choice; and, by ensuring that only those who pay for services get to use them, it eliminates free riding.

On the other hand, the market model *is* inefficient and inequitable in some respects. It perpetuates in the leisure world the class, race and gender inequalities found in the society at large; it provides individual benefits more easily than collective goods; it rarely generates leisure opportunities requiring long-term planning and heavy capital investment; it is unable to transfer between present known uses (e.g. motorcross racing) and unanticipated future uses (e.g. soil conservation). Perhaps most important of all from the standpoint of the politics of leisure, the market model cannot distinguish between price value and use value; land will be converted to theme parks if the price is right regardless of the long-term social utility of the land (Burch, 1984).

These deficiencies in the pure market model are only one reason we can anticipate a continued role for government in leisure, and an even more prominent role in the world of sport. First, professional sport is becoming increasingly competitive—off the field—with rivalry not only between leagues in the same sport but between sports, a rivalry intensified by stakes offered by the mass media. This competition heightens the 'big-business' aspect of sport and thus generates more frequent disputes, for example, over possible violation of anti-trust laws or over the public duty owed by a sport corporation to a community. The trend in sport away from 'local' individual ownership toward corporate (often absentee) ownership undermines the claim by sports promoters that theirs is essentially a 'hobby' or a private pastime and reinforces the idea that sport is a business to be regulated like any other. Third, labor relations in modern sports now resemble those in other industries and become subject to the law pertaining to all collective bargaining and employment rights.

Second, the increasingly 'mass' or public character of sports makes them more vulnerable to general statutes pertaining to civil rights. Indeed, in the dispute over civil rights for athletes, the state can play an active role in helping decide whether sport is private or public. A case in Canada in 1976 nicely illustrates this point. A team in the

Ontario Softball League was refused permission by the League to play a 9-year-old girl. The coach of the team filed a complaint against the League with the Ontario Human Rights Commission. The Commission agreed that discrimination had occurred. Failure to reach a settlement resulted in the establishment of a Board of Inquiry. The principal legal question being addressed was not whether a girl should be allowed to play on a boys' sports team but whether an amateur sports organization like the Ontario Rural Softball Association fell within the definition of public services and facilities in provincial human rights legislation. The Board found that the Association was public, in large part because it received government funding for its work and played on municipal parks. The fact that this case was lost on appeal on the grounds that the ORSA *was* private only points up the active role of the state in defining the nature of sport in democracies. Under amendments to the Ontario Human Rights Code made in the early 1980s, sport was specifically exempted from regulations that prohibited sex discrimination, thus placing it firmly back into the private sphere—and signaling a defeat for feminists (Hall and Richardson, 1983, p. 19).

Finally, increased international competition in athletics, and the improvements in mass communications technology that make the results of this competition instantly and widely known, will further involve the state in sports. Although government supervision and subsidy of international sport has a long history, the decision by the Soviet bloc countries to use this method of gaining a voice on the world stage has necessitated a response by Western countries. The long delay of the United States in fully mobilizing sports for diplomatic purposes testifies to the strength of its commitment to the market model of leisure provision and to the ideology of amateurism. However, there are clear signals that United States will in future search more diligently for methods of assuring respectable sport performance in international competition, albeit methods that do not violate the spirit of capitalism.

We can expect leisure to become increasingly politicized in the future. Despite recent efforts to privatize many aspects of social life, there is little sign that collective consumption will diminish in importance. State-managed or at least state-regulated amenities—transportation, housing, utilities and education—have become central elements in the lives of people, especially those living in cities. Leisure services—parks, museums, pools and playgrounds—now occupy a secure place among this list of necessary amenities. Struggle continues to take place over the provision of these amenities, a struggle that is ultimately a conflict between capital and labor over the proportion of wealth produced by the economy going to collective provision, but this struggle is now in many respects more important than that which occurs in the workplace. The 'contested terrain' is often literally a field. Many groups in society now have nowhere else to turn except to the state for the satisfaction of their more active needs. So long as collective consumption is vital to the well-being of large groups in the population, there will be a politics of leisure even in societies that continue to propound a philosophy of keeping politics out of sport.

# 5
# Leisure in the Welfare State: the United Kingdom

Social democratic states like the United Kingdom have 'mixed economies' in which some aspects of production and distribution have been nationalized. In such regimes, support is given to the notion of the 'public household' which exists alongside the private household and the market; it is the agency for the satisfaction of public needs and public wants, as against private wants (Bell, 1973, p. 220). As 'head' of the public household, government is essentially involved in the direction of the national economy through tax and monetary policies, transfer payments to redistribute income, social security schemes and various forms of subsidy. The government commits itself to redressing the impact of economic and social inequalities and in so doing creates a welfare state. Inevitably, the welfare state becomes an arena for the fulfillment not only of clearly public needs but also of private and group wants. Claims on the community take the form of 'entitlements'—to decent housing, affordable health care, old age security, unemployment compensation and the like. 'Entitlements' is another word for what T. H. Marshall (1950, p. 11) called social rights, 'the whole range from the right to a modicum of economic welfare and security to the right to share to the full in the social heritage and to live the life of a civilized being according to the standards prevailing in society.' Social rights thus include an equal claim to a 'style of life' as well as money income. The recognition that everyone has a right to a certain style of life interferes with the market principle of capitalism—just as an increase in the naked function of the market interferes with the enjoyment of egalitarian social rights.

In the welfare state, leisure also comes to be looked upon as an entitlement, a service to be delivered by the state, much like health care. The enjoyment of leisure is considered a basic individual right. The public expects state intervention in leisure and sees leisure provision as an important social service, even if people do not make full use of the amenities available. The leisure citizen, to whom benefits accrue as of right, stands in contrast to the leisure consumer, who must earn them in the marketplace. However, in such 'mixed economies' there is rarely any coherent leisure policy or program at the national level, many 'taste publics' exist, and private commercial organizations still dominate the provision of leisure services, while the state plays a secondary role. The state is torn between improving the cultural level of the public on the one hand (a kind of paternalism to which welfare statism is subject) and allowing the public to find its own level on the other. The result is a kind of cultural democracy providing 'entertainment' rather than culture.

## The Entitlement to Free Time

The state makes its impress on leisure to the extent that it helps determine the length and distribution of the time available for leisure. In other words, working-hours legislation has been an important shaper of leisure.

> The greatest 'social control'—if one wants to use the words—available to capitalism is the wage relationship itself—the fact that, in order to live and reproduce, the worker must perpetually resell his or her labor power. The necessity to obtain work, to remain fit enough for work and to make ends meet is far more important than any packaged consumer ideology which succeeds in intruding upon the worker's weekly or nightly period of rest and recuperation. Leisure time is clearly constricted by the type and hours of work.
> 
> (Stedman-Jones, 1983, p. 48)

Working-hours legislation rarely has the provision of leisure as its primary motive. Instead, it is chiefly intended to protect the vulnerable segments of the population from exploitation or to spread limited employment opportunities among a greater number of workers. However, a secondary motive has usually been to combat the immoral behavior long working hours are thought to encourage, especially among youth and women. Working-hours legislation thus has both direct and indirect effects on leisure.

The organization of work into the factory system did not so much save time, since it took both work and spare time out of their homogenized state and separated them into chunks. Where previously work and play had been tied together through community relations, the social organization of work through the wage contract decisively split labor time from non-labor time. The legislation that followed merely legitimated this, being intended more to regularize and synchronize working time than to reduce its overall amount. The 'ten hours' movement, in crystalizing the working day and rendering it more suitable for a machine age, also crystalized leisure time.

In the first half of the nineteenth century the typical English working day lasted twelve hours, even in the best regulated factories. As a result of reform agitation, Parliament established a 60-hour maximum work week for female factory operatives in 1850, which was reduced to 56 hours in 1874. The building industry adopted a 54-hour week for all workers in the 1870s, and engineering followed suit in the 1880s. The general trend of working-hours legislation since then has been to reduce the number of hours that work is permitted before overtime has to be paid or before another shift must be recruited.

Since the turn of the century, English working-hours legislation has been more or less in step with that of other industrialized countries. By 1914 legislation had reduced the industrial workday in North America and Europe to ten hours. The 48-hour week was general practice in Europe by 1922, in industry at least. The socialist government in France introduced a 40-hour week for industrial workers as well as twelve days' annual paid leave as early as the 1930s, but the reform did not survive the beginning of the Second World War.

The vast majority of modern capitalist countries now have statutory limitations on hours of work, applicable to both industry and commerce. In a few countries there is no generally applicable legal limit, but collective agreements, wage orders, or practice have effectively limited hours of work (Evans, 1969, p. 45). The policy of the International Labor Organization of encouraging legislation to settle hours of work by collective bargaining means that hours of work are longer where unions are weak.

Holidays, or vacations, have also been legislated. In Britain the Bank Holiday Act of 1870 gave at least one holiday in addition to Christmas Day and Good Friday.

> The very concept of the bank holiday was a significant step forward in the provision of a nationally and legally determined leisure time for all. This was not the only provision for free time (most of which was secured by industrial agitation and local custom), but the importance of the Bank Holiday Act was that it secured free time even for those without the collective and industrial muscle to insist on it...It was a major innovation in

establishing the principle that the state had a role to play in safeguarding free time.

(Walvin, 1978, p. 66)

The extension of the Bank Holiday Act in 1875 to cover docks, Customs houses, Inland Revenue offices and bonding warehouses made it much more likely that the parliamentary holidays would become nationally observed (Cunningham, 1980, p. 143). By 1938 most European countries had legislation providing for one week of paid vacation a year. By 1969 some thirty-five countries were providing by statute for a minimum holiday of two or more weeks (Evans, 1969, p. 50). The French, already enjoying a month's vacation, were guaranteed five weeks of vacation in 1983, with the stipulation that one week be taken separately from the other four to avoid August crowding. In Britain the Holidays with Pay Act (1938) made available by statute what had been common in professional and white-collar occupations since the 1870s. The relatively affluent 1960s saw some dramatic improvements in holiday benefits. As late as 1963 only 3 percent of manual workers covered by national agreements or statutory wage orders were entitled to a basic holiday of more than two weeks. By 1971 this figure had risen to 72 percent (House of Lords, Select Committee on Sport and Leisure, 1973, p. xiv).

The impact of the state on working hours should not be exaggerated. British working hours have been largely settled at the local level by collective bargaining. The general introduction of the forty-hour basic working week in the late 1960s and the increase in the proportion of industrial workers entitled to three weeks' holiday with pay during the same period did not come about by legislation but by negotiation at the local level (White, 1980, p. 3). Much the same could be said for the United States, where the eight-hour day, the two-day weekend and the two-week vacation were achieved largely through a combination of collective bargaining and changes in wage rates and the demand for labor (Owen, 1986, p. 4).

States can also shape leisure time by determining the age at which individuals can cease full-time work and still enjoy pension benefits. In Britain, while the state pension age (65 for men and 60 for women) has remained the same for forty-five years, the average age of retirement has decreased as fewer people choose to work beyond pensionable age.

## The Political Organization of Leisure Services

Throughout most of its brief history, the state's involvement with leisure has been highly decentralized and indirect. Local governments have been given the major role in administering leisure services; and whenever the state has become involved, it has chosen to do so indirectly, through voluntary organizations or quasi-public bodies. In this section I shall discuss both of these features of the relation between the state and leisure because they help us understand the role of leisure in the welfare state.

*States and Local Governments*
Historically, political intervention in leisure in the United Kingdom has been chiefly the responsibility of local government. Cities were the first suppliers of, and exercised the most control over, public leisure services. It was natural that the growing need in late nineteenth-century Britain for publicly owned leisure facilities would be met by local authorities.

> The public order functions of borough councils had long enabled them to regulate, control and even prohibit entertainments in public places (especially streets and markets) or those connected with the drink trade (and subsequently music and dancing)…towns increasingly sought special by-law powers from Parliament and Local Government Boards for the regulation of stalls, shows and processions, and for more effective control of the large music halls and other manifestations of an increasingly capital-intensive entertainment industry, which were proliferating rapidly and spreading even into the small towns by the 1890s.
> (Walton, 1983, p. 160)

City fathers came to believe that urban discontents could be resolved by the more assiduous public provision of leisure services. The cities, and not the national government, were forced to play this role because rural interests were reluctant to see urban unrest as their problem. It is also probable that the heavy reliance on local philanthropists in the nineteenth century made an especially strong case for local control. Only in the 1890s did 'the private philanthropists who identified a duty to spread "liberal culture" and social harmony begin to give way to, or work through, municipal bodies' (Walton, 1983, p. 162).

In the last quarter of the nineteenth century, municipal authorities took on the role of civilizers and educators for the urban masses. Outdoor recreation did not take the lead in this effort, nor was it considered the most important. That place was accorded museums, libraries and galleries because these fitted best the reformers' opinions about properly uplifting leisure-time use. However, recreation was included in efforts to improve hygiene, sanitation, housing, education, utilities and transportation. By the turn of the century, cities like Birmingham, Manchester and Liverpool had become important employers in their own right, and they could draw on expanding financial resources to fund leisure services as their ratable values and borrowing powers rose. Until 1945 their political supremacy in the provision of leisure services was unchallenged.

The involvement of the British government in leisure services before the First World War was therefore extremely limited. The most ubiquitous form of leisure, music, was virtually untouched by the state. 'In music in its various forms the English people found a pleasure and a recreation which surpassed all others, and it was not to be seriously dislodged until the inroads of broadcasting and cinema after the Great War' (Walvin, 1978, p. 97). Most music was private—informal singing in homes, clubs, choral societies and institutes—and much of it was communal: church music, works bands and choral societies. 'Sheet music was everywhere' (Walvin, 1978, p. 108). Only the music halls were essentially public and likely to bump up against the forces of law and order.

Nor did the rise of mass sports owe much to the state. Urbanization, the spread of mass transportation (particularly within cities) and increasing affluence and free time, seized upon by entrepreneurs anxious to capitalize on a growing market for sporting goods, were the major causes of the rise of mass sports such as soccer and cricket. Indeed, the scarcity of municipal parks probably contributed to the growth of spectatorism. The new commercialized, bureaucratized sports represented a tamer and more disciplined form of the ancient games and fitted well the discipline and rigors of a clock- and machine-dominated life. The forces of industrialism, combined with free Saturday afternoons and entrepreneurial guile, led to this social revolution, and politics hardly entered into the picture at all.

In the management of leisure services the United Kingdom lagged far behind those countries, like France, with a long history of centralized government. 'It may be suggested that French Governments over the last half century have come nearer to devising and implementing a more comprehensive and coordinated leisure strategy and have sought to exercise a tighter control over leisure than their counterparts in Great Britain' (Hantrais, 1984, p. 131). And yet even in France there was no national sports program before the Second World War, although the *loisirs populaires* of the Popular Front era did attract considerable support. The socialist Blum government offered cheap holiday travel and undertook a major construction program to improve sports facilities. A junior minister for leisure and sport was included in the administration. These initiatives were explicitly designed to steal a march on Hitler's 'strength through joy' program and Mussolini's *dopolavoro*. For the first time 'the recreational activities of the working class...received official sanction and support' (Holt, 1981, p. 209). The Second World War and the fall of the socialist government put a halt to these efforts to organize people's free time, and state policy toward leisure in France remained in disarray under a succession of conservative governments until 1977 when a report was issued calling on the administration to adopt a more active policy on leisure, chiefly by encouraging the staggering of vacation periods and the improvement of tourist amenities. The socialist government that assumed power in 1981 increased the attention given to leisure. It aimed at reducing leisure inequalities by channeling resources to underprivileged groups. A Ministry of Free Time was created in 1981.

With some considerable lag in time, the political administration of leisure in the United Kingdom has followed that of most other Western European countries, although it has not centralized to the degree found in France. Most European governments exercise closer supervision of local government officials, who often take on an additional role of agent for the national government in the community, usually in return for grant aid. 'The general pattern in European nations has been to view leisure as a national or federal responsibility, as a means of promoting ideology and serving important national goals' (Kraus, 1978, p. 198). One result has been that European countries have far outstripped the United Kingdom in expenditures on leisure. Expenditure on physical recreation per capita between 1945 and 1973 averaged 50 pence a year in the United Kingdom, a third of the amount spent in France and West Germany and a quarter of the amount spent in the Netherlands (House of Lords, Select Committee on Sport and Leisure, 1973, p. lvii).

Local governments in Britain are still the major public sector providers of leisure resources. But changes in political thinking and in the relation between central and local governments, especially since 1945, have expanded the role of the state. The central government is now likely to include generalized oversight of leisure services in its mandate to local governments and to make the provision of leisure facilities a condition of grant aid. Thus the central government can demand that certain matters be covered in local government land-use planning. The Education Act of 1944 had already placed a duty on local education authorities to secure the provision for their areas of adequate facilities for leisure-time pursuits. The Town and Country Planning Act of 1968 required that local authorities always consult the Countryside Commission to ensure that leisure facilities be protected or provided.

Centralization was also the goal of the 1973 House of Lords Select Committee on Sport and Leisure. It complained about the chaotic state of sports organization in the United Kingdom, with over one hundred governing bodies, each managing its own affairs, competing for resources and facilities, and only very inadequately coordinated through the voluntary efforts of the Central Council for Physical Recreation (CCPR): 'The coordination between these bodies is weak, sometimes non-existent, and they have little sense of common purpose' (p. xxvi). A stronger central coordinating body, conceivably a regular department of government, was urgently needed to resolve this problem. On the other hand, the last thing the Committee wanted was a highly centralized sport directorate similar to that found in communist societies. 'Within the public sector, local government is better equipped to assume...responsibility [for recreation] than central government—they are closer to the people whose demands call for their assistance and they respond to local wishes' (p. xxxii).

Despite the growing power of the Sports Council and the recent appointment of a Minister for Sport, no political party has formulated a coherent policy for sport, although each has been more forthcoming on the arts—a topic closer to middle-class concerns. 'So policy is formed by a combination of Sports Council action, ministerial whim and —crucially—local authority policy and spending patterns' (Whannel, 1983, p. 92). Government officials tend to cater to existing demand (usually articulated by more active and 'elite' users) and to ignore latent demand or the wider infrastructural supports necessary to meet it. For example, the Sports Council is able to fund the building of sports centers but can do little about the local government reluctance to fund mass transportation necessary for their widespread and equitable use. 'Only 2 per cent of the visitors to Rugby sports centre go by bus: the centre is so poorly served by public transport that a journey there often entails not only switching buses but also a long walk: on the other hand over 25 per cent of visits made to the Islington sports centre, which has many convenient routes serving it, were by public transport' (Hillman and Whalley, 1977, p. 35). In rural areas, recreation facilities are almost inaccessible after the contraction of rural rail and bus routes. When only two-thirds of British families own a car (in inner-city areas the proportion falls to between 20 and 50 percent) access to public pleasure grounds will be restricted to the wealthy (Groome, 1985, p. 100). 'Leisure effects' are caused (often unintentionally) by a range of ostensibly non-leisure pursuits: 'it is obvious that decisions concerning transportation, housing, education, broadcasting, income, unemployment and welfare have fundamental implications for the nature and content of modern leisure' (Coalter, 1984, p. 21). The Sports Council acknowledges that many groups lack access to sports centers, but it clearly does not look upon them as community resources. So long as it simply sees them as being 'for sport,' they will be used by those for whom sport is a conventional and attractive cultural choice (Clarke and Critcher, 1985, p. 136). Ironically, the House of Lords Select Committee on Sport and Leisure (1973, p. xxiii) argued that, precisely because it was so difficult to predict how people would like to spend their leisure time, private enterprise would always be able to meet leisure needs most efficiently, all but ignoring the fact that much leisure activity is 'supply led.'

The drift toward centralization of leisure policy and practice has no doubt been impeded by the low political priority of leisure issues, by the diffusion of leisure concerns through many other established government ministries, by the largely uncontroversial nature of most leisure policies and, not least, by the long tradition of decentralization of leisure provision, stretching back to the Baths and Washhouses Act of 1846 enabling local authorities to provide baths for swimming and recreation. Ironically, local government efforts on the leisure front tend to have been well integrated, especially since the administrative reforms of the 1970s. But central government direction of these scattered efforts, other than in the field of educational facilities, has been permissive. Only recently and only in Scotland and Northern Ireland has a legal obligation to provide physical recreation been imposed upon local authorities.

*Voluntarism*

As had been true at the local level, the national oversight of leisure service relied heavily on voluntarism, on inputs from private individuals. Leisure policy at the national level suffered badly from a political reluctance to become directly involved in providing leisure opportunities. Before 1945 the Labour Party, despite the influence of the Fabians, had no official policy on culture and leisure. In any case, during its two short terms in office Labour was plunged into the management of economic crises and unemployment. The activities of Hitler, Stalin and Mussolini further weakened the Fabian case for state and local government planning of any kind. The Conservative governments were more than content to rely on private initiatives in the sphere of leisure.

The attitude of 'the establishment' toward the role of the state in leisure is nicely illustrated by the early history of radio. The airwaves were looked upon as a public trust, and the BBC was from the outset determinedly non-commercial. In that sense, the BBC was anti-capitalist and had no parallel in the United States. Service was, however, very limited. There was no Sunday morning service, so that people would not be tempted to refrain from going to church, and there was no news before 6.00 p.m., so that newspapers would not suffer 'unfair' competition.

The BBC was not, then, expected to cater to popular taste. But neither was it a government agency. Instead it was a quasi-public body given a mandate to educate the public in core British values regarded as being so self-evident they needed no justification. Radio was not expected to be entertaining. The 1928 *BBC Handbook* insisted that 'each individual member of an audience...must give his or her best receptive faculties if the full entertainment value is to be received and appreciated.' The BBC discouraged background listening: 'the BBC deliberately left silence between programs to discourage casual listeners' (Frith, 1983, p. 107). The government also used the radio to structure people's leisure time. 'The BBC Sunday, for example, reflected not only Reith's Protestantism, but also his staff's wider set of assumptions about the place of the weekend in the organization of family life' (Frith, 1983, p. 112). Sundays were assumed to be a time of quiet relaxation around the family hearth, a reward for the week of hard work just completed and preparation for the week ahead. The state was therefore playing a very active, albeit understated, role in molding a national community along middle-class lines.

> To become a BBC listener was to join a club (children could do so literally) which clearly excluded people with bad radio manners— the tap listeners, the passive consumers. The I/we/you of the BBC announcer was, therefore, subtly arranged. The message was that the BBC was honoured to enter your home; the assumption was that your home was a particular kind of place; the promise was that if it wasn't, the BBC, by entering it, could make it so...Children's Hour with its BBC Aunts and Uncles is the most direct example.
>
> (Frith, 1983, p. 122)

The BBC set the tone for the Arts Council and Sports Council formed after the Second World War. The BBC promoted the idea of a public service corporation, established and licensed by the state, but distanced from direct day-to-day control by the government. This kind of self-governing professionalism, with its equality between colleagues, ethical stance toward clients and apolitical character, was thought to transcend class divisions without at the same time encouraging state bureaucracy. The BBC was, in fact, the result of a bargain struck between state and capitalist interests in terms of a limited separation of powers. The more typical solution in Western European societies of a similar size was direct state regulation of broadcasting, leading, in many cases, to direct state regulation of broadcasting production.

This unique 'public service' definition of the BBC lasted until the mid-1950s, when it was challenged by, and made competitive with, a commercial television network. The Independent Television Authority, later the Independent Broadcasting Authority (IBA), was another kind of 'bargain,' in this case weighted much more heavily in favor of private capital. The Authority was public in legal status but depended for its income on its contracted companies to whom it leased airtime. Both the BBC and the IBA are intended to be independent of the government of the day, although each is staffed by a complicated patronage system that ensures neither will be democratic or representative of popular opinion in any straightforward way.

State policy toward outdoor leisure was very similar to that adopted for radio, except that there was even more reliance on voluntary input. Efforts to establish a national sports directorate for the United Kingdom began in 1935 with the establishment of the Central Council for Recreation and Training, later renamed the Central Council for Physical Recreation (CCPR). Although it received a small grant from the Board of Education and enjoyed royal patronage it was actually a private body made up of volunteers who regarded outdoor recreation as something for which people needed proper education and from which they could derive moral improvement.

> The rise of fascism in Europe prompted British establishment figures to compare the nationalistic fervour of fascist youth movements with the supposed listless, apathetic state of Britain's youth. Within the ruling classes, both those who admired and those who feared the rise of fascism felt some need for action. These half-formed feelings combined with the growth of a consciousness about physical culture stemming from the medical and physical education professions. The many existing voluntary bodies also felt the need for a forum to coordinate activities.
> (Whannel, 1983, p. 89)

The Depression had hit school-leavers particularly hard, leaving many young people with a lot of free time on their hands; at the time the CCPR was set up only 10 percent of children stayed in school beyond 14. The events of the 1930s in Europe heightened the British establishment's concern about the physical fitness of the working class. The chaotic and amateurish operations of the governing bodies of sport, such as the Marylebone Cricket Club and the Royal and Ancient Golf Club, only made solving this problem more difficult. A National Fitness Council was finally established by the Physical Training and Recreation Act of 1937. Significantly, the Council's secretary was an ex-Army officer rather than a physical education instructor. By 1939 nearly a hundred national governing bodies were affiliated with the CCPR.

The Second World War increased the degree of political control over all spheres of life, leisure included. State funding for the arts, for example, ceased being given on an ad hoc basis and was placed on a more systematic footing by the establishment of the Committee for the Encouragement of Music and the Arts, which became, at war's end, the Arts Council. This marked something of a change from the state's policy during the First World War, when many leisure pursuits were forbidden on grounds that they diverted attention and resources from the war effort. By 1939, perhaps through the example of fascism, the government seemed to have become more perceptive of the need to provide people with a healthy balance of rest and work, and consequently tried to encourage a sensible attitude toward leisure pursuits. 'It was as if leisure had finally come of age and been accepted as an essential part of the national effort, and it was sometimes allowed precedence over more pressing matters' (Walvin, 1978, p. 148). The 1938 Holidays with Pay Act finally began to take effect only after war had ended. By 1945, 80 percent of the working population were paid during their holidays.

Another result of the postwar reconstruction drive in Britain was the establishment of a national park system. The Ministry of Town and Country Planning (established in 1943) began work on a National Parks and Access to Countryside Bill immediately after the war ended. The Bill was enacted in 1949, setting up a National Parks Commission to oversee the purchase and management of a national parks system which would, in principle, equalize access to scenic areas and recreational facilities. A White Paper, *Leisure in the Countryside*, published in 1966, reflected the new conventional wisdom for an enhanced level of recreational facilities around the major centers of population, acknowledging the expanding travel and recreational needs of the newly affluent postwar generation. The Countryside Commission replaced the National Parks Commission in 1968, with a broader mandate to protect the countryside for recreational purposes. The Wildlife and Countryside Act of 1981 strengthened the protection of natural habitat and landscape against the ravages of new agricultural technologies (Cherry, 1985).

Physical culture did not fare quite so well as the arts in the new welfare state. The CCPR found its private status an impediment in the competition for resources during the build-up of the welfare state. Much of its mission was taken over by the state with the passage of the 1944 Education Act, which not only raised the school-leaving age but also institutionalized physical education in the curriculum and established the principle of making educational facilities available to community groups for play. Its most significant achievement in the immediate postwar period was the establishment of seven national recreational centers providing residential facilities for training in a variety of sports for elite athletes. In the 1950s, as a result of growing apprehension about not only the intensification of international competition but also the CCPR's ability to meet, simultaneously, the needs of elite athletes and the general public, a push was made to establish a national sports authority on a statutory footing.

The CCPR set up the Wolfenden Committee in 1957 to recommend ways in which the national government could promote sport and leisure for the welfare of the community. That Committee's report, *Sport and the Community*, concluded that the national effort in sport was underfinanced and administratively misplaced in the Ministry of Education. It recommended a sports council on the lines of the existing Arts Council. It is significant that the Committee (itself a private body) was at this time opposed to the idea of a Ministry of Sport and affirmed its faith in voluntarism by recommending that the council be made up of 'six to ten persons of varied experience who have a general knowledge of the field and such personal standing as will give them accepted authority and influence' (Evans, 1974, p. 151). It is also characteristic that the executive committee of the CCPR could not muster a majority vote in favor of the recommendation concerning the establishment of the Sports Council. Other bodies, such as the British Olympic Association, also seemed to be reluctant to cede power to the government (Evans, 1974, p. 159).

In the run-up to the general election of 1959 both major parties published manifestos in which a sports council was suggested. The Conservative government did not follow through on this promise, although it did designate Lord Hailsham, then Minister of Science, as 'Minister with Special Responsibility for Sport.' The Labour government which assumed power in 1964 accepted the Wolfenden Committee's recommendation and set up the Sports Council without, however, giving it statutory powers. This decision reflected the government's desire to prevent institutions like sport from appearing to be state controlled. 'A Minister of Sport would be answerable to Parliament, whereas a quasi-independent council, even if appointed by the government, would be outside the parliamentary political process' (Whannel, 1983, p. 91).

A period of uneasy relations between the Sports Council and the CCPR ensued as a struggle over control of sport and leisure between public and private agencies took place. Personnel of the CCPR were 'seconded' to work for the Sports Council (Evans, 1974, p. 209), shifting, in a sense, from the quasi-public to the public sphere and back again. To the stalwarts in the CCPR the government appeared to be coopting its essentially private work. However, the increasing reliance of the CCPR and its constituent organizations on government funding left it with little choice but to accede.

The transfer of the Labour minister responsible for sport (Dennis Howell) from Education to Housing and Local Government promised a more rational administration of sport and leisure services by linking them with government agencies responsible for land-use planning. In 1971 the Conservative government supplemented the statutory powers of the Sports Council by giving it grant-aiding functions similar to those of a government department and it moved the Ministry of Sport to the Department of the Environment. The Sports Council assumed the role of dispenser of funds to local authorities (typically for larger-scale projects such as sports centers) and to voluntary organizations for training, management and the provision of facilities. Closely resembling it in structure was the other quasi-government organization with responsibility for the direction of outdoor leisure services, the Countryside Commission. It also channeled grant aid to local authorities and private individuals and organizations concerned to enhance and preserve landscape beauty at the same time as ensuring the provision of countryside recreation.

The direction of leisure policy was thus invested in the hands of a quasi-government organization or 'quango.' This device for dealing with frequently awkward or controversial leisure issues effectively absolved legislators of the responsibility of making difficult decisions while at the same time giving partial control or self-regulation to dominant institutions and their elites (Jessop, 1980, p. 61). Although a 'quango' might ostensibly follow popular democratic reform programs it none the less reinforced the separation of the people from control over the state in the area of political and ideological domination as well as imposing a framework of bourgeois social relations upon popular participation. Leisure policy therefore came to resemble arts policy in which, while general directions are determined by the government in power, specific policies are left in the hands of patronal or intermediate bodies, most of which are dominated by members of the nation's elite or by leisure professionals. This strategy reflected not only elitism but also the belief that both sport and art were essentially apolitical and should therefore be immunized from political control. It also reflected the typically British commitment to amateurism and the abhorrence of members of the establishment toward too much government control. The House of Lords Select Committee on Sport and Leisure (1973, p. xxv) pointed proudly to the 'British tradition' of trying to ensure that everyone was *able* to take part in leisure rather than *making* everyone participate, an obvious allusion to more totalitarian regimes.

Political direction of leisure policy has gradually shifted out of the hands of volunteers from elite groups and into the hands of civil servants, hired leisure experts and influential members of the private leisure industry. The CCPR went into voluntary liquidation in 1972, and all its staff and assets were transferred to the newly formed executive sports councils. In England the CCPR was re-established as the representative body of sport and recreation with the status of consultative body to the Sports Council. But the Sports Council, and behind it the government, was now exerting a greater degree of control over this volunteer body than ever before: 'it pays 75% of the salaries of 400 full-time officials; provides many of the governing bodies with their headquarters accommodation; pays for travel, training and preparation for international events and for the development of national squads; it makes large capital grants for facilities; it runs the National Centres that these bodies mostly use' (Hargreaves, 1986, p. 194).

The trend away from voluntarism and reliance on private initiative in leisure policy must not be exaggerated. The Sports Council has demonstrated its independence of the government of the day with respect to South African sporting ties and the question of boycotting the Olympics. The CCPR continues to function (with royal sponsorship) as a powerful and reasonably well-supported 'leisure lobby,' with seats reserved for it on the Sports Council. And the government has shown little inclination to favor major professional sport to the extent shown, for example, in the United States. 'Tax exemptions for sponsorship, charitable status for sports bodies, more generous transfers to sport via the betting tax and a levy on the football pools have all been called for and resisted' (Hargreaves, 1986, p. 117).

## The Government and Leisure Policy

Just how active the national government has been in the formation and execution of leisure policy has depended somewhat on the party in power, although the long-term trend has been toward more centralization and toward statutory powers and away from voluntarism. By the late 1960s both political parties had begun to appeal to a newly affluent working class and to college-educated professionals on the basis of their policies toward leisure. Conservative governments preferred to minimize government control over, or subsidy of, leisure, espousing a form of cultural democracy of the dollar in which the market regulates supply and demand. Labour governments have been more concerned to achieve equality of leisure opportunities through collective action. However, even the Labour government has not pursued the goal of leisure equality directly through the administration of leisure but rather through equalizing conditions of work.

There can be little doubt that public bodies like the Sports Council and the Countryside Commission have underrepresented working-class people and reflected mainly middle-class leisure interests. However, the impact of this bias on leisure behavior is far from clear. It has been limited by the fact that the marketplace has been the major determinant of leisure activities in Britain. Public providers of leisure have no captive audience. The public picks and chooses, and if the government seeks to compete with private enterprise in the bid to be the chosen provider, it must do so on terms dictated by the market and by consumer choice.

Battling both commercial interests and working-class apathy, the members of the sports and leisure establishment have sought to win approval of a leisure policy that would combine the goal of equality of access with the preservation of individual freedom. The Minister for Sport wrote in 1972 that 'the provision of sport and recreational opportunities is indeed a social service that in its own way is almost as important to the well-being of the community as good housing, hospitals and schools' (McIntosh and Charlton, 1985, p. 13). The House of Lords Select Committee on Sport and Leisure (1973, p. xxiv) declared that 'Providing for leisure is a service which public authorities now have a duty to undertake.' It was claimed that properly planned and supervised leisure would reduce the incidence of heart disease, reduce boredom and 'urban frustration,' combat 'hooliganism and delinquency among young people' and, through international competition, raise national morale. Committee members believed recreation to be one of the community's everyday needs, and declared that provision for it should be 'part of the general fabric of the social services.'

The Committee sought to justify government intervention in leisure on the usual grounds. The government must seek distributive justice ('leisure services should be available to all, whether they can afford to pay for them or not, and whether their neighbourhood is rich or poor': p. xxix); the government will always be needed to fill in the gaps left by the market (private enterprise is 'not concerned to see that an adequate range and location of facilities are available': p. xxix); government is necessary to protect public amenities and collective goods (to 'prevent the increased pressure for countryside recreation from damaging both agriculture and the countryside': p. xxix); government must come to the aid of voluntary work (which will usually be underfunded when it comes to major projects); the welfare state idea has established a sense of entitlement among the citizenry: 'The public in this country are not accustomed to paying the full economic rate for their facilities, and the American example of commercial sports halls will not be followed in the near future' (p. xxxi).

The Committee thus adopted an integrative approach to leisure policy, seeking to absorb all social groups in the life of the nation, 'to make us all participating citizens' (Clarke and Critcher, 1985, p. 139). In pursuit of a European-wide 'Sport for all' policy, the Sports Council likewise sought to make recreational facilities available to as many groups as possible. Special groups, referred to as 'sports illiterates,' were targeted for special attention. These included the elderly, women, the disabled and those who had never been exposed to sport educationally (McIntosh and Charlton, 1985, p. 16). 'Sport for all' was justified not only for its own sake, but also as a means of spreading health and social benefits and promoting social solidarity in inner-city areas.

Government priorities are usually reflected in budgets. The importance attached to leisure by postwar United Kingdom governments is difficult to gauge from budget figures because of the diffusion of responsibility for this provision across many government departments and because some departments, such as Education, do not list leisure expenditures separately. Expenditures on sport are recorded by the Sports Council and show a steady growth in support for sport until 1980. The amount of money the central government spends directly on sport is minuscule, but spending on sport by all government authorities is nearly twice that spent on the prison service or passenger subsidies to rail, bus, underground and ferry services in any given year (McIntosh and Charlton, 1985, p. 41). Dissatisfaction with the amount of expenditure by central government on sport has from time to time been expressed; but in principle and in financial terms, the aim of treating sport as a social service like housing, health and education has been achieved. Funding for sport at the state and local level has kept up with inflation as well as has funding for housing, health, or education.

Political differences in the approach to leisure are not hard to discern. Most conservatives favor a kind of cultural democracy, allowing people to express their leisure wants through the operation of the free market. They believe in the essential autonomy of leisure and are angered by attempts to use leisure for other purposes. They find the encouragement of leisure as disturbing as its censorship or suppression. Socialists, on the other hand, see leisure as being inevitably political and seek to make it serve the right political ends short of imposing a homogeneous leisure culture on what they see as an essentially pluralistic system. In this respect they differ from conservatives, who believe in the essential homogeneity of culture.

Despite these philosophical differences—representative, perhaps, of the more extreme viewpoints—Labour and Conservative governments have been strikingly alike in their willingness to invest money in leisure opportunities (Bramham and Henry, 1985, p. 16). Conservatives tend to approach leisure from the standpoint of economic efficiency and 'wastage of talent,' whereas Labour is more concerned with the amelioration of social inequality and an increase in social mobility. With enabling legislation and financial assistance under the Countryside Act of 1968, local councils and other agencies have embarked on major programs of developing rural land for recreation and protecting existing facilities from urban sprawl (Groome, 1985, p. 97). However, the economic stagnation of the 1970s and 1980s and the attendant government spending cuts have resulted in fewer new facilities being planned or built, the closure of old buildings and reduced opening hours for existing ones, and have exacerbated the problems caused lower income groups by the absence of mass transportation.

In the 1980s leisure policy in the United Kingdom came under the influence of a 'new Right' politics in which leisure is seen preeminently as an area of sovereignty of the individual best left untouched by the state. The Thatcher government's policy toward leisure was an integral part of its drive to reprivatize the economy and minimize the role of central governments. The Sports Council, which had already assumed the role of a clearing house through which potential commercial sponsors could be put in touch with sports bodies requiring funding, was restaffed to be more sympathetic to the government's 'new right' economic philosophy; the BBC came under increasing pressure to tolerate the use of commercial sponsorship in the sports events it covered; joint public–private ventures were encouraged; 'user fees' were instituted and other means explored (e.g. vending machines) to make leisure facilities self-supporting. Attempts to make local government more rational and cost effective also seriously affected the leisure component.

Under a new system in which the central government requires local authorities to draw up 'structure plans' justifying broad land-use policies—a reform which in principle could serve to better protect recreational opportunities—local governments are expected to emphasize a number of 'key issues' (e.g. housing). Leisure, however, is not one of the issues thus identified; it is treated as a residual concern in this new land-use planning procedure, best catered to by private industry.

## Can Leisure be Administered?

The political management of leisure services in a mixed economy will almost inevitably run the gamut from a policy in which the state is seen as stimulating and smoothing the working of the market for leisure to one where the state is intended to compete with and perhaps eliminate the market for leisure services. The first position is exemplified by the English Tourist Board (a government agency), which sees itself as enhancing people's leisure lives by stimulating private sector economic growth and employment. A spokesman for the Board approaches tourism and leisure as a marketing issue: 'We want to provide a product people want to buy' (Thorburn, 1984, p. 14). The second position is exemplified by a spokesman for the socialist-run Greater London Council (abolished in 1986). He points to the vast sums of money being earned by the 'culture industries,' money spent on gambling, home entertainment equipment, sports and sports equipment, books, toys and the like, and sees in this demand something to which the state could cater as well as private industry. Furthermore, public catering to these needs would avoid the kind of neglect of disadvantaged groups for which private enterprise is criticized (Tomkins, 1984). Mixed economies such as that of the United Kingdom therefore show no consistent or integrated policy toward leisure. In some respects this policy is closer to that found in the United States; in other respects it comes closer to the total elimination of the private market for leisure services in the interests of the state, a policy found in the kind of regime to be discussed in Chapter 6.

While we can expect the welfare states to become more and more involved in leisure, and particularly in sport, it is unlikely that any will endorse the view that the state itself should provide leisure services on any significant scale. Leisure cannot be equated with education, medicine and shelter as a state function because there is an inherent contradiction in the planning on which the welfare state must depend on the one hand and the freedom necessarily entailed in true leisure on the other. Leisure is, by definition and general consent, set apart from work, a kind of 'idleness' to which people claim the right; and yet the state must encourage productivity and reinforce the work ethic. Leisure means people doing what they want, without constraint or supervision; and yet the state must ensure a measure of conformity and order. Free choice of leisure opportunities means open access, but the government must look after the long run and protect the people themselves against the social costs of excess demands on leisure amenities. These are contradictions inherent in the social democratic state. Without full nationalization, and without the kind of colonization of leisure attempted in totalitarian regimes, these contradictions will continue to generate political conflicts over the use of leisure.

# 6
# *Leisure in Totalitarian Regimes*

Leisure in totalitarian regimes is unusual in the extent to which this aspect of life, like all others, is believed to be essentially political. Work and play, leisure and labor, are treated as a unity properly administered by the state. Little is made of the distinction common in liberal democracies between the public and private spheres. All aspects of life, including how people choose to define and spend their free time, are assumed to have political significance and usefulness.

As we shall see, it would be a mistake to assume that all totalitarian regimes are alike in their approach to leisure. We shall examine differences between fascist and communist regimes and encounter differences within these two categories. We shall also see that state policies toward leisure in totalitarian regimes have not always been consistent; they have changed over time and have rarely worked as planned.

## Leisure in Communist Countries

The most important distinguishing features of leisure in communist countries are as follows. 'Proper' leisure is defined in rational, utilitarian terms; leisure is a right, not a privilege; leisure use is centrally planned and organized; leisure activities are closely tied to school, college, or work; physical education is compulsory, its curriculum standardized and ideally lifelong, the culture of the body being just as crucial as that of the mind for the harmonious development of the individual and, ultimately, for the health of society; higher education in physical culture is a common and honored path of advancement, on a par with music and art; a nationwide system of honors links sporting achievement and political status; science and medicine are rationally applied to leisure practices;

sport festivals are typically used to commemorate political events and express national unity.

It goes without saying that many forms of leisure found in communist regimes are also popular in democracies. But the distinguishing feature of the leisure sphere in communist countries is the heavy emphasis on organized play. Leisure is neither the preserve of a moneyed elite not the commercialized pastime of the masses. It is, instead, a collective expression of political loyalty and national solidarity. The result is an overwhelming preoccupation with 'physical culture' or, more lately, sport. As we shall see in this chapter, the politics of leisure in communist countries is, in large part, the politics of sport. This is understandable in light of the intense suspicion shown by communist leaders for free, unorganized and unsupervised street or neighborhood play and the absence of any of the myriad private enterprise leisure opportunities found in capitalist regimes. Sport is the most regulated and predictable of leisure pastimes. Sport is also ideally suited to political manipulation:

> It has proved to be of peculiar utility by reason of its inherent qualities of being easily understood and enjoyed, being apolitical (at least superficially) and permitting emotional release safely. It has thus an advantage over drinking, sex, religious ritual and other forms of emotional release and companionship-formation by being officially approved and therefore less guilt-inducing and yet being relatively free of rigid official sanctions. It has had an advantage over literature, theatre and other forms of cultural expression by being more readily comprehensible to the mass public as well as less amenable to direct political control over style and content.
> (Riordan, 1978, p. 49)

In other words, sport can function as a political tool in part because it is apolitical and relatively free of the kind of close control and censorship which would alienate a subject population.

*Leisure is Rational and Utilitarian*
The interpretation of the body and its potential for athleticism by a political ideology is rooted in basic assumptions about the essence of human nature. For Marx, man's 'species being' was to be found in his productive capacities. Man is essentially *homo faber*. Marx wrote next to nothing about leisure. But this should not be taken to imply that he saw man as a worker and nothing else. He rejected the distinction between 'unfree' labor and 'free' play on which so much of today's exaltation of play over work is based.

The idea of an autonomous leisure sphere (e.g. hobbies) is

considered to be applicable only to capitalist societies, where it is believed to be a sign of false consciousness. Work and play are not antithetical categories, play being not an alternative to work but its creative element. The goal of communist policy is to reunite work and play. In the words of two Soviet leisure experts, 'Leisure in a communist society is not a fleeing from work but one of the transitional forms to a truly communist form of work, at which point the latter becomes enjoyment and the primary vital need' (quoted in Hoberman, 1984, p. 35). Leisure will become part of the ideal state of all-round human development, part of the 'new Soviet man.' To work to this end, 'production gymnastics' (i.e. physical exercises at work closely geared to work needs) were taken up on a massive scale in Russia with the onset of the first Five-Year Plan in 1925 and continue in use today. In Hungary the success of the revolution begun after the Second World War is believed to hinge on the development of proper leisure services for the workers. A Hungarian writes: 'Socialist revolution is introduced by political revolution, and followed by the revolutionary transformation of production relations; but without cultural revolution and the shaping of socialist man, advanced socialism cannot be achieved' (quoted in Sapora, 1981, p. 31).

Second, Marxism accords priority to the training of rational faculties and seeks to suppress the emotional, irrational side of human beings. The impulsiveness and spontaneity associated with play must be controlled and channeled so as to enhance the individual's intellectual capacities rather than impair them. Post-revolutionary Soviet sport ideology contained three themes reflecting this emphasis. First, physical culture replaced bourgeois sport to condition people for the spartan conditions following the revolution and to encourage the idea of the 'hardened revolutionary ascetic.' In the immediate post-revolutionary period, the ignorance that was the cause of so much disease, starvation and misery, and hampered both military effectiveness and labor productivity, was to be combated by a broad program of physical exercise and sport. 'Physical culture' lacked the element of competition present in sport (a theme we see best preserved in Communist China) and did not exalt physical perfectionism (because of its elitist implications). Instead, it sought the harmonious development of the body and mind. Second, public health was given a political dimension by the hygienics movement which opposed, among other things, 'irrational,' 'unedifying' and 'dangerous' sports such as boxing and weightlifting. The First Trade Union Games, in 1925, excluded soccer, boxing, weightlifting and gymnastics from its program, even though these were four of the most popular sporting pursuits in the country at the time (Riordan,

1978, p. 20). The hygienists 'had virtual control over the government body for sport (the Supreme Council of Physical Culture), the sporting Press, the Health Ministry and the physical education colleges' (Riordan, 1980, p. 29). Their influence lasted well into the 1930s. Time-budget studies carried out in the Soviet Union during that period significantly employed a category of time called 'wastes of time' in addition to the 'free time' and the 'work time' they allowed their respondents to check (Moskoff, 1984, p. 4). Here, as in the West, moral improvement was linked to 'appropriate' leisure.

As a third element of the rationalization of play, 'proletkultists' condemned all sports associated with capitalism, particularly those encouraging competition, as decadent and degenerate. In a book called *New Games for New Children* the proletkultists advocated such new games as 'Swelling the Ranks of Children's Communist Groups,' 'Rescue from the Fascists' and 'Helping the Proletarians.' Although this hostility to competitive sports did not last long, official approval was always contingent upon their being oriented to collective rather than individual achievements and subject to appropriate medical and pedagogical controls to avoid 'excesses' of fandom. Russian writers were quick to condemn any signs of athletic egocentricity or 'stars' and any inkling of the 'dandified culture of the body' (Hoberman, 1984, p. 192).

During the 1930s the Soviets decided to stratify sport, to distinguish a more or less professional group of sportsmen and sportswomen from the main body. This was fully in keeping with Stalin's strategy of social development at the time. The ordinary people were to be inspired by the efforts of the outstanding performers, with whom they could identify. Competitive activities could be useful, it was reasoned, as a means of generating support for political programs, in raising the level of work skills and in promoting international class solidarity. Competitive sports with mass appeal, such as soccer, basketball and volleyball, were officially encouraged, with regional and national leagues, stadiums, cups, championships and popularity polls. Watching these sports helped in no small way to provide general recreation to the fast-growing urban population.

Communist China originally discouraged competitiveness, especially in its international forays. Winning was subordinated to participation and consciousness-raising. Radio Beijing announced in 1971 that

> Whether or not a team or individual is victorious and gains honor depends on whether or not he gives prominence to proletarian politics during the competition, whether or not he wins in the

realm of ideology, whether or not he can lose without losing the spirit of sportsmanship, and whether or not he puts proletarian politics in command of the tournament and participates for the sake of proletarian politics.

(Kanin, 1981, p. 74)

More competition-oriented athleticism became respectable only after the death of Mao. 'The result has been an expansion of the sport school system, rewards for good performance, the introduction of scientific sport medicine, and even the importing of professional athletes from West Germany to serve as tutors' (Hoberman, 1984, p. 227).

The change in China's attitude is reflected in this official statement concerning the People's Republic's participation in the 1984 Los Angeles Olympic Games: 'To win competitions and glory for our country, we must first win a gold medal...If we are just participating, yet unable to achieve outstanding results, the dignity of both our nation and our people will be impaired and the people will not be satisfied' (Hargreaves, 1984, p. 68).

*Leisure Is Not a Privilege but a Right*
Efforts to link the democratization of leisure to a socialist political program (i.e. rather than leisure being democratized through market forces) can be traced back at least until the 1890s with the rise of the workers' sport movement in Germany. The movement aimed at more equality of opportunity to participate in sport and less emphasis on 'antisocial' competition. It was intended to be an alternative to the 'capitalist pleasure industry' which was seen as dissolving class identities by its sensationalism and over-refinement of the performance principle and its 'cynical and aimless thrill seeking' (Hoberman, 1984, p. 178). The workers' sport movement never managed to attract more working-class members than the 'bourgeois' sports clubs it roundly condemned. Just as important, it never won over the left intellectuals in the socialist movement. By the time the movement had formed an alliance with the German SPD it was 1929, and too late.

Modern communist regimes assert that sport is a right and not a privilege, that sport is equal in status to science and art, that sport shall no longer be the preserve of the universities and colleges. Thus, for example, in Cuba today the slogan declares that sport is 'the right of the people,' and mass participation is encouraged at every level. Article 25 of the Constitution of the German Democratic Republic states:'For the full and distinctive development of the socialist personality and the growing satisfaction of cultural interests and requirements, the participation of citizens in cultural life, physical culture and sport is guaranteed by state and society.' And Article 35 of the Youth Act of 1974 reads, in part: 'The Socialist government guarantees physical education and sport for young people in all walks of life, and promotes the activity of the German Gymnastics and Sports Union as the initiator and organizer of sport.' Everyone in the GDR has the right to join the Deutscher Turn und Sports Bund, the association of mass recreation sports clubs, and any collection of seven people within any enterprise or living unit has the right to form a DTSB sports club (Gilbert, 1980, p. 50). In Hungary, district, city, town and village councils are required by central government to operate cultural and leisure services as a basic social service. It is assumed that a 'precondition for self-realization is equal opportunity' (Sapora, 1981, p. 35).

This 'right' is not, of course, interpreted in the same way than an 'entitlement' under law might be interpreted in social democracies, as a 'claim' the individual has the right to make on the state. Rather, it is interpreted, as is the case in China, in the context of the slogan 'serve the people,' where the state (or party, which is much the same) should take care of every aspect of its citizens' lives. Thus Mao declared in 1953:

> New China must care for her young and show concern for the growth of the younger generation. Young people have to study and work, but they are at the age of physical growth. Therefore, full attention must be paid both to their work and study and to their recreation, sport and rest.
> (Clumpner and Pendleton, 1978, p. 112)

Making the right kind of leisure opportunities available to each person is justified in terms of developing the well-rounded individual and helping them contribute to the political program of the regime rather than being justified in terms of maximizing the individual's freedom of choice. Furthermore, the ideal is that leisure should not be consumed individually but as part of a group. The politically proper leisure is that which is engaged in jointly, as an organized group activity. The Soviet Union still distinguishes between organized and unorganized holiday-makers.

> Organized holiday makers are those who spend their leave at state or trade union facilities. These are facilities for which passes are required, such as houses of rest or sanatoriums and pensions... Organized tourists are treated much better than those who operate on their own. For example, it is much more difficult to find hotel

rooms or camping facilities if you are an unorganized tourist than if you have the official status associated with a pass from your enterprise or local trade union.

(Moskoff, 1984, p. 119)

The leisure activities of people in the Soviet Union are much less expensive, much less consumer-oriented and much more communal in character than the leisure activities of people in the West.

All communist countries seek mass participation in physical culture, but all modern communist regimes also place considerable emphasis on the development of elite athletes. Thus, although the GDR has its mass recreation clubs, it also operates twenty-seven elite sports clubs, many of which run special sports schools. Coaches are rewarded with time off from work with pay for volunteering to help with these activities. Elite and mass sports are not seen as incompatible aims. As usual, the Chinese have a catch-phrase for this–'walking on two legs.'

> Popularization of sports for the masses must exist alongside high level training for the few. Mass advancement on the upper levels provides incentives for the masses and in turn raises the entire national level of performance. In terms of professional training, the phrase 'walking on two legs' means that physical culture training courses should be offered on the highest planes in university level physical education institutes and normal universities for some, and on a spare time or short-course basis for others. Athletic meets should be held on a local small-scale basis as well as on a grand national scale. Traditional sports should coexist with modern sports...In short, the policy of 'walking on two legs' commits the Chinese to pursue a policy of sports for everybody.
> 
> (Kolatch, 1972, p. 94)

Equal opportunity policies are also part of the notion that leisure is a right guaranteed by the state. Most communist countries give as much official encouragement to women as to men, backed up in material ways by the allocation of approximately equal time, facilities, funding, coaching, competition and media coverage. The amount of attention paid to elite female athletes in communist countries is much greater than that accorded women in capitalist democracies, with results that are clearly evident in the world of international sporting competition, where women's teams from communist countries usually win a higher proportion of their meets than do communist men.

It is not altogether clear, however, just how far the principle of equality of leisure opportunity extends in communist countries. There is a possibility that communist countries have rather cynically used women in Olympic sports because they know that capitalist democracies are typically weak in that area and medals are relatively easy to come by. There is an even stronger possibility that equality of opportunity does not extend very far down the skill ladder. The accomplishments of a few female communist athletes should not mislead us into thinking that all communist women enjoy equal access to leisure opportunities. Under conditions of grave labor shortages and chronic failure to meet production goals, the wage structures of most communist countries oblige both men and women to work in order to make ends meet. This means that nearly all women effectively have two careers, as homemaker and wage-worker, with very little time or energy left over for leisure, particularly its more active forms.

*Centralization*
When a country decides that the enjoyment of leisure is a right and not a privilege there must be massive government intervention at both local and national levels to make that idea an actuality. In Hungary it is taken for granted that the conduct of activities that involve as much attention and time of people as culture, leisure and sport cannot be left to chance. The state must play as central a role in providing leadership in the provision of leisure services as it does in other areas of society (Sapora, 1981, p. 27). Planning for leisure at all government levels is considered necessary to ensure that leisure time is not wasted. 'People, it is theorized, do not normally diagnose their leisure needs . . . leisure, work and education must serve in close connection and unity with each other for the full development of the individual' (Sapora, 1981, p. 30). To ensure that leisure serves its political purpose, control over policy and planning is vested in the Council of Ministers and, specifically, in the Ministry of Education and Culture and the Ministry of Sport. Centralization is considered to be an integral part of the administration of leisure in communist countries; all other forms are backward. Thus, one Czechoslovakian writer approvingly observes that, despite a long history of interest in sport but little international success, 'it was not until February 1948, when Czechoslovakia took the socialist path of development, that the entire sports movement was unified' (Kostka, 1978, p. 60). Communist China, likewise, moved quickly to centralize leisure policy, soon after the founding of the Republic. The Physical Culture and Sports Commission, set up in 1952, brought all leisure policy-making and administration under one roof. The centralized

direction of physical culture is 'inherent in the Chinese concept of a national physical culture' (Kolatch, 1972, p. 89).

In the Soviet Union the definitive statement on the role of sport in Soviet society, to which all subsequent policy statements were to refer, was issued in 1925 under the heading *On the Tasks of the Party in Physical Culture*. In 1930 an All-Union Physical Culture Council was established. It was, in effect, a Ministry of Sport because it was attached to the USSR Council of Ministers. It continued pretty much unchanged until 1957. The administrative reforms of the 1957–60 period did not in any way decentralize sports administration in the USSR. Rather, the basis of affiliation of the sports clubs under its jurisdiction was changed from that of unions (which are organized on an industry-by-industry basis) to a republic, i.e. one of the fifteen territorial units formed during the late 1950s. A separate rural sports society was also to be set up in each republic. Four more non-territorial sports societies found a home in the reorganized Council: Burevestnik (students), Spartak (health, civil service, trade, food, culture and education workers), Lokomotiv (railway) and Vodnik (river and canal transportation) (Riordan, 1978, p. 33).

> Each society has its own rules, membership cards, badge and colors. The societies are financed out of trade union dues...and given responsibility for building sports centers, acquiring equipment for their members and maintaining permanent staffs of coaches, instructors and medical personnel. All members have the right to use the societies' facilities for a nominal fee of 30 kopecks a year and to elect and be elected to their managing committees.
> (Riordan, 1980, p. 44)

A revamped and more powerful Committee for Physical Culture and Sport, attached to the Council of Ministers, was created in 1968. The Committee has the stature of a regular ministry, with organs at all federal levels. Its resolutions and decisions are binding on all ministries and public organizations. 'Within the confines of a single Moscow building are housed the heads and offices of every national sport-governing body' (Jeffries, 1986, p. 52). The chairman of the Committee is *de facto* Minister of Sport. The Committee is the ultimate employer of an administrative staff in excess of 20,000 people and supervises the activities of well over 52 million sportsmen and -women, six million trainers and coaches, and various physical culture institutes producing 28,000 graduates annually. In addition it oversees the construction and maintenance of stadiums, the conduct of international competitions and the activities of individual sports federations (Hazan, 1982, p. 29).

Centralization of control over leisure also occurs indirectly in important ways. To a degree unknown in social democratic regimes, working hours and wage structures are set by central governments. The Soviet Union, for example, stipulates nationwide legal minima for holidays with pay, limits the length of working days (to eight hours) and sets the retirement age. This is not to say that these directives are everywhere and always obeyed, but is a reminder that leisure planning is highly centralized. Leisure is also centrally planned to the extent that party officials are able to regulate leisure consumption through control over production decisions; leisure goods typically are accorded low priority. Soviet planners engineer a shortage of leisure opportunities in order to lower the opportunity costs of additional work. 'After all, if there is not enough to enjoy when one is free from work, then perhaps people will be willing to work more' (Moskoff, 1984, p. 198).

Although communist leisure, especially sports, is highly centralized in comparison to Western countries, it would be misleading to overemphasize this point. As in Western countries, there is no 'leisure ministry,' simply because the leisure function is so diffuse once we leave sports behind. Thus, although the state owns all the land in these countries, a situation which would seem to be most advantageous in planning leisure, there is typically no category of recreational land used, and the 'leisure lobby' within the party has to compete with the much more powerful industrial ministries. The result is a provision for 'open spaces' in urban areas and their vicinity that is much lower than in Western countries. Here centralization has helped hardly at all (Shaw, 1980, p. 200).

Centralization is also inhibited by the competing pulls of socialism and democracy. The sports program of the German Democratic Republic, for instance, is more centralized than is the case in Western nations. Leaders and workers in the sports program are bound by law to enforce regulations passed by the Central Committee. However, the East Germans themselves believe that their version of 'democratic socialism' is not so highly centralized as that found in the Soviet Union. Manfred Ewald, president of the German Gymnastics and Sports Union, believes that the strength of the sports system of the GDR is its foundation in a municipally based system built around local enterprises and town and village communities (Gilbert, 1980, p. 40). The same is true in Hungary. Most of the funding for leisure services (68 percent) comes from local councils. The county (the equivalent of a state in the United States) is a very important intervening unit in the administration of leisure services. Advisory committees are expected to oversee leisure activities at the local level. And it is an established principle that the state does not initiate leisure ventures; these must originate in a plan of operation drawn up at the grass-roots level (Sapora, 1981, p. 50). There is no doubt that, in times of domestic and international crisis, communist regimes have the power and resources to centralize administration to a degree unknown in the West. But it is far from clear that this is typical of the mundane and more routine administration of leisure, when considerable latitude is enjoyed by local governments and enterprises.

*Productivism*

Communist regimes seek to forge a link between work and play by ideologically and structurally uniting them. Success in work is related to physical fitness and health, while physical culture is based on and organized around work organizations. One of the first acts of the Bolsheviks was to attach formally organized leisure to the workplace. 'In future, all local sports clubs were to be organized on a production basis, all the people belonging to a particular factory, office or college (and members of their families) being eligible for membership of the sports "collective" at their place of work' (Riordan, 1978, p. 23). Today, 'Work is still considered the most important category in the life of the individual. It is certainly viewed as more important than leisure...In the strictest sense the end of life is work and time off or leisure is for the purpose of getting ready for work again' (Moskoff, 1984, p. xiv).

The head of the Physical Culture Faculty at Leningrad's Lesgaft Physical Culture Institute believes that 'there is no other means in society save physical culture through which people can be trained physically for the new [automated] production' (Ponomaryov, 1981, p. 53). This same authority also sees physical education as enabling a person to 'master new specialisms' and believes that 'people who take part in sport acquire work habits and skills more quickly and skillfully, their work capacity is greater, their organism more quickly adapts to work conditions.' Similar efforts to harness leisure to work have been made in other communist regimes. In China, Mao declared that physical culture must be made to serve productive labor. A stronger, healthier worker would do a better, more efficient job. In Czechoslovakia 'the entire activity' of the sports movement is to prepare citizens for work (Kostka, 1978, p. 66). The continued popularity of sanatoria in communist countries, long after they have declined in Western Europe, is partly due to the poverty of alternative forms of holiday accommodation but it is also testimony to the official desire to tie leisure to recuperation and restoration for work (Shaw, 1980, p. 197).

Recent increases in free time and discretionary money pose an ever-worsening 'leisure problem' for communist leaders. Their task is to make sure that this new leisure is not divorced from the production process. The growing popularity of television has created special difficulties in the Soviet Union. The goal of the Soviet leadership has always been the molding of the creative individual, who should be an active contributor to society. 'Yet one of the undeniable results of the introduction of television on a mass scale in the Soviet Union is that the so-called creative activities have declined...the Soviet sociologists have had to coin a new word to describe this process of passive leisure: *relaksatsia* (relaxation)' (Mickiewics, 1981, p. 38). During the 1970s irrational pursuits such as body-building and yoga were banned, showing that the state was still interested in controlling the public's use of its non-work time even though leisure pursuits were no longer so closely tied to production organizations.

*Didacticism*
Leisure has always been expected to serve didactic purposes in communist regimes. Leisure pursuits are taken up not simply to provide pleasure and entertainment but to serve an educational purpose, principally that of instilling the ideals of the Communist Party. Radio and television, even the popular quiz shows, are used to teach the values of hard work and sacrifice on behalf of the party. The party frowns upon entertainment that seems to be purely escapist and without pedagogical content. The popularity of television has been especially welcomed because of its didactic potential and because, in its scope, it offers the opportunity to transmit standardized lessons to all Soviets. The same can be said for reading books, magazines and newspapers, which is very popular in the Soviet Union. Not only does this encourage a generally high level of literacy (and thereby help boost productivity) but it also facilitates 'the transmission of the system's values' (Moskoff, 1984, p. 82).

It also follows logically from this argument about the didactic functions of leisure that it can have seriously pathological consequences if misused—if it teaches people the wrong lessons. There is therefore no subscription to the view that leisure contains its own values. The creation of leisure is good, its consumption is bad; activism in leisure time is good, passivism is bad; collective forms of leisure are good, solitary forms are bad; activities that elevate are good, those that degrade are bad. The assumption that the individual cannot be trusted to spend his or her leisure time in a socially beneficial way is as strongly embedded in the psyche of modern communist planners as it was in the minds of the Progressives in the United States at the turn of the century.

The didacticism of leisure in communist regimes helps explain the close integration of physical education into the school and factory system. The socialization function of school and factory life is not impeded by leisure activites as is so often the case in Western countries. Physical activities are seen as a natural adjunct to the learning of appropriate communist ideals. All Soviet students take physical education and sport as a compulsory part of the curriculum for the first two years of college or university. 'They must have a record of full attendance and must pass their preliminary examinations in the subject before being permitted to continue into the third year of their normally five-year degree course' (Riordan, 1980, p. 86). The GDR instituted a program in 1970 which made swimming compulsory for all schoolchildren from age 9 to 19. Schools without pools must arrange summer camp swimming.

The Chinese, who retain many of the marks of the privation occasioned by guerrilla warfare, also use physical education didactically. Unlike Western societies, where the distinction between sport and physical education is sharp, the Chinese embrace them under the general heading of 'physical culture.' Sports are not differentiated from home, educational, or work settings and are not associated with particular age categories or social statuses. The involvement in physical culture is expected to be universal and lifelong.

> The Chinese child, when he begins primary school, starts what is theoretically hoped will be the first step in a lifelong continuous process of physical culture. Every morning, like workers and students throughout the land, he will engage in 'broadcast' exercises to radio music. He will participate in regular physical education classes plus 'voluntary' after-school programs which expand upon the class-time work and pay more attention to games and athletics. Beginning with middle school, the 'labor-defense system,' participated in by men and women in all walks of life throughout China, will become his focus of attention. In place of the regular after-school sports program, the more qualified will be able to play on school teams or attend spare-time sports schools. If he has such inclinations, the student might qualify for a special sports high school or university-level physical culture training. The worker will often find a complete sports program at his place of employment, as will the soldier on his army post, and it is fully expected that participation will not be voluntary.
> 
> (Kolatch, 1972, p. 76)

In theory, after-school physical education classes are strictly voluntary, but in fact hidden pressures leave the student no choice but to 'volunteer.'

The Chinese copied the 'labor-defense system' from the Soviets, who had devised it in the 1930s. The Soviets' program *Gotor K Trydu I Oborone* (GTO—'Ready for Labour and Defense') is still considered the foundation of the sports system. The policy objectives were to engage people in sports from an early age, supply military-type training, reduce absenteeism from work and channel youthful energies in constructive directions. GTO consists of a prescribed set (the number varies from time to time) of activities in which regular instruction is provided, tests administered and certificates of achievement awarded. The activities (e.g. swimming and camping) are geared to national defense needs. China preserved this idea of 'everyone a soldier' until the Cultural Revolution. During the Quemoy-Matsu crisis of 1958 the boundary between military training and physical education virtually disappeared. 'Sports' like telegraphy and rifle shooting were included in the numerous local and national athletics festivals.

*Physical Culture as a Career*
Communist countries make no distinction between the professional and the amateur. It is, of course, possible to engage in a host of leisure pursuits without getting paid to do so, and in that sense there are 'amateurs;' it is also true that there are many athletes who are paid to train and perform as athletes, these being 'professionals.' However, the distinction as it is made in the West has no meaning because communist countries do not draw the boundaries between the public and the private sphere in the same way. Thus they would see no meaning in distinguishing those who 'play for pay' in the commercialized sector and those who 'play for love' for their own amusement, because both make sense only where leisure is considered to be a private affair. To the communist, all play is public.

Where the state is the ultimate employer and also responsible for the administration of leisure, 'broken-time' payments are no problem. In order to qualify for the 1952 Helsinki Olympic Games, Soviet athletes were given one of three occupations: student, serviceman/-woman, or physical education instructor. It is not true, then, that there are no full-time athletes; rather, these athletes will have been trained and are employed by the state.

> All leading Soviet sportsmen are 'state professionals' whose financial rewards depend largely on the level of their performance. To maintain the impression of amateurism, leading sportsmen are

on the payroll of various plants, institutes, universities, offices, and the army, but these salaries are paid for their sports achievements only. Soviet sportsmen are among the best paid groups in the country, and their regular income is no less than double the average income of an ordinary Soviet citizen.

(Hazan, 1982, p. 43)

Ironically, many of the Olympic athletes of communist countries are to be found in the same place as their American rivals, in colleges and universities. The major difference is that communist athletes will probably be enrolled in or on the staff of one of the many physical culture institutes that have been set up to train physical education instructors for schools and universities, as well as coaches, researchers and sports administrators. These institutes provide qualified athletes with the time and supervision necessary to reach world-class performance levels. It is this specialized training, as much as the full-time support, that accounts for the success of communist bloc countries in the Olympics. If an athlete is not part of the physical education establishment he or she is likely to be a member of a sports club attached to a factory or government agency. Thus, of the 287 members of the German Democratic Republic's team in the 1976 Olympics, 25 came from ASK (the armed forces sports club), 58 came from Dynamo (the club of the People's Police), 20 came from Leipzig's University for Physical Culture and 21 came from the club for state employees (Childs, 1978, p. 95).

Obviously, these are professional athletes in all but name, given ample time to train, superior facilities and a measure of freedom from financial insecurity. Olympic prospects who do have a job in industry are reimbursed for time off from work so that they can have adequate time for practice. The Olympic effort is boosted by a Central School for Sports which trains promising boys and girls for high-level international sports in an accelerated program. The GDR has been highly successful in Olympic competition. In 1976, the last time the USA and the GDR competed in the Olympics, the United States won a medal for every 2.2 million people in its population; the GDR won one medal for every 188,000.

*The Leisure Meritocracy*

Achievements in the field of leisure, principally in the area of athletic and sporting prowess, are sought for and prized as much in communist countries as in the West. But whereas in capitalist countries athletic merit might yield largely financial rewards, in communist countries such rewards are smaller, and successful athletes are obliged to draw comfort from the bestowal of honors in the name of party and country. The leisure meritocracy is intended to motivate athletes and act as an inspiration to others, but its major purpose is to reaffirm political values, to signal the accomplishments of which only true believers are capable.

A uniform ranking system for individual sports, setting levels of superior achievement, was developed in Russia in the 1930s. The topmost rank is Master of Sport of the USSR (International Class), with five ranks below this before the junior rankings begin. Political honors also flow to successful athletes. In recognition of the successes at the 1976 Olympic Games in Montreal, athletes, trainers and officials were rewarded by decree of the Supreme Soviet Presidium, 8 of them receiving the Order of Lenin, 27 the Order of the Red Banner, 93 the Badge of Honor, 124 the medal for Working Valor and 60 the medal for Working Excellence. Awards were also bestowed by the winning athletes' home republics and by the enterprises for which they worked. Athletes in the armed services were promoted. Public recognition for service to sport is also given in Czechoslovakia, with the titles Merited Master of Sport and Master of Sport (Kostka, 1978, p. 64). China, too, honors Masters of Sport and First, Second and Third Degree Sportsmen. In Hungary each of thirty-seven recognized sports is governed by its own sports branch of the National Office of Physical Education and Sport. All athletes in each sport are classified and ranked nationally in accordance with past performance.

*Science and Medicine*
Socialist-bloc sport ideology promotes the ideal of human adaptation to an evolving technology. Sports-related activities must conform to the principles of science. It is assumed that all programs will be well conceived according to the principles of physiology, hygiene, anatomy and physics. Riordan (1980, p. 57) notes that medical supervision is an integral part of Soviet sport. 'Every Soviet athlete must have a medical card and a personal care history which is registered at his local sports clinic or club.' The production of champions is systematically engineered by the identification, isolation and coaching of young athletes. Scientific tests are devised to assess the body-type, physiological characteristics, psychological traits, intelligence and competitive drive of future Olympic champions. Nowhere is this approach taken further than in the GDR, where sport has achieved a futuristic scientism; when the president of the West German Sport Federation toured the major East German sport research facility in 1975, he noticed in particular one unusual piece of equipment—a corpse (Hoberman, 1984, p. 207). GDR sport research has required huge expenditures by the state. Responsibility

for the conduct of sport medicine research and care is, significantly, given not to the Ministry of Health but to the Minister of Sport, who is responsible for sport science, the College of Physical Culture in Leipzig and, in conjunction with other ministries, all educational aspects and matters relating to the production of sports equipment. In Hungary elite and advanced training in sports medicine is provided by the Hungarian Academy of Physical Education.

*Political Integration through Physical Culture*
Leisure in communist countries is expected to be more homogeneous and unitary than in democratic regimes. There is no conception of 'taste publics.' Leisure culture 'unites all classes, strata and groups' (Iovchuk and Kogan, 1975, p. 173). There are, admittedly, remaining occupational, regional and ethnic differences in leisure culture, but progress in communist regimes is measured by the extent to which these differences are obliterated and individuals are integrated into one socialist culture.

Physical culture in communist regimes has always been linked to national integration. The many parades and pageants in Russia in the 1930s were intended to create and reinforce national unity as well as to evoke feelings of patriotism. It became the custom in the Soviet Union to mark political anniversaries with physical culture demonstrations. Thus a Russian sports magazine pointed out that 'contests, festivals, spartakiads and other types of sporting competition have played an important part in cementing the friendship of the Soviet peoples' (quoted in Riordan, 1978, p. 19). A prominent Soviet sports philosopher described the tasks of the sports spectacle as follows:

> to help mass education in the spirit of the moral code of the builder of communism; the constant improvement of socialist social relations; demonstrations of the socially valuable qualities of the individual (collectivism, courage, daring, initiative, discipline, friendliness to teammates and respect for them, selflessness, and staunchness when facing an opponent); propaganda of specific sports; and the formation of examples for emulation in the social conduct of young people.
> (Ponomaryov, 1981, p. 204)

The theme of patriotism is given special emphasis as a prophylactic against exposure to foreigners. 'Before major competitions, Soviet sports delegations are taken to Lenin's mausoleum and the grave of the unknown soldier so that they can once again feel the responsibility for defending the sports honor of the Motherland' (Hazan, 1982, p. 39).

Other Soviet-bloc countries also use sports festivals to focus political celebrations. 'It is a rule that Spartakiads should be associated with anniversaries commemorating the national liberation struggle and Czechoslovakia's liberation by the Soviet Army in the last war...they are simultaneously a spontaneous manifestation of the political unity of our nation and peoples' (Kostka, 1978, p. 62). In addition, all Soviet-bloc countries send trainers and coaches abroad on goodwill missions, just as they provide free education for trainee coaches from Third World countries.

## Similarities and Differences

The politics of leisure does not vary much by communist regime. All share a basic doctrine laid down very early by the Soviets and not much altered since. The system of administration, the rationalism, the didacticism, the leisure meritocracies and the emphasis on mass and continuous participation are themes to be found in all countries of the Soviet block and its acolytes. There are, however, a few differences worthy of note because they reflect the different national histories, cultures and rates of modernization of the countries of the communist world. These differences are evidence of the failure to subordinate leisure experiences completely to a common political philosophy.

The regime which has emphasized physical culture most, and the regime which in many ways comes closest to accepting the Western definition of sport, is the GDR. This is due in some part to the activities of Walter Ulbricht, who 'resolved just after the establishment of the GDR on October 7, 1949, to create an exemplary performance-oriented sport culture that would serve as a model for other sectors of East German society' (Hoberman, 1984, p. 202). It is also due to the rivalry between the two Germanies and the decision on the part of the GDR to compete on the international stage as a means of triumphing in this rivalry. The GDR has also signaled its partial independence from the Soviets in spheres outside the Olympics. Although it joined the Soviets in the boycott of the Los Angeles Olympics and, of course, ignored the Americans' boycott call in 1980, it has not followed the Soviet example in international soccer. The Soviets refused to play Chile in a World Cup qualifying round in 1974 as a result of the overthrow of Allende and were disqualified by FIFA. In response the USSR called for a boycott of the World Cup but only managed to get Bulgaria, Poland and Yugoslavia to withdraw. The GDR attended. The closest model to that of East Germany in the communist bloc is Cuba, which has also consciously harnessed sporting achievement to the assertion of national independence and prestige.

Squabbles among communist regimes for leadership of the communist movement are also reflected in differences in approach to sport. The Soviets for a long time championed the cause of the People's Republic of China in its claims to be the 'true' China in the Olympic Games. But after the Sino-Soviet split it came to oppose the PRC's efforts. It was still doing so in 1979 when the PRC was finally admitted, only to have the Chinese join in the US-called boycott of the 1980 games.

Until recently the Chinese have not pursued this strategy of promoting international socialism through sporting competition as vigorously. Maoist sport specialized in an etiquette based on the eradication of hostile feelings toward an opponent. During the Cultural Revolution, as might be expected, this hostility toward competitiveness intensified. The Physical Culture and Sports Commission was put under the control of the General Political Department of the People's Liberation Army. After the collapse of the revolution, as part of a general effort to modernize, a more systematic competition-oriented athleticism has been encouraged. However, China still lacks the resources available to heavily industrialized and urbanized European communist regimes to encourage sophisticated sporting achievements. Chinese physical culture is still stamped by the largely rural and agricultural character of the country's population and economy.

China is also different from the Soviet Union in its claim to care more about the person in the athlete.

> The Chinese have the same respect as the Soviets for scientific training methods. They try to learn the most modern methods in each sport from whoever is the best at it. However, while the Soviets greatly stress scientific training and Pavlovian repetition of skills, the Chinese care more about the human will. The Soviets expect their athletes to be well-rounded physically and intellectually, but the Chinese place special emphasis on constant positive ideological reaffirmation on the part of the athlete wishing to demonstrate his or her loyalty.
>
> (Kanin, 1981, p. 73)

On the other hand, countries like China and Cuba, where the standard of living is relatively low, have not had to face some of the leisure problems encountered in European communist countries, where a rising standard of living and increasing free time have meant that leisure is increasingly looked upon as a consumption item, much as in the West. This means that the state must increase its efforts to control the way in which leisure time is used so that it continues to be edifying and to prevent it being 'antisocial.' Thus in 1966 the Soviets, alarmed at the wasteful way in which people were spending their increased free time and discretionary income, felt obliged to issue a resolution 'On Measures to Promote Physical Culture and Sport' which reiterated the utilitarian and political functions of sport first spelled out in 1925: 'there still is, particularly at the level of ideal patterns or official value prescriptions, a heavy puritanical residue appropriate to a rapidly and forcibly industrializing society, a society of scarcity as far as consumer goods is concerned' (Hollander, 1966, p. 184). In the GDR the concern about the increasingly privatistic use of leisure (e.g. television watching) is if anything even more intense (Childs, 1978, p. 95). These communist-bloc nations are faced with a number of tensions as far as leisure is concerned—between work and play, leisure as free time and idleness or leisure as political education and activity, between free time as 'license' and leisure as social discipline, between free time as 'individual' and free time as 'collective.'

## Leisure in Fascist Regimes

Fascism is totalitarian because it subjugates all areas of life, both public and private, through the use of terror. Thus, in Hitler's Germany all individuals and all organizations had to be 'nationalized' in the sense of making them subject to Nazi Party control. Individuals were organized in groups which sought mastery over their private lives outside their work, from the Hitler Youth to the organization for 'German mothers.' 'The boundaries between public and private activities were abolished, just as the dividing line between politics and the totality of life had ceased to exist' (Mosse, 1966, p. xx).

Leisure in fascist regimes is in many ways similar to that experienced in communist countries. They are alike in seeking to politicize leisure and in the deliberate employment of sport and leisure for political purposes. Neither Hitler nor Mussolini were behind Stalin in their use of sports festivals for nationalist purposes. Indeed, this activity most directly derives from the gymnastics movement of nineteenth-century Germany. The fusion of rhythmic bodies into a symbolic whole was a standard element of all totalitarian liturgies.

*The Sportive Temperament*
The totalitarianism of the right known as fascism structures leisure

rather differently than the totalitarianism of the left as it is practiced in most modern communist societies. As we have seen, Marxism attempts to subordinate the human capacity for violence, aggression and competition to the rational faculties. Leisure must have a rational base and utilitarian function. Communists condemned the irrationality, perverseness and wastefulness of undirected leisure. Fascism, on the other hand, celebrated the human capacity for violence and saw in the utilitarianism and labor fetishism of the communists slavery, boredom and confinement. Hitler, addressing the German Gymnastics Festival in 1933, declared that 'Life will not proceed by weak philosophies, but by strong men' (Hoberman, 1984, p. 165). Politics, for Hitler, 'was the consciousness of race, blood, and soil, the essence of the Nazi Definition of human nature' (Mosse, 1966, p. xx).

The German fascist anthropology of the body can be traced to twentieth-century conservatives like Scheler, for whom

> the body and sport constitute either a salvational vessel containing a vital force which is more important than work—which is beyond redemption—or, in their debased form, they represent a form of leisure which is ultimately utilitarian rather than ludic in character because it offers recuperation from work, or just the boredom pervading society, and nothing more.
> (Hoberman, 1984, p. 39)

It also has its roots in the doctrine of Friedrich Ludwig Jahn (1778–1852), founder of the gymnastics movement in Germany in 1811. It was Jahn who first seized upon the concept of *Volkstum* to denote a cultic and racial nationalism which would require little improvisation on the part of the Nazis. The dream of dynamic virility has been a theme of every fascist culture: 'the body has signified a domain of the irrational, in that it has been interpreted as the sphere of instinct and as the tangible, if illusory, embodiment of racial substance' (Hoberman, 1984, p. 79).

The primary significance of the body for Nazi ideologists thus lay in its racial rather than in its specifically sportive properties. However, there were subthemes within fascist ideologies of leisure. The body metaphor connoted naturalness, growth and, in the context of sport, heroic self-testing. The 'sportive temperament' was characterized by competitive aggressiveness, self-conscious physicality, ascetic indifference to pain and ethical disinterestedness. The hero for the Nazi was not a man of knowledge but one who has developed his power of will to the fullest in order to activate his 'healthy' instinct for what is right.

Especially in Italy, the metaphor of the athlete was applied to fascism's leader (a political athlete) and to the body politic itself in a fashion never encountered in communist regimes. Mussolini's conspicuous athleticism (horseback riding, boxing, car racing) was not simply a publicity trick but derived from a profound physical narcissism which fed energy into public display. There was, then, a distinct physical anthropology in fascist ideology which exalted the sportive temperament.

A second subtheme within fascist ideologies of leisure was a critique of bourgeoise culture. Both communists and fascists accused bourgeois politics of depoliticizing whole areas of public life, in effect of privatizing them. Leisure was a conspicuous example of one of these areas which the communists and the fascists felt obliged to recolonize. But whereas the communists rejected bourgeois sport because it exploited the masses and dehumanized its participants, fascists rejected it because its encouragement of spectatorism made it too passive, its intellectuality robbed it of virility, and its emphasis on intrinsic motivation robbed it of its necessary political role. The fascists refused to accept that leisure could be an end in itself and were always ambivalent about individual record setting and about the importance of success in international competition.

A final subtheme of fascist ideology linked sport to a total aesthetic of dynamism and virility. Hoberman (1984, p. 91) reminds us that fascism was, 'as much as anything else, a political aesthetic and therefore a phenomenon of style.' In Germany this took the form of the exaltation of the warrior-athlete, the 'hard' and virile physical specimen exemplified in the SS officer. In Italy this subtheme was expressed in the writings of the futurist Filippo Marinetti and echoed by Mussolini himself. For the futurists, the present age was dynamic, and speed was of the essence. A dynamic age was ripe for the imagery of sport, especially motor sport, where speed was an intoxicant, 'an apotheosis of irrational experience' that expressed perfectly the fascist style of politics (Hoberman, 1984, p. 62).

*The Administration of Fascist Leisure*
The actual practice of sports in fascist regimes was never focused so directly on the achievement of specific political or military ends as it has been in communist countries. This has something to do with the differences in structure between the two regimes; fascism encourages private enterprise up to a point and must filter its political directives through these private institutions or otherwise make use of them. Nevertheless, National Socialism implied the colonization of its citizens' free time. No one could be allowed to stand aside. Beginning in 1933, fascist organizations in Germany absorbed or

coopted most private leisure organizations, swallowing school, family and many church groups. All the various German sporting associations were merged into and subsumed by the Reich Federal Sports Association (Mandell, 1971, p. 60).

The Hitler Youth movement was designed to absorb all youth leisure activities and orient them to the needs of the party. Not all pre-fascist youth movements willingly complied with or joined the movement, Catholic organizations proving to be remarkably resilient. However, even these were worn down by 1936, when a law was passed making membership in the Hitler Youth compulsory. Even though the executive order needed to make this law effective was not passed until 1939, the fact that having been in the Hitler Youth was made a prerequisite for party membership and for most civil service jobs effectively ensured compliance from all except the most hostile political and religious groups. By 15 March of the year in which he or she reached the age of 10, every German youngster was obliged to register with the local state youth headquarters. There was a division for boys and a division for girls. The League of German Girls had as its cornerstone physical health for the purposes of 'efficient motherhood.' The paradigm was far different from that later seen in communist countries like the GDR. 'The ideal female athlete must be a *female* athlete, which means eventual motherhood is the chief criterion of fitness. As early as 1935 nearly half a million girls participated in over three hundred sports festivals designed to further the process of "buxomisation"' (Becker, 1946, p. 187).

For boys, 'The ideal was to produce youths who were slim and strong, swift as greyhounds, tough as leather, and hard as Krupps steel' (Stachura, 1981, p. 144). Pursuits which had rather innocuously occupied the time of youth groups before 1933, such as camping and hiking, were invested with direct political significance by the Hitler Youth. 'Hiking...ceased being a merely pleasurable ramble by a group of friends around the countryside; it became an exercise in physical and ideological development' (Stachura, 1981, p. 140). More competitive sports also attracted considerable interest. By 1939 the Reich Sports Competition was attracting nearly 7 million participants. Sporting instincts were also harnessed to the needs of industry. A scheme of vocational training was structured around 'championships.' Constant propaganda appeals were made to persuade German youth to 'train' for victory in the skills of bricklaying, carpentry and the like, and a system of 'preliminaries,' semi-finals and finals was directly borrowed from the world of sport. Of course, vocational skill alone was not to be allowed to determine victory; 'personality, family background, physical appearance, and other attributes were considered to an extent relevant to the tasks at hand' (Becker, 1946, p. 185). Adults were not ignored, although the bureaucracy involved was somewhat less complex. State construction projects would usually have associated with them supervised leisure-time activities. The highway construction camps of the State Labor Service were cared for by the 'Office of Leisure Time' of the 'National Socialist Community of Strength through Joy,' which maintained its own 'State Highway Theatre' (Stollman, 1978, p. 43).

*The Culture of Consent*
The National Socialists made even more use of mass rallies than did their Soviet contemporaries. The mass meeting became one of the most important techniques of the Nazi movement for mobilizing support, especially in its early years. Indeed, daily life was permeated by celebrations, ceremonies, artificially created customs and staged folklore. 'Analogous to the calendar of celebrations of the Christian Church there was a "calendar of National Socialism" with a number of holidays which were all more or less ritually observed' (Stollman, 1978, p. 43).

The National Socialists also made excellent use of the most resplendent rally of them all, the Olympics. For the 1936 Olympics the Germans organized an Olympic Exhibition which lauded the achievements of National Socialism. The Nazis seized this opportunity to link the Aryan culture to the culture of the ancient Greeks. A German newspaper said of the Olympics, 'It is the supreme achievement of the totalitarian state' (quoted in Mandell, 1971, p. 281). After the Olympics were over, 'thousands of ordinary tourists left with a sense of aesthetic fulfillment, a conviction of German efficiency, and a vague impression that National Socialism was not the horror that they had imagined it to be' (Guttman, 1984, p. 79). Most were content to ignore the exclusion of Jews from the rosters of the participating fascist nations and only feebly protested the difficulties placed in the way of countries with Jews among their athletes.

The fascists in Italy practiced what might be described as a selective totalitarianism. However, they did make a number of efforts to colonize leisure for political purposes, and these often involved the state in the supervision and control of everyday leisure pursuits. The approach of Italian fascism to leisure can be understood only in the context of that regime's need to 'nationalize the masses' in a country which had not long been united and where a civic culture was almost non-existent. On assuming power, the fascists were faced with the task of making the working population as a whole respond to and endure the pressures of a distorted economic growth in a country where the distance between the government and the governed was vast, regional differences sharp and political divisions especially bitter. In this they were aided by two forces. One was the advances in mass communications technology, especially radio and film, which did much to facilitate the emergence of a national civic culture. The other was the emergence of what in the United States came to be called 'welfare capitalism'—programs of business-guided and -sponsored social activities ranging from child-rearing practices to social activities such as sports—all designed to combat unionism, lower absenteeism and increase productivity. The paternalism of the nineteenth century was replaced by a science-based, technocratic approach to the regulation of the workers' free time, an approach the fascists encouraged and themselves employed. Leisure was thus related to the welfare of the nation in a technocratic way, properly managed and designed leisure being seen as a means of improving the efficiency of the worker and the economic health and political strength of the country. The fascists at first simply endorsed company largess. However, as we shall see, welfare capitalism worked better when what began as a private managerial operation, through its public character, became more acceptable to the workers.

The Italian fascists' principal effort to colonize the free time of the populace was the Opera Nazionale Dopolavoro (OND) or the National Agency on After-Work, set up in 1923. The *dopolavoro* was initially organized as a paragovernment foundation including both public and private appointees. Its quasi-autonomy from the state allowed it greater flexibility with regard to its financial arrangements and its relationship to local and private initiatives. By 1926, however, it had become a full-fledged auxiliary of the Fascist Party and became the regime's chief weapon in its battle to win the consent of the governed. In 1937 the regulation of leisure was further centralized when the OND was finally changed from a paragovernment organization in which membership could be held to an agency under the direct control (nominally, at least) of Mussolini. It became a public service, and the local affiliates which until then had enjoyed considerable autonomy were absorbed fully into the state apparatus.

*Dopolavori* were recreation circles, organized on a local scale, serving to coordinate and mediate popular entertainments, sports and outings, which in liberal democratic societies waxed and waned in response to market demand and supply. Each was a club in which people could enroll. The OND negotiated discounts with retailers and offered insurance in an effort to attract members but also to stimulate rational consumption and thrift. Discounts to cinemas and theatres and traveling entertainment caravans helped democratize exposure to culture.

*Dopolavoro* sports 'reached out to the masses' rather than seeking champions or grooming exceptional athletes to break records. Team efforts to promote solidarity were combined with competition to teach discipline. 'The ideal *dopolovorista sportive* was indeed the disciplined mass man; not overly competitive, yet with a well-developed "self-confidence" and a sense of "fair-play," "fit" and "virile" with a profound sense of team spirit' (De Grazia, 1981, p. 173). It need hardly be added that *dopolavoro* sports were overwhelmingly male-oriented.

Sports subsidies became increasingly lavish and, from the late 1920s, increasingly propagandized by the fascist regime. The Fascist Sports Charter of 1929 put the national Olympic Committee in charge of all professional, competitive and international sports and the OND in charge of essentially noncompetitive games, amateur associations and the 'low sports' like *bocce* and tug-of-war. The 'high sports' were financed both by lavish government expenditures and by private sports promoters. The state paid for public soccer stadiums, granted generous tax incentives to sports impresarios and subsidized international travel for sports teams. This political support for the mass spectator sports served the regime's propaganda purposes well, and their popularity was thought to act as something like an opiate, but it did not sit well with the attempts to achieve disciplined solidarity and physical fitness through the *dopolavoro*.

OND propaganda was directed at 'uplifting' the status of popular pastimes (such as bowls, bands and amateur theatricals), sanctioning their practice as contributing to the formation of a new national culture that would transcend class or regional boundaries. National competitions were organized for pastimes as different as drama and *bocce* in order to destroy their class character. Popular pastimes were thought to represent opportunities to sustain old allegiances. Unless they were in some way detached from the social forms that shaped them, or were infused with an entirely new meaning, the fascists could not expect to break down resistance to their rule, much less inculcate a new sense of national unity. Strenuous efforts were therefore made to nationalize these popular pastimes. 'Formal regulations for traditionally unstructured games and prescriptions on content and rules of conduct were enforced by official supervision and incentives in the forms of subsidies, critical acclaim and a hierarchy of contests' (De Grazia, 1981, p. 170). Tourism was not exempted from this nationalization strategy. The regime promoted tourism to instill in a parochial public the sense of a 'greater Italy.'

However, group activities were strictly controlled; all outings had to be registered with *dopolovaro* officials. Although regional differences were a concern, the major object of these initiatives was to destroy class allegiances.

Although fascist groups mounted attacks on socialist recreation clubs in the struggle for power, once the fascists were firmly in place the use of leisure for purposes of destroying working-class allegiances was always indirect. In contrast to communist policy, *dopolavoro* strategy was to divorce leisure from production, to attach leisure to the community rather than the workplace. The *cultura dopolavorista* was a policy of diversion from political concerns rather than a program designed to implant fascist principles. Escapism was officially encouraged. Lando Ferretti, first fascist president of the Italian Olympic Committee, considered sports 'the best distraction for youth otherwise tempted by political activities' (De Grazia, 1981, p. 171). This is not to say, however, that sanctioned leisure activities were ethically neutral. Conformism, moralism, social individualism and modest achievement—quintessentially petty-bourgeois values— were given public sanction and universal application.

The success of the fascists in securing the consent of the governed through the colonization of leisure time must be judged in terms of the goals they set for themselves and in the context of more general social developments in leisure time. The Italian fascists were not generally inclined to expend excessive energy regulating groups that posed no obvious threat to their rule. Nor did they seek to extend state or party control into areas of civil life where a responsive audience would have served no immediate political or economic purpose. And the efforts by the fascist regime to act as midwife to the emergence of mass leisure in Italy were only separated by degree from the more private efforts being made in liberal democracies to deal with the increasingly severe 'problem' of worker leisure created by the reduction in the working day and increases in discretionary income. In the United States this leisure problem was attacked by a combination of business, voluntary and state initiatives. In Italy it took the form of direct government intervention, and in Nazi Germany it took the form of the 'Strength through Joy' organization set up in November 1933. Similar organizations were set up in Portugal and Spain.

That the fascists were not always successful is indicated by the reaction of peasants to the *dopolavoro* organization, especially in the South, where membership remained low throughout the interwar years. Its own officials were forced to admit, by the late 1930s, that it conducted 'no political propaganda whatsoever among the masses' (De Grazia, 1981, p. 227). Complaints of corruption and inefficiency were frequently heard, and party officials bemoaned the lack of political content to the programs of the recreation circles. De Grazia (1981, p. 243) points to much more serious obstacles to the success of the OND. These include the remarkably low level of popular consumption, official indifference to traditional concepts of culture, the government's solicitous respect for private enterprise, the failure of social reform movements to appease the working class or erode support for the communists and, ultimately, participation in a highly unpopular war. The regime's effort to use leisure to overcome class conflicts ultimately failed, accentuating capitalists' dependency on the state while leaving the industrial working class highly skeptical about the unpolitical nature of the national culture.

## Consent Denied

In both fascist and communist countries leisure was thoroughly politicized. But in neither has leisure been a central part of government planning and practice. Fascist ideology, coupled with its tolerance of capitalist enterprises, meant that its colonization of leisure must always be less ambitious and less complete than that either planned or achieved in communist countries. In the latter, industrialization and rising consumer affluence with its attendant privatism have created increasing problems in the political administration of leisure. And the increasing importance of international sporting achievement on a world stage more brilliantly illuminated by the mass media polarizes elite and mass sports, and encourages the adoption of bourgeois notions of sport that are professional in all but name. It is with this world of international sporting competition that Chapter 7 will deal.

# 7
# Leisure and Nationalism

The years between 1870 and 1914 can be regarded as the period when state, nation and society began to converge. Seen from below, the state increasingly defined the largest stage on which the crucial activities determining human lives as subjects and citizens were played out. Political elites became increasingly aware of the importance of 'irrational' elements such as national holidays, ceremonies and festivals in binding the loyalty of people to this new entity and for marking the boundaries between 'us' and 'them'—aliens, foreigners, strangers. As we shall see, all manner of leisure pursuits, and sport in particular, have played an important role in these affirmations of identity and unity.

Regardless of political regime, modern societies now routinely use leisure to make claims for nationhood, to establish the boundaries of their nation-state, to establish an identity for their people, to deny the claims of other peoples for nationhood, to integrate existing conglomerates into national communities and to symbolize and reaffirm hierarchies of power and status among the nations of the world. Modern communications technology makes sporting competitions of national interest immediately available to citizens at home, who are much more likely to identify with the elite athletes representing their country than they would identify with artists, or even politicians.

The topic of leisure and nationalism can be considered under a number of subheadings. Leisure activities can be used by newly emerging nations to establish a presence on the world stage; they are a means of achieving nationhood, which requires not only recognition of the legitimacy of the nation by its own peoples but recognition by other countries. Leisure activities can also be used internationally for the same purposes they are used intranationally, to symbolize the distribution of rewards in the world system and as a surrogate for economic and military competition between established nations. Pastimes can also be used by states to strengthen their hold over the allegiance of the people, to unite and solidify the nation. Popular pastimes can equally well be used by groups seeking to resist this integration. Finally, nationalism plays a role in the internal organization of leisure activities. For example, the international sporting order helps shape how a nation's sporting associations operate and how sport resources are distributed within the country.

When we think of leisure in an international context we tend to think of sport. Leisure is more deployable as a symbol of the nation the more it is seen as a central, deliberately contrived national institution, rather than as an individual, spontaneously generated, unserious activity. Leisure has to reach a certain stage of incorporation to be usable; its use for nationalistic purposes, in turn, alters its character, rendering it more formal and more centralized. It is bureaucratized play, or sport, that is used as a weapon in international conflict, not the more amorphous world of leisure.

## Achieving Nationhood

In a new nation, sports have a dual function in the building of national identity and national competence. Nation-building is ultimately connected with social mobility, which implies people moving physically, but even more mentally, as they broaden their horizons. Social mobilization starts from the center of a social system and spreads outward to the periphery. Sporting activities do likewise. Sports can thus play a role in the mobilization of peripheral countries to new awareness and hence in social development. In the case of nations forged out of many formerly constituent units, the demarcation of the nation-state requires a show of strength and unity. Sporting success in the international arena, which is highly visible and easy to quantify, is ideally suited for this purpose. The use of sport to inculcate political loyalties to the system as a whole, transcending bonds of kinship, language and locale, has been widespread in the Western world and, after the Second World War, in the communist-bloc countries and their non-European satellites.

Even countries that do not use sport to achieve a sense of national unity find it useful when making a claim for international acceptance. Almost literally, the arena in which the credibility of this claim is judged is usually the Olympic Games. The games are available for this purpose because, ironically, the Olympic movement has pursued two contradictory goals. The Olympic Charter declares the non-political purpose of the Olympic movement. Supporters of the Olympic movement have attempted repeatedly to preserve Olympism by diminishing nationalism within amateur sports. They have constantly sought to restrict the use of national flags and anthems and the use of official 'points' tables.

On the other hand, the revival of the Olympic Games had strong nationalist motives, a series of early reforms paved the way for subsequent nationalist manipulations of the games, and most modern participants have blatant nationalist motives. Pierre de Coubertin himself saw the Olympics as helping restore the vigor of French youth and building loyalty to and pride in France. The 1896 Olympic Games in Athens were primarily used as a tool for achieving national unity by a Greek dynasty under domestic pressure. In the games of the 1900s, political identification of competitors soon led to national teams, a tendency encouraged by Coubertin's insistence on a parade of athletes by nation at the beginning of the games and the raising of the flag and playing of anthems during the victory ceremonies. Olympic rules actually allowed medal tables between 1896 and 1914. The 'First New Nation,' the United States, was also the first to advertise itself through its victories in the modern political sport system; as early as 1906 the American press was scoring the Olympics on a national basis (Kanin, 1978, p. 249). Soon thereafter no athlete would be allowed to compete as an individual or appear in Olympic events out of national uniform. The original Olympic Charter calls for the 'support of Government' and gave nations the task of holding elimination trials. The International Olympic Committee (IOC) has persisted in using national Olympic committees as its base, refusing requests for recognition from sports organizations not affiliated with these national committees; and the committees, in turn, have identified themselves with the nation-state in order to establish their claim to legitimacy.

It comes as no surprise, then, that problems of national identity arose almost immediately after the revival of the Olympic Games and have continued to plague the movement as nations and would-be nations use this forum to stake a claim to legitimacy on the world political stage. The Finns protested at having to compete under the Russian flag in 1908 and 1914. Bohemia, one of the founding members of the Olympic movement, was prevented from participating by Austria-Hungary after 1912. In the early 1920s both Morocco and the Philippines wanted to enter the games under their own emblems and flags but, because they were not self-governing, were forced to compete as part of their governing nation's teams. Special dispensation had to be sought from France and the United States to permit these countries to compete as autonomous bodies.

The emergence of the People's Republic of China on to the world stage was also symbolized by its acceptance into the system of international sport competition. The issue was greatly complicated by the continued existence of a rival claim to the title of China, from the government on Formosa. In its first vote on this question, in 1954, the IOC opted to recognize both Chinas.

> In this way they followed the political developments of the day. Their ruling, for all intents and purposes, recognized two separate states: Peking-China and Formosa-China. To that extent they did not sacrifice their rules, for the rules stated that their could be only one committee per country. By recognizing two committees they recognized two countries.
>
> (Espy, 1979, p. 45)

Despite its claim to be the one true China, the PRC seems to have accepted this ruling and prepared in earnest for the 1956 Melbourne Olympics, only to withdraw at the last minute because of Nationalist China's participation. In 1958 the PRC severed all connections with the IOC. It did not immediately return when, in 1959, the IOC removed Nationalist China from its rolls as a body representing all of China. The Nationalist Chinese competed as 'Taiwan' for the first time in the 1960 Rome games. By the 1960s the PRC was more concerned with the threat of the USSR to its security than the threat of the West and used sport to underscore differences within the communist camp itself. It organized a military sport meet in 1964 which involved thirteen communist states but gave pride of place to Albania, Romania, Mongolia, North Korea and North Vietnam—all acolytes of China and hostile to the Soviets (Kanin, 1978, p. 269).

Sport is used to make gestures of international hostility and rejection which, if other means were used, might be too provocative or disruptive of alliances. The sport boycott of South Africa is a case in point, where countries which cannot agree on commercial sanctions can unite to withdraw sporting relations. Conversely, sport can be used to give a sense of 'normalcy' when international tensions are high. Between the two world wars, English soccer touring teams, along with many other sporting organizations, traveled abroad and played along guidelines laid down by the Foreign Office. The Football Association was given firm instructions concerning which countries they should visit and which they should avoid, although in public the government presented a totally different face, and spokesmen openly denounced the idea of political interference in sport (Walvin, 1975, p. 126). These visits helped reinforce the normalcy of the fascist regimes in Germany and Italy.

In the 1958–66 period of the cold war Soviet-American track and field meets were one of the few arenas in which members of the two countries met. They survived the U-2 incident, the second Berlin crisis, the Cuban missile crisis and the abrupt changes in both superpower regimes in 1963–4. The athletic meets became a victim of the American escalation of the air war in Vietnam when the Soviets refused to attend the scheduled Los Angeles track meet in 1966. Sporting ties have not been sufficient to repair relations between Cuba and the United States. Even though sport exchanges between the United States and Cuba have received a fair amount of publicity, they have not served to break new political ground for the two countries.

Countries can use international sport to resume a place on the stage after a period of being an international pariah. Germany's return to international respectability after the First World War was signaled in 1928 with its readmission to the Olympic movement. The Federal Republic of Germany was readmitted to the Olympic movement in 1951 only after its national committee had 'publicly apologised for World War II and the German atrocities' (Espy, 1979, p. 29).

The Soviets were admitted to the Olympic movement in 1952, but on terms negotiated by the Soviets that would clearly indicate their difference from the Western nations that had dominated international sports between the wars. For example, they demanded that Russian be made an official language of the Olympic movement and that Soviet officials be guaranteed a seat on the executive committee of the IOC. The culmination of the Soviets' efforts to achieve respectability in the international sporting arena was their hosting of the 1980 Olympic Games, which gave them a chance to show off not only on the athletic field but also in technology and social organization.

Sport was an important tool in the guided restoration of Japan after 1945. 'Olympic veteran McArthur ordered baseball competition renewed and arranged for the participation of Japanese swimmers in American meets' (Kanin, 1981, p. 83). Sport was one of several ways the United States government tried to make sure that American values took hold at all levels of Japanese society. A measure of the extent of the incorporation of Japan's sport into the international order was the country's hosting of the Olympic Games in 1964. By then the games had become truly pan-national events, part of the global village and only loosely attached to the people of the hosting nation. 'The 1964 Olympic Games were a typically Western event, barely touched by elements of Japan's own cultural heritage' (Kanin, 1981, p. 84).

Long before then, the hosting of the Olympic Games had become perhaps the most dramatic means for a country to stake its claim to be at the center of the world stage. The Japanese were not concerned about the 'unJapanese' character of their games because their interest was in gaining acceptance as a legitimate trading partner, a modern nation, at the core of the world's economy. Mexico's hosting of the 1968 Olympics in Mexico had a similar purpose. The Mexicans deliberately sought to overcome their status as a Third World, debtor nation by agreeing to host an expensive event. Hosting the games would signal their parity with and independence of the United States. They also sought, in the cultural events surrounding the games, to revive the spirit of revolutionary independence that had founded the nation. Mexico's hosting of the 1986 FIFA World Cup amidst a mounting debt crisis had a similar aim.

There can be no doubt, then, that sport is a popular tool for the assertion of nationhood. But we should not exaggerate its importance on the world scene. Highly bureaucratized competitive sports are a creature of the Western capitalist world, and their role has not been so salient in the birth and development of the many new nations that have emerged with the collapse of colonialism. In both Africa and South-East Asia, elite athletes have been trained to act as ambassadors for their countries, and regional confederations (e.g. the All-Africa Games, GANEFO) have been formed to provide an arena for non-Western ideas about sport. But sport has been placed on the back burner when it comes to allocating resources for national development, physical culture being secondary to providing shelter, clothing and nourishment. African countries have viewed sport in a 'lethargic manner' (Uwechue, 1978, p. 546), while those in South-East Asia have fine programs for sport 'on paper—and little else' (Uwechue, 1978, p. 538). Sport *can* be a tool of national integration, but the human and material resources needed to make it perform this task are usually unavailable or otherwise committed in newly emerging nations outside the West.

## Sport and the World System of Exchange

Sport is such a communicative marker of international placement and standing because, unlike so many other forms of international exchange, it is inherently competitive. Art works can be exchanged without *necessarily* leading to a comparison of national heritage, whereas sport demands that comparisons be made. Sport, unlike most art, is a phenomenon of the masses, who understand its rules and recognize its players, with whose successes and failures they are likely to be thoroughly conversant. Sport competition can also be finely tuned to symbolize the state of relations between countries. Sport competition between two intense political rivals tends to be equally intense, while between two allies of unequal strength it tends to be gauged so that the bigger party does not humiliate the former. The beauty of sport for the politician is that the same sport can be used both by the dominating country and by the country struggling for equality, because it has no intrinsic political value. It can be used to justify any political claim, any political philosophy.

International sport can be looked upon as a ladder, reaching down from countries in the center of international affairs to those on the periphery. For example, it has always been very clear that Olympic success is distributed roughly in the same manner as any other reward in the international system—according to GNP, per capita income and so on. It is a ladder well used by centrally planned countries such as the GDR, who use sporting elites to acquire a position in the sporting arenas of the world, usually far above their achievements in economic, political, military and cultural spheres. Conversely, powerful nations have seen their leadership threatened by sporting challenges, and declining nations have seen their fall affirmed on the playing-field.

The break-up of the British Empire is poignantly marked by the rise to supremacy of former colonies in international competition in games 'exported' to colonies by Britain. West Indian cricket is a vivid example. Tours by the England side began to generate overt hostility as early as the 1950s. James (1963, p. 49) writes that the English team seemed intent on giving the impression 'that it was not merely playing cricket but was out to establish the prestige of Britain and, by that, of the local whites.' Riots during the Test matches of 1960 expressed the hostility of blacks seeking independence against local whites and their black 'retainers.'

Colonies populated mainly by settlers from England were placed in an especially excruciating dilemma. They sought to assert their equality with the mother country but not necessarily on Britain's own terms. As early as the 1880s cricket matches between England and Australia were riddled with a mixture of brotherly competition and political rivalry. 'On the one hand, victories over Englishmen were deemed by some as a demonstration of the strength of Australian abilities, while on the other, the fact that Australia played the English game of cricket demonstrated the basic "Englishness" of Australians' (Caldwell, 1982, p. 174).

The sport 'world system' of exchange and cooperation corresponds only roughly to the world system of exchange and production in trade. The Olympic movement marks the outer boundaries of this sport world but it is rivaled by international networks set up by individual sport organizations such as FIFA, which every four years mounts the World Cup soccer tournament. Nations also organize themselves into regional tournaments, such as the European Games and the Pan-American Games, and organize competitions between members of pan-national units such as the Friendship Games between countries of the Warsaw Pact and the Commonwealth Games among former members of the British Empire. These smaller networks of relations often shift the balance of sporting power in ways meaningful to less powerful nations. For example, Cuba has devoted much of its energies to the Pan-American Games (first held in 1951) because there it does not have to compete with many of the world's greatest athletic states. Even though it must compete head to head with the United States, the latter does not always field its strongest team, enabling Cuba to make its mark where it most keenly desires to do so, in Latin America.

The idea of international athletics being used as a demonstration of a country's prowess is foreshadowed in the 'exposition,' the first of which, held at the Crystal Palace in 1851, was frequently imitated in the next one hundred years, especially in France and the United States. The founder of the modern Olympics, Pierre de Coubertin, 'was seduced by the exposition tradition' (MacAloon, 1981, p. 138). It is no accident that the third, fourth and fifth Olympics (1900, 1904, 1908) were attached to World Fairs.

The Olympic Games' early association with expositions and World Fairs came back to haunt them. The fairs and the games were among the first international markets—of objects, ideas and people. The first Olympics dealt not only with sports but with the arts too. Under the leadership of Coubertin, the games began to serve as a public reinforcement of the myths of Western civilization's superiority over colonial peoples. In both the Olympic and the Commonwealth games, the latter of opportunity—becoming more like the West—was carefully described.

IOC policies have continued to serve the West better than the East. The IOC recognized the Federal Republic of Germany in 1951. Possessing by far a larger population and having more widespread political acceptance, Bonn quickly came to dominate the unified German teams celebrating the Olympiads from 1952 to 1964. This policy fitted very nicely the interest of the NATO countries in affirming their position on Berlin (Espy, 1979, p. 78). Ironically, this strategy of containment only served to increase the East Germans' desire to have their own representation. Until 1956 the GDR had hoped to spread its ideology and power into the Western zones and for this reason agreed to joint participation with West Germany. 'However, when it became obvious that the union of West and East

Germany under Soviet bloc control was a lost cause all effort subsequently went into a drive for sovereignty and independence' (Carr, 1974, p. 124). The two Germanies participated jointly in the 1960s Olympics in Rome, but relations soured in 1961 with the erection of the Berlin Wall. A joint team was sent to the 1964 games, but it took an enormous amount of diplomatic efforts to ensure this. By the 1968 games the IOC was anxious to secure a compromise, so it recognized two German Olympic committees but stipulated that all Germans march under a neutral flag and that Beethoven's 'Ode to Joy' be played on the occasion of a victory by either West or East Germans. The IOC Congress in 1968 finally and officially recognised the German Democratic Republic. As late as 1962 GDR athletes seeking to attend the World Wrestling Championship in Toledo were denied visas on the grounds that they traveled under a passport not recognized by the United States. 'When in 1972 the East Germans marched into the Olympisches Stadium in Munich, they achieved their ultimate objective; they quite literally flaunted their flag before their hosts from the Federal Republic, who had publicly to acknowledge East Germany's legitimacy as well as East German athletic prowess' (Guttman, 1984, p. 157).

No tactic of international public diplomacy, not even trade embargoes, has attracted so much attention, nor been so extensively used, as the sports boycott. Boycotting a sports event is an especially appealing diplomatic strategy because it rarely costs the state money, hurts only a small constituency directly (athletes) and can be interpreted (if this is found expedient) as an attack on an organization other than the state (e.g. a sports federation or the Olympic committee).

Communists and socialists tried to organize boycotts of the 1932 and 1936 Olympic Games, but the practice of organizing a boycott of the Olympics began to occur on a wide scale only after the Second World War as a consequence of the conflicts generated by the rise of the Soviet bloc and by decolonization. The Netherlands, Spain and Switzerland boycotted the 1956 Melbourne Olympics to protest the Soviet invasion of Hungary (both the Soviets and the Hungarians took part), and the same games were boycotted by Egypt, Lebanon and Iraq to protest the occupation of the Suez Canal by Britain, France and Israel. Just how complicated and intricate boycotts can become is illustrated by the 1976 Olympic Games in Montreal, when thirty countries boycotted the games because New Zealand, which had earlier played rugby against South Africa, was participating. Even the African members of the IOC opposed this boycott. The IOC protested that it had nothing to do with the question of the rugby matches; rugby is not even an Olympic sport, and the IOC had already expelled South Africa from the Olympic movement. Interestingly, by 1979 the IOC had seemingly come to adopt the position of the 1976 boycotting nations, warning France that a scheduled tour of France by the South African rugby team would result in its expulsion from the Moscow Games. The United States threatened to boycott these same games because Canada would not allow Taiwan to fly its flag. The threat was not called because the Taiwanese refused the compromise of marching behind the Olympic banner.

The United States did better four years later when it used the boycott to protest the Soviets' invasion of Afghanistan a few days before Christmas 1979. This case is of interest not only because of the size and effectiveness of the action but also because of what it reveals about the 'independence' of national Olympic committees in Western capitalist countries. In January 1980 President Carter delivered a major address to the American people in which he stated that the United States might not take part in the Moscow Olympic Games if the Soviet Union continued its 'aggressive action' in Afghanistan. Carter also threatened to embargo grain sales, ban the export of high-technology goods and curtail scientific and cultural exchanges. The Soviets were given an ultimatum of withdrawing by 16 February or facing a boycott of the games. Strictly speaking, the Carter administration had no power to make this threat because American participation in the games was a decision for the United States Olympic Committee (USOC) to make. On 20 January, Carter sent a letter to the USOC, urging it to lobby the IOC to cancel the games, or at least move them. This pressure was increased by a congressional resolution that the games be boycotted. In March, Carter personally lobbied the USOC, claiming that 'national security' was at stake and asking it not to compete. In April the USOC voted two to one not to go to Moscow.

Lord Killanin (1983, p. 179), then president of the IOC, noted that the timing of this crisis was unfortunate for the USOC.

> Unhappily, the USOC was not as independent as it had been in the past because of the Amateur Athletics Act of 1978, passed by the US Congress, making the USOC virtually the official governing body of all sports in the United States. The constitution of this committee is a complex one in that through the act it is answerable in some ways to the government.

Killanin (1983, p. 175) believed that Carter's 'glib ideas about moving the Games were neither politic nor desirable, and the idea of postponing events for a year took no account of the complexity of the international sporting program or the strict IOC rule that the Games take place in the last year of the Olympiad.'

Political pressure on the Canadian national Olympic committee was, if anything, more intense. Canada's Minister of External Affairs declared that 'the Soviet action in Afghanistan makes it wholly inappropriate to hold the Games in Moscow' (Cantelon, 1984, p. 145). The government did not go so far as threatening to revoke the passports of participating athletes, but it did withdraw financial support. After having initially voted in favor of attending, the Canadian NOC succumbed to political pressure and voted to boycott in April 1980. This action reflected not only political philosophy but the dependence of the NOC on state funding, as spelled out in the 1961 Fitness and Amateur Sport Act. 'Since that time, the federal government has become a dominant factor in Canadian sport, particularly at the national and international levels' (Cantelon, 1984, p. 147). Over 90 percent of the funding for amateur sports in Canada comes from the federal government.

In Britain, although political pressure was just as intense, the absence of strong linkages between amateur sports and the state made compliance with the Thatcher government's directives less predictable. After the invasion of Afghanistan, a newly formed hands off Afghanistan committee of MPs wrote to the British Olympic Association chairman (Dennis Follows) urging a boycott of the games. The House of Commons voted 315 to 147 in favor of a boycott. Prime Minister Thatcher called on the BOA to approach the IOC and suggest a movement or postponement of the games. She even offered three sites in Britain and £50 million toward the expenses of moving the games (Riordan, 1984b).

Intense pressure was brought to bear on the television networks to reflect the official government line on the boycott. 'Coverage as originally planned by the TV networks was scaled down drastically, and the media as a whole sought news angles consonant with the conventional political definitions and stereotypes' (Hargreaves, 1986, p. 157). However, there was also considerable opposition to joining in the boycott, and £800,000 was raised to fund athletes who wanted to attend. In March the BOA voted to defy the government and send a team. Consisting of 326 people, it was the fourth largest at the games.

Eventually, 80 out of the 146 member countries ignored the boycott. Those who sided with the USA did so for a variety of reasons. The Supreme Council for Sport in Africa counseled against the boycott, but some African countries nevertheless joined in. Several countries close to or sympathetic with the Afghanistan people supported the boycott (e.g. Pakistan, Indonesia, Malaysia and

Egypt). The monarchies of the Middle East supported the boycott for reasons of anti-communism, as did Israel, but the more radical secular states (e.g. Syria) did not. Countries of Southeast Asia split along ideological lines, with Japan, the Philippines, Singapore and Thailand supporting it and Vietnam, Laos and Kampuchea opposing it. China joined in the boycott for its own anti-Soviet reasons. In Europe, only West Germany, Norway and Turkey supported the boycott. Here, a country's position on the boycott said something both about the prevailing political sympathies and the degree of control the government exercised over sport, with the former probably being more important. In France, Minister of Sport Soisson promised to permit French sporting authorities complete control over the participation of their athletes in the games. But more influential was the position of the French government that Afghanistan was a South Asian rather than a European problem.

According to Lord Killanin (1983, p. 221), 'The boycott of the Moscow games was the most damaging event since the games were revived in 1896.' It had no discernible effect on Soviet foreign policy.

Predictably, the Soviets refused to participate in the Los Angeles Olympic Games in 1984—although at no time did they refer to their actions as a boycott. In April 1984 the Soviets first raised serious question about the security of their delegation to the games and voiced their disapproval of the 'uncontrollable commercialism' of the games. On 9 May 1984 they announced that they would not be participating, giving a number of reasons for their decision. They charged the United States with violating the Olympic Charter, in first demanding visas of visiting Soviet Olympians and then, when this was successfully protested, asking to be provided with a list of all athletes coming to the United States. They repeated their doubts about the security measures taken to protect Soviets and also complained that the Reagan administration was using the games for political ends. On 9 May, Bulgaria also announced that it would not be attending the games, followed by East Germany on 10 May. By 17 May, Poland, Vietnam, Mongolia, Hungary, Czechoslovakia, Laos and Afghanistan had joined the boycott. Eventually, South Yemen, North Korea, Iran, Albania, Libya, Cuba, Ethiopia and Angola added their names to the list of eighteen countries not participating in the 1984 Olympics. This was a small fraction of all countries invited, but without the Soviets, East Germans and Cubans, many victories were hollow.

There can be little doubt that politically inspired boycotts of international sporting events are here to stay. In 1986 the Commonwealth Games in Edinburgh were boycotted by thirty-two of the fifty-eight invited countries, most of them from Africa and the Carribean. The reason for the boycott was the British government's failure to impose strong sanctions against South Africa. The games were an athletic and financial failure. In that same year the North Koreans headed a small boycott of the Asian Games in protest at the awarding of the 1988 Olympics to South Korea and the refusal of South Korea to share the role of host.

## The World Order of Sport as a Political System

The structuring of sporting competition along national and international lines has slowly created a world order of sport in which the trend is toward the homogenization of sports and the centralization of control over them. This was an imperative present in the very beginnings of international sporting competition, origins in which the British played a prominent role. In many respects the distinction between the amateur and the professional with which international sport has struggled for a century was created by the British system. In order to compete with Britain, then the most prestigious sporting nation, nineteenth-century athletics organizations had also to distinguish between amateurs and professionals. Indeed, the creation of international sporting organizations was necessitated by the need to ensure that no professional athletes participated and that no cash prizes were awarded. These international organizations had to struggle against not only local traditions, which often permitted cash prizes, but also international sports entrepreneurs. 'Unless a national sports organization could guarantee to the corresponding British organization the amateur status of its members, contacts with Great Britain were not possible' (Stokvis, 1982, p. 203).

The original Olympic ideal was that national Olympic committees would be entirely independent of internal politics. Indeed, this was made a requirement for recognition by the IOC. But this idea was based on the nineteenth-century liberal conception of the supreme importance of private as opposed to government institutions and was much easier to enforce when this philosophy was hegemonic. In a sense, the period between the founding of the first national and international sports organizations (around 1870) and the 1952 Olympic Games (when the Soviets finally entered the movement) can be defined as a stage of transition in the social organization of sport, during which traditional ties with local life disappeared and ties with local and national governments were still too weak to influence sports significantly. International sports were truly private and amateur, controlled by aristocrats and members of the business elites with the time and money to travel internationally who formed a tightly knit and mutually supportive network of 'old boys.'

All this began to change after 1945. 'In the postwar period, many governments realized the political implications of sports and began to assert direct government control over their national Olympic committees, often in the form of a ministry of sports' (Guttman, 1984, p. 135). By 1954, the majority of the then eighty national Olympic committees were state financed, the state demanding some say, at least at the international level, in how its money was spent (Espy, 1979, p. 51). The IOC was forced to turn a blind eye to the control by the state over national Olympic committees not only in the communist bloc but also in many parts of the Third World. However, it was the communists, specifically the Soviets, who broke the tradition whereby the IOC itself nominated the person to 'represent' a given country (many had no such 'representatives'), demanding the right to appoint their own representative. The Soviets obviously recalled that the IOC refused to acknowledge the Bolshevik revolution and allowed the old tsarist Russian Olympic committee to 'represent' that country for many years after. Such Russian Olympic Committee members as General Butovksy, Count Ribopierre, Baron Vilebrandt and Prince Urosov all served on the IOC between 1917 and 1932 (Riordan, 1978, p. 52).

Once the Soviets had broken the mold, members of the IOC slowly changed from being ambassadors of a movement to their countries to being representatives from a country on the IOC. From this time it was obvious that more and more members of the IOC would serve less as individuals and more as political representatives of a given administration or ideology. The position of the Olympic movement on this whole question is contradictory and illustrates the impossibility of keeping politics out of sport. The Olympic ideal demands that nations mixing sport and politics be barred from participating in the games. On the other hand, the Olympic ideal also demands that political considerations should play no part in determining whether or not a national Olympic committee be recognized.

Believers in the Olympic ideal subscribe to the idea that the games can help overcome international obstacles to peace and even that the movement can do something about inequalities between rich and poor nations. Thus, the opposition of the IOC to professionalism has been based partly on the grounds that this would increase differences between rich and poor nations. The Soviets demonstrated in the 1950s that the task of new nations was not simply to secure acceptance into a predefined system but to change that system so that they need not compete at a disadvantage. When they entered the movement, the Soviets upset the Western capitalist categories of professional and amateur. To compete with communist-bloc countries, Western athletes had to resort to a variety of 'illegal' stratagems. In 1974 this situation was acknowledged in a change in the Olympic rules permitting 'broken time' payments, thus allowing Western athletes to enjoy openly the same subsidies as those paid to communist athletes. To his credit, Avery Brundage had long railed at the hypocrisy of the West, especially of the United States, in complaining about the professionalism of Soviet athletes while supporting their own athletes on academic scholarships (Espy, 1979, p. 6).

The Olympic movement was founded by Western capitalist nations and espoused largely Western capitalist values. As the most attractive and prestigious arena in which to compete for international influence, the Olympics have proven irresistible to new nations but they have also occasioned considerable resentment at their perceived political biases. The modern Olympic movement is actually made up of three organizations. The IOC is the oldest (established in 1894) and has been the most powerful in the past. It was also the most oligarchic, choosing its own members and deciding who should represent it in any given member country. The power of this unit within the Olympic movement, heavily weighted with Western European and North American interests, began to wane only in the 1960s as a result of pressure from the Soviets and Third World countries. In the 1920s the IOC had delegated to various sport federations responsibility for conducting competitions in their respective sports in the quadrennial games. As the number of sport federations multiplied and as the international structure of each sport federation became more complex, they began to seek to exert more control over the direction of the Olympic movement. The General Assembly of International Sports Federations was established in 1967 with the purpose of improving cooperation between federations and more equitably dividing the burgeoning television revenues. The second major change to occur in the 1960s was the formation in 1968 of a Permanent General Assembly of National Olympic Committees. As a result of pressure from the Soviet bloc, NOCs were no longer the creatures of the IOC and had closer ties with host nations than the Olympic Charter had formerly tolerated. Besides the issue of independence, one matter of controversy between the IOC and the national committees had been the distribution of aid for the development of sport in underdeveloped countries. At the 1973 Olympic Congress, a new Tripartite Commission was founded consisting of members of the IOC, international federations and national Olympic committees. Well before that time elections to the IOC executive board 'had become thoroughly politicized' as each bloc of nations sought to seat its representatives on this major decision-making body (Guttman, 1984, p. 173).

There can be little doubt that the reforms of the 1960s were in some degree a consequence of the pressure brought upon the IOC by organizational competition from countries of the Third World, who had been attempting to set up their own games. The first Asian Games were held in 1951, under the supervision of the Asian Games Federation, whose founding members were Afghanistan, Burma, Ceylon, India, Indonesia, Pakistan, the Philippines and Thailand. They were part of a more general effort to promote Asian unity against Western colonialism. These regional games have experienced their own internal weakness. The 1962 games were controversial because the host country, Indonesia, responsive to pressure from the PRC, denied entry visas to Taiwan and Israel. In turn, the IOC suspended Indonesia from the Olympic movement for political discrimination. Indonesia withdrew from the IOC in 1963 and turned its attention to organizing a rival to the Olympic movement in which Third World countries would play a more equitable role. As we have already seen, the 1986 Asian Games were boycotted by the North Koreans.

Another rival to the Olympic Games had its base in the Conference of the New Emerging Forces, which was intended to establish a Third World United-Nations-style organization. Founding members consisted primarily of Asian, African and Latin American countries. They organized the Games of the Newly Emerging Forces (GANEFO). The first GANEFO were held in Jakarta in 1963, with forty-eight Third World countries participating. The GANEFO were a very serious challenge to the hegemony of the IOC. If the IOC alienated Third World countries, they now had a viable rival, supported by a superpower (China), to turn to. The GANEFO threatened the Olympic movement with a loss of its monopoly over the accreditation and recognition of sporting federations and even its monopoly over the recognition of new states.

Despite the fact that GANEFO I were considered a great success, GANEFO II never came to pass. This was in part due to the overthrow of Sukarno, the Indonesian leader most sympathetic to communism, and the return of Indonesia to the Olympic movement in 1967. It was partly due to the withdrawal by Egypt of its offer to host the games because of its war with Israel. And it was partly due to the withdrawal of support and participation by the PRC as a result of the Cultural Revolution. Third World countries instead turned their attention to reforming the Olympic movement itself.

In 1978 the non-aligned nations took another step in the formulation of a sports policy of benefit to poorer nations. In Algeria a 'Manifesto and Plan of Action for Cooperation in and Development of Physical Education and Sports among the Non-Aligned Countries' was signed. It attacked 'zionism' and 'racism' in international sports, seeking to democratize the decision-making structure in international sports, encouraging the exchange of athletes, coaches and experts, promoting competition between non-aligned countries and strengthening the position of the non-aligned countries in UNESCO's Intergovernmental Committee for Physical Education and Sports. This manifesto had its roots in the decolonization process of the 1950s and 1960s, and drew direct inspiration from GANEFO and from talk in the United Nations of the 'New International Order.' At the time, the IOC had 150 member countries, 26 of them having been recognized since 1970, but the IOC had appointed representatives in only 70, few of them from the Third World.

## Sport, National Integration and Disintegration

Nation-building demands not only the delineation of national boundaries but the integration and unification of the new state into a cohesive unit. Nationalism thus also has an inward-looking aspect as the new nation seeks to homogenize its population. Immigration is restricted to those who 'fit,' new immigrants are subjected to socialization into citizenship values, domestic culture is standardized and a distinctive national character molded.

Sports and leisure in general have been extensively used in this aspect of the nationalization process. In the United States, for example, baseball was said to be 'only second to the public schools as a teacher of American mores to the second generation' (Riess, 1980, p. 25). Only games and pastimes that affirmed the new national character were promoted, while 'alien' pastimes were frowned upon. Sports which emerged as mass spectator events in the United States during the final quarter of the nineteenth century did not appear haphazardly: 'the sorting process was aimed at finding games that recalled the basic traditions that had formed "Anglo-Saxon" personality and character' (Mrozek, 1983, p. 166). In the nationalization process, ancient games, or 'imports,' are taken over and adapted to better fit the national character. 'Qualities that were supposedly American were imputed to football and baseball, which, in turn, were presumed to generate those values in the players' (Mrozek, 1983, p. 160). Each sport had created for it a myth of national origins, located in a specific time and place.

The Americanization of games was taken very seriously, although motives were often as pecuniary as they were patriotic. The drive to Americanize baseball was led by Albert Spaulding, an early professional star who later owned the Chicago Cubs and ran a sporting goods company that came close to monopolizing the market. He managed to create such an interest in the origins of baseball that a blue-ribbon committee of seven prominent citizens, including two United States Senators, was set up to decide once and for all where the game had begun. The committee concluded in 1907, on the flimsiest of evidence, that baseball had indeed originated in America in 1839 when Abner Doubleday supposedly laid out the first baseball diamond in Cooperstown, a site which has since become a 'shrine' of baseball fans. In 1939 the US Post Office placed its imprimatur upon this history by issuing a commemorative stamp to mark the centennial anniversary of the birth of 'America's game' (Riess, 1980, p. 16).

Political elites were quick to associate themselves with the rise of sports. Senator Henry Cabot Lodge, scion of two distinguished New England families, together with Theodore Roosevelt and Elihu Root, then Secretary of War, linked sport to a general program for renewing their society and reordering world affairs. Roosevelt, although an indifferent athlete, made much of his interest in sport and encouraged the armed services to use sport as part of their training programs to improve fitness, agility, strength and agression (Mrozek, 1983, p. 47). Roosevelt was of the opinion that 'Sport did not imitate other experiences that yielded values which society favored; it actually produced them by means that occasionally resembled activities other than athletics' (Mrozek, 1983, p. 32). Here we see that same coupling and merging of military training and national defense as we see in the 'physical culture' programs of communist countries.

We have already observed how national elites identify themselves with the Olympic Games in order to enhance their role as national symbols. The Greek royal family were enthusiastic supporters of the idea of the revival of the Olympic Games: 'the royal family were always on the lookout for chances to demonstrate their "Greekness" and their prowess at embodying it' (MacAloon, 1981, p. 187). Nineteenth-century English political elites also recognized the value of sports in forging bonds of national loyalty.

By 1890, sport was an almost obligatory interest of leaders of society. This was not always so. In a letter to his mother sent from Malta in 1830, Disraeli told her how he had once been in a gallery of a racket court where he was struck by the ball which then lay at his feet. Elegantly dressed as ever, his response was to hand the ball to a rifleman standing nearby. 'I humbly requested him to forward its passage into the court, as I really had never thrown a ball in my life.' By 1890, no British Prime Minister, whatever his private feelings, would have made so damaging and 'un-English' an admission.

(Dobbs, 1973, p. 21)

Many English people who hold the monarchy in contempt identify strongly with the national cricket and soccer teams. 'Terms like "English" or "British" derive much of their significance from national sporting traditions' (Whannel, 1983, p. 27). Luckily, most Britons do not have to choose between the monarch and their favorite sport because the monarchy and the political elite in general have exploited this interest in sport to establish themselves as national symbols by taking up various sporting pursuits and by conspicuously attending popular sporting events.

Nationalist spirit intensifies the desire for there to be 'one voice' speaking for a given sport—or indeed for sports in general. The demand that a nation speak with one sporting voice usually stems from a desire to improve the nation's international competitive position. Thus, in amateur sports in the United States, the chronic struggle for control over sports between the AAU and the NCAA has been in part a struggle for control over sport policy for the United States as a whole. The AAU and the NCAA were also fighting over what American sports should be. The president of the AAU complained that, under the direction of the NCAA, 'Our school athletic programs are all directed toward the "star" system where an extremely limited number make the final squad' (United States Congress, Senate Committee on Commerce, 1977, p. 195). The AAU also complained that the NCAA directed American youth toward football and basketball, only the latter being an Olympic sport and the former having no real world presence at all. It was not surprising, in the opinion of the president of the AAU, that the United States seldom won a medal in over half the Olympic sports. The AAU saw itself as standing up for a more truly American way of sports, more democratic in its organization, populist in its appeal and pluralist in its catering for minority groups.

The call to speak with one sporting voice in an increasingly competitive sport world is especially urgent in countries with federal polities. Canadian sport is generally considered to have suffered from that country's strong tradition of federalism. For example, until the mid-1960s the Canadians selected their amateur ice-hockey representatives by a method whereby the team competing successfully against other city teams won the right to represent Canada in international competition (Caldwell, 1982, p. 177). The domination of Canadian sport by American sports which are not prominent on the international stage, such as football and baseball, was largely responsible for this state of affairs, but the failure to overcome regional rivalries has also been partly responsible.

More recently Canada has begun to make a more serious effort not only to achieve a national sport policy but to use sport to achieve a greater measure of national integration. In 1969 the government established Sport Canada, a non-profit organization funded both privately and publicly, to administer and support Canadian sport growth. However, it is important that in both the United States and Canada the intervention of the state in the administration of sport is limited and falls far short of using the state to achieve equity in sporting opportunities. 'The extent of sport involvement on the part of...government elites does not go beyond attempts to maintain system stability through the promotion of Canadian national unity and international prestige' (Helmes, 1981, p. 222).

States also use sports as part of the national defense effort. Indeed, the exploitation of the sporting interest for the purposes of military training has a long history. Even in societies with weak states or societies which were highly decentralized, leisure pastimes were frequently geared toward military preparedness (Mandell, 1984, p. 43). French leaders turned to gymnastics after France's humiliation by Germany in 1870 to better prepare the nation's youth for future battles. They cleverly exploited the fact that gymnastics had firm roots in the popular street culture of juggling and acrobatics (Holt, 1981, p. 45). Holt notes that 'much of their propaganda fell on deaf ears' and that gymnastics served chiefly as a source of good fun. The more serious purpose of organized fitness regimens was revived after the First World War, but it was not until the fascist regimes began to set examples through their fitness programs that the French were able to organize their Fédération Sportive et Gymnique du Travail.

We have already witnessed the use of sports for this purpose in communist countries. Its role in capitalist countries is rather more limited but nevertheless accounts for much of the involvement of the state in leisure. The formal involvement of the federal government in sport, fitness and recreation in Canada began in 1943, with the National Fitness Act, passed in order to improve the fitness of recruits to the Canadian Army (Helmes, 1981, p. 213). In England the Football Association did not hesitate to put its organizational clout behind the war effort in 1914, being responsible for half the volunteers in the first year of the war. 'Football and its machinery offered the state a swift and acceptable entry into working-class communities which might otherwise have proved difficult to penetrate' (Walvin, 1975, p. 90).

So far I have written about the use of sport to achieve political integration. But sports are used to *resist* a larger nationalism and affirm autonomy. Popular pastimes, like language and religion, can solidify autonomous or separatist nationalism. Since they are elements of everyday life, they are bound to carry some awareness of their existence among those they characterize more, perhaps, than religion or language. They are already status communities, helping strengthen the popular belief in a unique and valuable culture that existed prior to any existing state and its boundaries. Although languages are perhaps more impervious to change, while popular pastimes are more vulnerable to direct political control, the action of the state against pastimes with regional identification often affects many more people who are attracted to the pastimes but do not speak the language on a daily basis.

Nation-states seek to suppress leisure activities with a strong regional identity, while regions, especially those in which nationalist movements are active, will seek to preserve, revive and affirm regionally distinctive leisure activities. Soccer competitions between Scotland and England exemplify the attitudes of many Scottish people to England. They are regarded as David-and-Goliath affairs, soccer being one of the few remaining institutions which maintain for the Scots a feeling of rivalry with England. Rugby was, and remains, an aspect of the national identity of Wales. During the resurgence of Welsh nationalism in the postwar period, rugby became 'more emphatically a national passion than ever' (Morgan, 1981, p. 348). During the formation of the Irish independence movement, Gaelic football was revived and popularized.

In France bullfighting is most popular in the southwest (e.g. Provence): 'the question of the *corrida* became involved in the revival of Provençal nationalism' (Holt, 1981, p. 120). The national government has chosen not to move forcefully against this highly controversial sport, despite pressure in Paris from interest groups, because of the intense hostility to this in the southwest, whose residents brand animal rights and humane society activists as 'deracinated metropolitan intellectuals.' 'The supporters of bullfighting argued their case in terms of the legitimate autonomy of regional traditions in an overcentralized state. The challenge to the *corrida* was interpreted as yet another affront to the identity and integrity of the Midi (Holt, 1981, p. 120). There is, however, a paradox in the strong identification of French bullfighting with a specific region. Bullfights are very popular with tourists, and there is no doubt this sport is also designed in large part to extract tourist money. However, converting the sport into a tourist spectacle threatens a total loss of authentic regional identity for this activity. The cockfighting which is popular in the Nord and which also has strong regional connotations in France is also considered best left alone by the central government. However, it is not likely to suffer the deracination of the tourist trade to the same extent as bullfighting.

## The relationship between International and National Organizations

The fact that sport now operates on a world stage with nation-states as actors means that the organization of sport within each country will be shaped by that country's place on this world stage. The countries of the world are now linked by over one hundred separate international sport federations (the most famous of which is FIFA), most of which belong to the Olympic movement. Indeed, it was the Olympic movement that called most of them into being. The relation between the Olympic movement and the sporting federations was symbiotic. Coubertin needed the federations so that each country could make a single input to his movement. The federations needed the Olympic movement to license their claim to be the sole governing body in that country.

A country finds it next to impossible to use sport for nationalist purposes without dealing with these sporting federations. This can frequently lead to intense debate and often paralyzing conflict when internal sport politics and international sport politics diverge. Thus, in the United States the NCAA has long been opposed to control over domestic athletes being granted to any central organization (such as the USOC). One reason is that the USOC is seen as tool of various national governing bodies which are, in turn, subservient to their respective international sporting federations entirely beyond the reach of United States law and public policy.

In large part, the whole structure of sport administration in the United States and the relation of sport organizations to the government can be explained in terms of the foreign policy needs of the United States. In order to use sport to help meet these needs the state must deal with an existing sport world order. It must seek to match the requirements of participation in that order with the administration of sport within the country. Where those who make decisions on foreign policy and those who make decisions on sport policy are the same, there is no problem. But where one is a public agency and the other a private body—and a highly disorganized body at that—then problems are bound to arise.

The United States government began to discover these problems in the early 1950s and particularly after 1952 when the strong second place showing of the Soviets in the Olympics generated considerable alarm at the propaganda values the Soviets were reaping from international sport competitions. Early congressional efforts were aimed at barring Soviet athletes from the Olympics on the grounds that they were not true amateurs. However, Bills were also unsuccessfully introduced in the early 1950s to reimburse American Olympians for expenses incurred. By 1960 the deteriorating competitive position of the USA was becoming so alarming that initiatives were undertaken to set up a National Sports Federation which, although privately funded, would help coordinate the international effort. Kennedy's assassination in 1963 aborted this initiative, but earlier that year he did sign an Executive Order establishing an interagency committee on international athletics, the purpose of which was to improve the country's international performance, its image abroad and the degree of coordination between various sport bodies within the country. One year later President Johnson appointed his own committee to consider the issue of how to organize athletics better in order to compete well internationally. This committee also suggested setting up a foundation, pointing to the acceptance in most other countries of the state's obligation to be involved in some way with the public direction and provision of sport. The committee's report was pigeonholed, no doubt because of Johnson's preoccupation with a larger international issue—the war in Vietnam. Until the establishment of the Presidential Commission on Olympic Sports in 1976, this was the end of centralized direction of international sports.

Since 1946 the United States government had available to it a vehicle that could have facilitated a vigorous presence on the international sport scene. Acts to permit and fund cultural exchange (e.g. Fulbright) did not exclude sport, However, the State Department did not typically encourage it. Permanent funding for sporting exchanges was requested and granted only in 1955, a year in which the Soviets sent 239 teams abroad, compared to the United States' nine. A separate Bureau of Education and Cultural Affairs within the State Department did not increase the number of teams sent abroad to more than sixteen. According to a report issued in 1971, the failure of the State Department to compete adequately with the Soviets was due to its belief that sport made negligible difference to international relations and that sport would lose its purity if tied too closely to the government (Clumpner, 1978, p. 433).

Canada has a much longer history of federal involvement in sports, but the motive has been much the same: to boost the international success of its athletes and thus the prestige of the country. Subsidies to athletes participating in the Olympic and Commonwealth games began in the 1920s. During the war, a National Physical Fitness Act was passed to try to improve the physical condition of conscripts to the Canadian Army, but inconsistency of the national effort in the sporting arena is indicated by the repeal of that Act in 1954.

> During the years immediately following the 1954 repeal, a strong lobby emerged advocating some type of reinvolvement by the federal government in the area of sport and fitness. One important factor which caused the federal sector to re-evaluate its position in this regard was the diminishing success of Canadian athletes and teams in international sporting contests such as the Olympics. Of special concern was the loss of world ice hockey supremacy, considered to be Canada's forte in the world of athletics.
> (Baka, 1978, p. 306)

The result was the Act to Encourage Fitness and Amateur Sport (1961) which set up a federal Fitness and Amateur Sport Directorate and increased federal funding for amateur sports.

A nation's decision to participate in the Olympic Games means accepting the terms and conditions of a world sport order that not only determines which sports will be given priority within the country but also channels resources to elite athletes who stand the best chance of winning medals. An even stronger impact is felt by the nation (strictly speaking, the city) that competes to host the games. This, too, will mean that sports funds will become concentrated in elite sports, and sports facilities will be geared to Olympic needs.

> Montreal's investment in the Olympics could have provided low-rent housing for 120,000 citizens, free public transportation for ten years, or free recreational programmes for a generation of young people. Instead, the Games benefited local and international commercial interests, middle class sports associations and bureaucrats, and the sports professions.
> (Gruneau, 1984, p. 14)

Clearly, the interests of a nation within the international sporting order do not always coincide the interests of all that nation's citizens.

The Olympic boycotts show that sport allegiances do not always gel with political allegiances. As we have seen, the participation of a 'country' in the Olympic Games is actually the decision of a private organization, the national Olympic Committee, which, under the charter of the Olympic movement, must operate independently of the state. We have also seen, however, that when the state deems the national interst to rest upon directing the actions of this or any other organization involved in international exchange, it will not hesitate to do so. The West is no less likely to do this than the East. In 1973 the PRC invited American swimmers to tour China. The AAU refused to organize the tour because China did not belong to the international sport federation for swimming. In the interest of improving diplomatic relations, the State Department undertook the organization of the tour instead, despite the certain knowledge that the swimmers and coaches participating would be suspended by the AAU.

Thus the compromises and frequent conflicts between national and international interests witnessed in the fields of trade, travel, communications and cultural exchange also occur in the field of sport. Governments can put this to good use if it suits their needs, for they can claim that they have little control over the rules, equipment, standards and even the outcome of play. They can, on the other hand, use sport as a diplomatic weapon when it suits their purposes. The United States opposed the 1976 African-led boycott of the Montreal Olympics on the grounds that politics should keep out of sports but four years later organized a boycott of its own on the grounds that some political acts were so heinous that they necessarily involved sporting relations. This double-edged nature of sport is the reason we can expect to see its continued political embroilment in the future.

# 8
# Conclusion: The Future of Politics and Leisure

What will be the future of the politics of leisure? Are we likely to see more or less political influence over how people spend their 'free time?' Is leisure likely to become more politically salient or will it become confined more and more to the private sphere? Will the state continue to expand its sphere of influence, and what will be the impact of such expansion on leisure activities? It is twice as difficult to anticipate the relationship between two institutions as it is to predict the future of either considered in isolation. The answers to these questions are thus doubly difficult to find. However, certain broad trends in politics and leisure are clearly enough established for us to be able to conclude by looking ahead and suggesting new research agendas and policy concerns for the serious student of leisure.

Leisure has proven to be a dangerous minefield for forecasters to tread. In the economic boom of the 1950s, visions of a future largely freed of work and abundant with varied and fulfilling leisure opportunities were commonplace. Shorter working weeks, longer holidays, earlier retirement, more sabbatical leaves, job sharing, plentiful part-time work and flexible work schedules would result from automated technologies and sophisticated management. Confidence in these predictions was in no way shaken by the fact that some believed this increased leisure time would become a burden for the individual and a social problem for society. Few would have disputed the notion that with modernization and industrial growth come shorter working hours and more time and money to spend on leisure.

In the interim a number of social developments have cast doubt on these predictions. While some groups of workers have seen their hours of employment decline, most spend as long on the job as their parents did before the Second World War. For some this is a matter of choice; they have preferred to trade increased productivity for more money. Others have had no choice; they work in industries largely unprotected by collective bargaining agreements in which overtime rates are agreed upon or by enforceable working-hours legislation. Looking to the future, then, it is most likely that white males, particularly those working in unionized jobs, will find their working week gradually shortening, their paid vacations gradually lengthening and retirement with pay beginning as early as 60 years of age. These workers, however, are a declining proportion of the population. Other groups—those working in the burgeoning labor-intensive service industries—must anticipate a future in which they will have to continue to work the same or even more hours to sustain their standard of living, must confront the likelihood of periodic and often lengthy lay-offs and must accept 'permanent' part-time work. The future free time of these people is much harder to predict.

Future trends in free time will be determined chiefly by economic forces. The *political* future of free time is uncertain because the extent to which working hours are regulated by legislation varies widely from one country to another. In Britain working-hours legislation covers only women, young people and those occupations (e.g. truck driving) where long working hours are considered hazardous. The free time of other workers is legislated only indirectly, through the laws regulating collective bargaining agreements.

We have seen that the length of the working day has always been a concern of trade unions, although this concern has rarely been primarily motivated by the desire for more leisure as such. There is no reason to think that working hours will be dropped from the agenda of collective bargaining sessions. However, trade unions, particularly those in the United States, have shown enthusiasm for more flexible work schedules only under highly favorable conditions. In labor negotiations, neither management nor labor has given work scheduling high priority unless both feel economically secure. Employers are much more disposed to 'be flexible' with working hours when the supply of labor is short in relation to the demand (as it was until the 1970s). Workers, too, are more disposed to consider innovative work scheduling and more leisure time when incomes are high and seem likely to rise. Under these conditions, also, governments encourage all kinds of part-time work arrangements in order to boost productivity. However, in times of depression and high unemployment the picture changes. Workers become insecure, their discretionary income falls, they seek the protection of traditional work schedules and become fearful of part-time work arrangements. Employers, on the other hand, find the supply of labor exceeding their labor requirements, try to force part-time work arrangements on their employees and spurn 'costly' and 'inefficient' experiments with flexitime and the like.

These adjustments to changing economic conditions take place rather slowly, however, in part because of past political actions. For example, laws passed to protect workers from exploitation by limiting the length of the working day become an obstacle to experiments with four-day work weeks of ten hours a day. Governments learn that, once the idea of flexible work schedules is introduced in times of prosperity, and legislation is enacted to clear the way for it, they have also removed safeguards against part-time work, homework and all manner of work scheduling designed to meet the convenience of the employer rather than the leisure needs of the employee. What begins as the promise of more freedom of choice becomes a threat of 'compulsory leisure' or idleness. The politics of free-time legislation, then, is inextricably caught up in the struggle between labor and capital for a share of expanding productivity and for security during economic slowdown. This struggle, in turn, takes place in the context of past working-hours legislation, which itself becomes a weapon in the war.

Future legislation of free time will not only have to take into account the structure of industrial relations. It will also have to take seriously the linkages between work, family and leisure. Governments must face the fact that working people, but rarely employers, see the work–leisure relation holistically. Most of their leisure is family-based; they regard leisure time detached from their family and friends as virtually useless. But legislation rarely extends to restructuring times when children are in school, or coordinating spouses' work schedules. This requires that working hours be seen as part of a whole pattern of work, family and free-time activities which comprise for the individual a meaningful whole. It is highly unlikely, however, that reforms will be instituted which acknowledge this fact. Future legislation is equally unlikely to extend to improvements in the quality of work, even though variety and choice in one's job are known to have positive effects on one's leisure.

The trend toward a more or less uniform reduction in working hours and more free time has thus not occurred as was predicted and is unlikely to take the form anticipated. The forecasters of the 1950s also largely failed to take seriously the entry of many more women into the labor force. Increasing numbers of women with children must work outside the home; some are the only wage earners in the family, while others need to supplement their husband's income. These women have dual careers, as homemaker and wage worker. Consequently, they have very little time for leisure.

It is not very likely that future democratic governments will do much to guarantee working women equal 'rights' to leisure. In order to do so, the state would have to re-examine its policy on working hours, because this policy is based on the assumption that one hour less of paid work is one hour more of free time, and this assumption holds only for men and not for women. The chief reason why women's leisure rights will not be improved is that the working mother's leisure deprivation is only partly caused by her working hours; even more damaging is lack of transportation, child-care facilities and discretionary income. Women suffer most of all from the prospect of leisure continuing to be treated by governments as separate from educational, housing and transportation issues. Ironically, women's future leisure will be best enhanced indirectly. The state must endorse the position that women's employment is as much a right as is that of men; it must guarantee freedom from sexual harassment to women in public places; and it must ease the burden of child care currently imposed almost exclusively on the mother.

Finally, leisure forecasters failed to foresee the extent of 'forced' leisure in the form of unemployment. Historically high rates of chronic unemployment, or the underemployment of obligatory part-time work, disguise even higher rates of idleness among youth and minority groups, particularly in economically depressed regions. Pervasive unemployment, combined with projections that the need for work in the future will far outstrip the supply of jobs, is likely to intensify demands that the government reallocate resources to the area of public sector leisure services, if only to prevent social unrest. But there are no easy answers to the question of the correct policy toward leisure when there are substantial numbers of people who are permanently without work and when conventional efforts to bring them back into the labor force are doomed to failure. Here, deep-seated values attached to work and the stigma attached to idleness present severe obstacles to the government helping people deal with and actually enjoy their 'unemployment.'

There are some indications that, in welfare states at least, the social safety net will be expanded into the provision of properly structured leisure for the unemployed. An example is the Sports Training and Research Scheme set up in Leicester, England, a project jointly funded and administered by central and local government agencies and specifically aimed at the unemployed. Its objectives are to encourage participation in sport, recreation and leisure and to promote the understanding of leisure opportunities on the part of the unemployed, to give structure to their daily life and retain for them networks of contact in semi-public life (Dawson, 1986, p. 173). This kind of scheme directly involves the state in education for unemployment rather than recreation for the return to work and it might be the foretaste of things to come. Many other government schemes can be interpreted as performing the same latent function, providing ways for the unemployed to 'pass the time,' even though their manifest function is to get their clients back into the workforce; these include 'training programs' for non-existent jobs, 'volunteer' schemes along the lines of the Peace Corps and many 'make-work' programs. Even school itself can be interpreted as a kind of 'holding tank' in which 'pastime' activities are provided for those who have little prospect of securing a job.

Two other leisure trends, much debated in the postwar period, need to be discussed, because their continuance promises to have profound effects on the relation between politics and leisure. The environmentalist movement of the 1960s convinced many leisure planners that future governments would have to play a more assertive role in the rationing leisure opportunities. Many leisure resources, they noted, were especially vulnerable to the 'tragedy of the commons;' population increases intensify the demand placed on parks and museums to the point where they lose their original aesthetic appeal and recreational potential. These social limits to growth present democratic governments with a dilemma. Unbridled access in the name of equality of opportunity threatens to destroy the very amenity to which access is desired; restrictions on use, however, place the government in the position of reserving public facilities for use by the privileged few.

Population trends in advanced capitalist countries would appear to make it inevitable that governments must restrain access to parks, beaches and the like in order to alleviate environmental degradation, overcrowding and the social conflict to which they can lead. There is other evidence, however, which would contradict this expectation. Recent research on the impact of crowding on recreationists' satisfaction suggests that people can be remarkably tolerant of environmental degradation and overcrowding. It seems that, however diminished the quality of recreational opportunities and environments becomes, a majority of recreationists adapt to it. This adaptability means that state-imposed rationing is either unnecessary or can be safely left to the private market; if the 'costs' of attending a particular leisure facility because of overcrowding exceed what people are willing to pay, they will simply go elsewhere or seek other diversions.

A second trend in leisure, whose political consequences are uncertain, is privatization. For more and more people, leisure is something they experience in private. It is not my concern here to account for this phenomenon, nor do I wish to argue that it will certainly be part of our future. However, the privatization of leisure does have considerable political significance. On one level, the privatization of leisure promises to diminish the extent to which it is politically controlled. It is to this threat that the authorities in totalitarian regimes feel they must respond. Privatization here seems to promise greater freedom of choice; we have more freedom in the choice of which video cassette to rent than we have freedom to select a television program or decide which cinema to attend. However, the continued privatization of leisure need not be so politically innocent. In some respects, the private sphere has been destroyed by consumerism and its attendant technologies. The market can now reach deeper into the home and into the regulation of individual leisure than ever before; and the individual no longer has home, street, neighborhood, or community alternatives, because the mass media have destroyed them. Having stood by and allowed the public sphere to be destroyed and the private sphere to be penetrated by the market so that even the most intimate of leisure pursuits are commodified, governments are well positioned themselves to become more intrusive in the leisure sphere than ever before. The mass media, being in many ways the least democratic of all the pleasure industries, threaten to monopolize our leisure time and thereby increase the extent to which we are 'unfree.'

The future of the politics of leisure will also be affected by political developments. In Chapters 4 and 5 I described the emergence of a political philosophy which would legitimate the state's role in the supply and supervision of leisure services. Leisure in the welfare state becomes an 'entitlement.' This would seem to have achieved for leisure the status of a 'social right,' the right to happiness. Unfortunately, this has occurred at precisely the same moment that the welfare state ideal has come under increasing political scrutiny.

In the eyes of its right-wing critics the welfare state has failed to ensure the continued accumulation of capital, upon which governments must depend for their revenues. Public ownership of the commanding heights of the economy has proven to be inefficient and costly, while the 'safety net' of the welfare programs seems to have sapped people's work ethic, diminishing productivity and discouraging savings and investment. Left-wing critics feel that the welfare state has lost its legitimacy, having largely failed to eliminate the social problems it claimed to solve because state officials have refused to listen to the needs of the people rather than the opinions of 'experts.' At the same time, it has led to the growth of unrepresentative bureaucracies and an interventionist and invasive state apparatus. Welfare officials have transformed themselves from enabling to controlling agents. Clients must not only demonstrate need but also show that they 'deserve' assistance.

The political economy of the rebuilding period after the Second World War was that of social partnership, especially in Western European democracies. Capitalist economies would benefit from a measure of government regulation and even the nationalization of certain essential but unprofitable industries, while individuals would enjoy the protection of an ever-expending net of 'social rights,' including the right to rewarding leisure. These assumptions have been seriously undermined by the events of the past two decades. It is no longer so obvious that the political economy of democracies should be social partnership. The implication is that in the future governments might well be much less involved in economic affairs, and the list of goods and services to which the citizenry is entitled would be abbreviated in such a way as to exclude altogether such 'luxuries' as leisure.

And yet the conclusion is inescapable that there can by no going back from the welfare state. The advanced capitalist economies have become heavily dependent upon the fiscal and monetary supports of the state. Their citizenry have built up expectations about their rights to the fruits of these economies that can be tempered only occasionally and briefly. Social rights are now as important as political or legal rights. Indeed, these social rights are looked upon by many as 'enabling rights' without which civil rights are useless. Politicians can rail at the 'excesses' of the welfare state but they do not propose to dismantle it. The question then becomes one of anticipating the future of leisure as part of the welfare state. What can we learn from what has been achieved to date? And how can we use this to anticipate future trends?

The future of public education, state-assisted health care, unemployment assistance, old-age pensions and the like does not seem to be in question, however much politicians and client groups worry about the fiscal soundness and administrative efficiency of these different programs. The right to an education, to treatment of sickness, to a 'safety net' in times of hardship and old age, is largely undisputed. But do we have an equivalent right to leisure? This question has always been a troublesome one, and answering it has been made no easier by recent attacks on the whole idea of entitlements and the escalation of expectations to which they lead.

Regardless of political changes, there are some reasons why the 'right' to leisure is less credible than the right to more 'basic' things like health, food, shelter and education. Welfare policy is bedeviled with boundary problems. Where, for instance, should health care extend? Should a national health policy take responsibility for clean air and pure water? Should unemployment policy concern itself with educational issues? But the problems of institutionalizing leisure services are even more profound. It is very difficult to decide where leisure begins and ends. This is reflected in the fact that, although most Western democracies have set up ministries of sport, they are a long way from coordinating all the leisure services under one administrative agency. For example, the United Kingdom still splits its management of the leisure function between the departments of Environment, Education, Health, Agriculture, Transport and Trade and the Home Office. Leisure is recognized as a fairly important component of housing policy, regional economic policy, education policy, health policy, environmental policy and so forth, and the call to develop a separate and distinct leisure policy is persistent. However, there is also a strong feeling among many leisure planners that to 'encapsulate' leisure policy as a totally separate budget item and administrative function would be to remove it as a strong and permeating force within corporate planning at the local, regional, or national level. These administrative difficulties reflect more deep-seated problems encountered whenever attempts are made to 'institutionalize' leisure. Leisure components exist in all activities to some extent—in the home, on the shop-floor, in the classroom, on the streets—and administrative efforts to 'provide' and 'manage' them tend to be self-defeating because they inevitably interrupt personal rhythms, fragment lifestyles and rationalize the essentially non-rational.

The idea of entitlement to leisure suffers also from the fact that there is little agreement on the 'basic' level of leisure services which the state ought to guarantee, nor is there any agreement on what kinds of activity should be provided. This is a problem which all welfare planners face. The difficulty of gauging the appropriate level of leisure is only by degree more difficult than the difficulty of assessing subsistence needs in the case of transfer payments or old-age pensions. But the case of leisure is more difficult to deal with because of the inherently limitless nature of leisure activities. It is very difficult to match government provision with public wants. Indeed, many of the population's favorite leisure-time pursuits (e.g. gambling) tend to be frowned upon by governments. Proponents of the idea of leisure entitlements are asked: if leisure is essentially an individual activity, freely chosen, why should the government be involved in providing it? The more leisure planners present leisure services as 'good fun' and the less they emphasize hygiene, health and hard work, the more insistently is this question put. It becomes very difficult for taxpayers to see why they should put money in the public purse for the enjoyment of others while they get their own fun elsewhere and pay commercial rates for it. Business interests see subsidized fun as unfair competition and add their voice to this complaint. The basic problem is that, almost by definition, leisure is defined by what it means to a person or group. State-provided services not only must be leisure to state officials but must mean the same thing to their 'clients,' just as state officials must be willing to take their clients' word that what they are requesting government funding for is 'really' leisure to them. This problem is not so acute in the provision of services like health care or old-age pensions where control over clients can be taken for granted more easily and where some consensus on what is a reasonable state of health or standard of living can be presumed.

A third problem is a tendency toward 'friendly fascism' in the delivery of leisure services. Most people regard their 'right' to leisure as a liberty, a right to participate or engage in an activity, to be left alone while they enjoy themselves. However, welfare states have a tendency to strengthen this right so that it becomes a 'claim,' to equal shares of the social wage. The problem here is that leisure is much too amorphous, too diverse for it to be manageable as a right in the second sense. To overcome this problem, advocates of leisure welfare policy have tended to stress what people need rather than what they are entitled to. The first campaign document on 'sport for all' which was issued by the Sports Council in 1972 used the word 'need' fifteen times in fourteen pages and the word 'want' only four times. It is no accident that leisure is conceptualized in this way. 'Need' implies obligation and necessity and is therefore better suited to concepts of the welfare state; 'need' suggests a real entity which is discoverable by scientific investigation and is therefore objective and 'technically' approachable; 'need' is more adapted to making distributional choices, for it is easier for a government to declare that people do not need a facility than to declare that they do not want it (McIntosh and Charlton, 1985, p. 21). These technocratic reasons for stressing needs do not conceal the fact, however, that there are as yet no clearly identifiable leisure needs which governments can help satisfy, no leisure deprivations the government can help eradicate.

Leisure is essentially self-determined. It is sullied to the extent that a higher authority initiates it or guides it. Protecting people's right to equal leisure can strike them as paternalistic or intrusive. Outdoor recreation is administered on the basis of what is considered good for society, which may or may not be what people desire, on the grounds that people do not always know what they want or what their true needs are. Worse, the citizenry must be protected from destroying, by its own irrational actions, what it does value. The people have every right to be alarmed. The line between 'recreational welfare' and 'recreation as welfare,' between the provision of leisure as a right and the provision of the right kind of leisure, is thin indeed (Coalter, 1984, p. 25).

Government leisure policies that are not paternalistic are frequently technocratic. A government official, seeking to defend an entitlement policy, discovers that his defense is greatly strengthened if it can be made on neutral, apolitical, technical grounds. This promotes a 'managerial' approach to leisure, based on a rather restricted view of leisure which recognizes active and public leisure (activities that are amenable to administration) more clearly than its passive and private forms, and fosters the professionalization of leisure supervision, which in turn encourages its specialization and technification.

These problems with the idea of leisure as an entitlement suggest that we should be skeptical of projections which envision the right to equal play as part of the future of democracies. Those governments strongly committed to the ideals of the welfare state are likely to choose to guarantee some measure of leisure satisfaction indirectly, by attaching leisure to something else that they *can* clearly identify as a right, such as health, education, or safe streets. Thus the provision of suitable recreation might be integrated into programs to retrain or simply keep occupied unemployed youth; fitness programs might be designed to play a part in rehabilitation schemes or in provision for senior citizens, and play treated as an integral part of good public education.

In those democracies where subscription to welfare state principles is hesitant, governments might still play a role in 'guaranteeing' leisure, but in the sense of protecting people's 'negative liberty,' or freedom from interference by others. This is an association of the right to leisure with the traditional idea of 'right,' in the sense of the power to choose or exercise one's will, and it is actually more congruent with the hegemonic view of leisure in countries like the United States. This political system would find little room for the idea that people have a moral right to leisure goods and services; for example, that the government fails its people if it does not provide adequate public transportation for car-less people to reach swimming-pools. It would, however, see as a proper function of the government the protection of wilderness areas so that people can, if they choose, enjoy them, or the regulation of mass communications so that the freedom to choose which programs to listen to or watch is unimpaired.

There is an alternative scenario to this 'hands-off' approach, foreshadowed in the command economies of the Soviet bloc, in which leisure might play a different political role. While the twentieth-century trend toward the decommodification of institutions has been arrested by the shift toward free-market political philosophies in the 1970s and 1980s, the reversals have been few, and there is little certainty that this change is permanent. It is unlikely, for example, that we would resume entrusting social services to religious, philanthropic and other private bodies; and there is even less likelihood that the expanding demand for these services could be met equitably by the private sector. This would seem to clear the way for a measure of state control over the economy, including leisure services. However, state provision of schooling, health care, housing and the like is not necessarily antagonistic to the advance of capitalism. Max Weber predicted long ago that the development of market forces and bureaucratic state control could go hand in hand, the one being necessary for the other. This implies an extension of both state and corporate control over not only political but private life. Thus mandatory workplace testing for recreational drug use can be legally justified by the corporation and defended by the state in the interests of productivity and national security. Control over sexual practices that might lead to debilitating illness or death can be defended on the grounds of the social costs incurred. 'Workfare' schemes to combat 'idleness' can be defended on the grounds of preserving the work ethic to ensure the country's competitiveness in the world economy.

Will leisure continue to figure in political protest as much as it has in the past? There are good reasons to think that it will. We have already concluded that the struggle over use of time will engender conflict; but just as leisure is necessarily implicated in the struggle over time, so too is it affected by the struggle over the meaning and function of space. New information technologies are breaking down the old spatial arrangements of work and home, restructuring cities and detaching subcultures from their territorial base. These new uses for territory are frequently resisted by neighborhoods seeking to preserve work–leisure unities, and by regional cultures seeking to protect their autonomy.

Leisure in the welfare state exhibits many of the inequities found in leisure provided by the private sector. Most benefits in the form of public services and 'amenities' flow disproportionately to the affluent and well educated. Indeed, this tendency seems to be more pronounced in the provision of leisure services and amenities than it is where welfare consists largely of transfer payments, because the latter can be much more precisely steered in the direction of those in most need. In the heat of party competition, promises of more and more benefits to more and more entitled groups lead to a gradual escalation in the 'social wage' and a 'benefits scramble' as different groups in the population compete for a slice of the pie. In this scramble, organized groups do much better than unorganized constituencies, producer groups are heard more clearly than consumer groups, and organizations seeking tangible, individual goods fare better than those seeking intangible, collective outcomes. The escape from the market does not therefore ensure justice for the leisure-deprived and does not encourage us to expect that this arena will be any less politically stable than it has been in the past.

Leisure will also play a significant role in political protest to the extent that conflict focuses on issues other than those having to do with the workplace. Social movements whose goals are not primarily workplace oriented are becoming increasingly common. Such movements are concerned less with the distribution of jobs and income than with the quality of the natural and social conditions of life their members experience. They target the domain of 'civil society' rather than the economy, raising such issues as the democratization of the structures of everyday life and focusing on forms of communication and collective identity. Their purpose is to defend the right to choose a certain kind of life and a certain identity. They see themselves as resisting the colonization of life by both the market and the state. These movements are not strongly identified with socioeconomic classes, although they do tend to recruit disproportionately from middle-class liberals, from peripheral groups such as students and (when their interests coincide) from production groups such as farmers and small businessmen.

The reason for the outcrop of these movements is the tendency for advanced capitalist societies to privatize production while socializing reproduction. Capitalism generates a series of social costs—unemployment, traffic congestion, pollution, occupational injury and community dislocation—which are not priced on the open market. The distributional struggle over who is to meet these costs is increasingly transposed to the state. Additionally, the state is forced to take over the supply of collective goods such as transportation and utilities because private corporations find them unprofitable. And workers tend increasingly to seek to compensate for their limited power in the labor market by attempting to increase benefits from the state—their share of the 'social wage.'

The common result of each of these trends is that social activism becomes focused more and more around 'consumption' problems, including those having to do with space for leisure. The state, not the capitalist class, is the target of the activists because it plays such a large role in the structuring of everyday life, especially among the urban population. 'The management of urban services by state institutions, while demanded by the labor movement as part of the social contract reached through class struggle, has been one of the most powerful and subtle mechanisms of social control and institutional power over everyday life in our societies' (Castells, 1985, p. 317). To the extent that the state becomes the actual manager of the collective services structuring everyday life, it will become the target when the management is deficient or unfair. The fact that these social movements focus around consumption rather than production issues—a concern with physical territory, space for action, the 'life-world' of the body, health and sexual identity, the vitality of communities and neighborhoods and the cleanliness of the environment—provides an opening for the political articulation of leisure demands. So, too, does their defense of individual autonomy and freedom, and their opposition to corporate and government manipulation, regulation and surveillance. Leisure demands thus seem likely to be 'relocated' in the political arena, no longer so closely tied to production issues in a straightforward class struggle but more intimately involved in the political struggle over collective consumption in which class alliances are formed and dissolved as the issue changes.

In the 'command economies' of the modern communist world, the future of the relation between leisure and politics is equally hard to anticipate. Communist regimes such as those in Poland, Hungary, Czechoslovakia, Yugoslavia and, more recently, the Soviet Union oscillate between the poles of extreme repression and cautious tolerance when it comes to cultural expression. This oscillation is set in motion by the economic need to allow room for creative expression and experimentation and by exposure to the West occasioned by the necessary transfer of technological knowledge. But too much freedom, leading to overt and flagrant departures from communist orthodoxy, provides fuel for the more conservative of the political elite to argue that the party is losing control over the people, and the cycle begins to swing toward repression once more. The moving forces here are economic need and political power, but the means is often cultural expression in the form of popular music, film and leisure-time reading.

The Hungarian system presents one possible future scenario, with considerable latitude for entrepreneurial activities both within state-run enterprises and outside them. Both the Soviets and the Chinese are experimenting with capitalism on a small scale in order to increase productivity and cater more responsively to palpable demand for a wider range of better-quality consumer goods. This promises not only to create a wider range of leisure goods and services (over which the state currently holds a monopoly) but also to differentiate the population into a wider range of 'taste publics' similar to that found in capitalist economies in the West. However, it also promises to postpone yet again any hopes of overcoming 'the perspective of bourgeois economy' in which work and leisure are opposed (Andrew, 1981, p. 154).

These trends must also be set beside an overwhelming manpower shortage being faced by most Eastern European societies, especially the Soviets. They are acutely aware of the fact that long-term economic growth across a broad front requires maximizing the quantity and quality of the work supplied by an adult population that is growing only slowly. Planners face enormous pressures to maximize the labor input of existing workers and are also forced to tolerate widespread moonlighting, a practice which cuts deeply into leisure time. The Soviets must also encourage the participation of women in the paid labor force on a scale unmatched in any other industrial society. Those same workers, because their incomes are indeed slowly rising, are increasing their demands for leisure items, particularly for home entertainment goods. This means that the scarce leisure time the Soviet economy will be obliged to permit for the foreseeable future is going to be spent on the consumption of increasingly privatistic goods and services. The optimistic vision of the well-rounded Soviet citizen, in whom work and leisure are finely balanced and mutually enhancing, has been postponed well into the next century.

As the nations of the world become more economically interdependent, we can anticipate seeing four trends, each of which will shape the international politics of leisure. Interdependence means more frequent and broad-ranging exchange of goods and services across national boundaries. These exchanges will undoubtedly include leisure goods and services, ranging from consumer items such as home entertainment equipment and sporting goods to activities and pastimes which are 'exported' (e.g. soccer in the United States and football in the United Kingdom), as well as events and images (e.g. athletic meets, horse shows and chess tournaments) which are intended for an international audience. The mass media will be part of this growing interdependence, permitting inhabitants of the new 'global village' to witness mass sporting events simultaneously. Events in one country will be timed, not for the convenience of the indigenous population, but to suit the timetable of the country with the largest viewing audience. The siting of events will be determined by the size of the television audience— hence serious talk of siting the soccer World Cup in the United States, not because of the minimal public appeal of soccer there but because of the size of the advertising revenues that could be generated. A shrinking leisure world will also mean the standardization of leisure identities. Most obviously, this will entail the standardization of the 'rights' of the athlete and of the status of 'professional.' It can be confidently predicted that the current Olympic distinction between 'professional' and 'amateur' will disappear—to the benefit of the First and Second worlds, where resources to pay athletes are more abundant. However, the universalization of athletes' rights also increases the chances of women and other minorities in the First World to gain equal access to leisure facilities. Where 'hidden payments' are no longer necessary and where competition from women in the Second World and blacks in the Third World threatens the sporting dominance of core countries, we can expect to see those countries respond pragmatically by opening up more sporting opportunities for minorities. Thus, while global interdependence might mean the creation of an international division of leisure labor, it might at the same time mean more equality of opportunity within countries.

Second, the increased trade in leisure goods and experiences will no more mean international equality of access than it does in other areas of economic life. The 'core' countries will more and more monopolize the production and distribution of leisure events and products. The 'exchange' of leisure will therefore be uneven, the more developed economies reaping most of the rewards of international athletic competition, the less developed countries trying to survive on the periphery of the world sport order. International sporting organizations will, in their internal structure and external functioning, replicate the international system of stratification. For example, athletes will be 'extracted' from the periphery for full exploitation in the leisure industries of the core. Tourism, likewise, will 'bring home' the 'raw' leisure experiences of the periphery for processing and reproduction (in the form of slides and video) in the core. Third World countries will become increasingly dependent on the living they derive from providing leisure experiences to visitors from the First World. Many of those visitors will stay in hotels and use facilities built by multinational corporations. In other words, even in an increasingly interdependent world, leisure relations will be asymmetrical.

Third, the 'globalization' of leisure implies its increasing capitalization or commodification. The United States, Western Europe and Japan all have a tremendous stake in the internationalization of production and an open trading system. A globally integrated world economy organized along capitalist lines means that leisure experiences will on an increasingly worldwide scale be homogenized and mass-produced as commodities. The 'market model' promoted by the advanced capitalist countries will encourage peripheral countries more and more to see leisure as produced and distributed by a few large corporations (perhaps absentee-owned), distributed on a local basis by many small and highly competitive enterprises and 'enjoyed' or received in private. This will be seen most strikingly in the homogenization of media cultures—films, television and radio programs, magazines and newspapers becoming increasingly alike regardless of indigenous culture and language. But this trend will also be evidenced in sports and popular pastimes which will 'flow' more readily along the conduits of world trade laid down by electronic links and rapid transportation.

Fourth, the asymmetry of global interdependence, and the vitality of the communist bloc and its satellites, means that sport will be more, not less, affected by international political struggles. Increasingly, the countries of the world find themselves woven into complex webs of economic, political and cultural alliances and blocs which diminish the autonomy with which they can enter into and transact leisure exchanges. They can no longer expect to be solitary actors in the world system of sport or assume that this system is unaffected by economic and political ties. The mass media, themselves increasingly internationalized, transform the globe into a single stage, tremendously amplifying the symbolism of sporting events as arenas for political struggle. Thus, at the same time the staging of events in this world theatre becomes more practicable—audiences of billions for the Olympic Games and the soccer World Cup—the probability of these events being politicized also increases. Ironically, nationalism, although it is rooted in economic competition, has as much to do with competing cultural claims—to superior styles of life—as it does with jobs and better living conditions. Nationalist claims on the basis of sporting achievement, more broadly the realization of individual and group goals through non-instrumental activities, promise to play a surprisingly important role in the future of international politics.

The alternative scenario is less plausible. It could be that sport and other leisure exchanges will be 'goodwill ambassadors,' the televizing of international leisure events a means of easing the tensions which stem from ignorance and blindness. But the recent past provides scant support to this idea. The mass mediation of sports on a global scale is used for the purpose of political propaganda by all parties concerned. The international sporting federations and the Olympic movement have become more, not less, riddled with political voting blocs, their members bound more firmly than ever to the interests of their country rather than the interests of their sport. 'Olympism' and the 'brotherhood of athletes' notwithstanding, neither 'sport' nor leisure in general have their own ideals; there is no world order of sport, no 'leisure world.' Each takes on the hue of the political system in which it is embedded, replicating rather than transcending the political conflicts in which it becomes embroiled.

# References

Alford, R., and Friedland, R. (1985), *Powers of Theory: Capitalism, the State and Democracy* (Cambridge University Press).
Andrew, E. (1981), *Closing the Iron Cage* (Montreal: Black Rose Books).
Archer, R., and Bouillon, A. (1982), *The South African Games* (London: Zed Press).
Aronowitz, S. (1973), *False Promises* (New York: McGraw-Hill).
Badie, B., and Birnbaum, P. (1983), *The Sociology of the State* (University of Chicago Press).
Bailey, P. (1978), *Leisure and Class in Victorian England* (London: Routledge & Kegan Paul).
Baka, R. (1978), 'Canadian federal government policy and the 1976 summer Olympics,' in B. Lowe (ed.) *Sport and International Relations* (Champaign, Ill.: Stipes), pp. 305–15.
Baughman, J. (1985), *Television Guardians: The FCC and the Politics of Programming, 1958–1967* (Knoxville: University of Tennessee Press).
Becker, H. (1946), *German Youth: Bond or Free* (New York: Oxford University Press).
Bell, D. (1973), *The Cultural Contradictions of Capitalism* (New York: Basic Books).
Blanchard, K., and Cheska, A. T. (1985), *The Anthropology of Sport* (South Hadley, Mass.: Bergin & Garvey).
Bland, L., McCabe, T., and Mort, F. (1979), 'Sexuality and reproduction,' in M. Barrett, P. Corrigan, A. Kuhn and J. Wolf (eds.), *Ideology and Cultural Production* (New York: St Martin's Press).
Boyer, P. (1978), *Urban Masses and Moral Order in America, 1820–1920* (Cambridge, Mass.: Harvard University Press).
Brake, M. (1980), *The Sociology of Youth Culture and Youth Subcultures* (London: Routledge & Kegan Paul).
Brake, M. (1985), *Comparative Youth Culture* (London: Routledge & Kegan Paul).
Bramham, P., and Henry, I. (1985), 'Political ideology and leisure policy in the United Kingdom,' *Leisure Studies*, vol. 4, pp. 1–19.
Burch, W. (1984), 'On public, private and personal approaches to leisure,' in A. Tomlinson (ed.), *Leisure: Politics, Planning and People* (London: Leisure Studies Association), pp. 48–66.

Caldwell, G. (1982), 'International sport and national identity', *International Social Science Journal*, vol. 34, pp. 173–84.
Cantelon, H. (1984), 'The Canadian absence from the XXIInd Olympiad,' in M. Ilmarinen (ed.), *Sport and International Understanding* (Berlin: Springer-Verlag), pp. 145–51.
Carpenter, L. (1985), 'The impact of Title IX on women's intercollegiate sport,' in A. Johnson and J. Frey (eds.), *Government and Sport* (Totawa, NJ: Rowman & Allanheld), pp. 62–78.
Carr, S. (1974), 'The use of sport in the German Democratic Republic for the promotion of national consciousness and international prestige,' *Journal of Sport History*, vol. 1, pp. 123–36.
Castells, M. (1983), *The City and the Grassroots* (Berkeley: University of California Press).
Cavallo, D. (1981), *Muscles and Morals: Organised Playgrounds and Urban Reform, 1880–1920* (Philadelphia: University of Pennsylvania Press).
Chandler, J. (1985), 'The Association for Intercollegate Athletics for Women: the end of amateurism in US intercollegiate sport,' *Studies in the Social Sciences* vol. 24, pp. 5–18.
Cherry, G. (1985), 'Scenic heritage and national parks lobbies and legislation in England and Wales,' *Leisure Studies*, vol. 4, pp. 127–39
Childs, D. (1978), 'The German Democratic Republic,' in J. Riordan (ed.), *Sport under Communism* (London: C. Hurst & Co.), pp. 67–102.
Clarke, J. (1979), 'Capital and culture: the post-war working class revisited,' in J. Clarke, C. Critcher and R. Johnson (eds.), *Working Class Culture: Studies in History and Theory* (London: Hutchinson), pp. 238–53.
Clarke, J. (1981), 'Subcultures, cultures and class,' in T. Bennett, G. Martin, C. Mercer and J. Woollacott (eds.), *Culture, Ideology and Social Process* (London: Batsford), pp. 53–79.
Clarke, J., and Critcher, C. (1985), *The Devil Makes Work: Leisure in Capitalist Britain* (Urbana: University of Illinois Press).
Clumpner, R. (1978), 'Federal involvement in sport to promote American interests or foreign policy objectives,' in B. Lowe (ed.), *Sport and International Relations* (Champaign, Ill.: Stipes), pp. 400–52.
Clumpner, R., and Pendleton, B. (1978), 'The People's Republic of China,' in J. Riordan (ed.), *Sport under Communism* (London: C. Hurst & Co), pp. 103–40.
Coalter, F. (1984), 'Public policy and leisure,' in A. Tomlinson (ed.), *Leisure: Politics, Planning and People* (London: Leisure Studies Association), pp. 21–31.
Cohen, A. (1982), 'A polyethnic London carnival as a contested cultural performance,' *Ethnic and Racial Studies*, vol. 5, pp. 24–41.
Cranz, G. (1982), *The Politics of Park Design* (Cambridge, Mass.: MIT Press).
Cunningham, H. (1980), *Leisure in the Industrial Revolution* (New York: St Martin's Press).
Dawson, D. (1986), 'Unemployment, leisure and liberal-democratic ideology,' *Scoeity and Leisure*, vol. 9, pp. 165–79.
Deem, R. (1986a), *All Work and No Play: A Study of Women and Leisure*

(Philadelphia, Pa.: Open University Press).
Deem, R. (1986b), 'The politics of women's leisure,' in F. Coalter (ed.), *The Politics of Leisure* (London: Leisure Studies Association), pp. 68–81.
De Grazia, V. (1981), *The Culture of Consent: Mass Organisation of Leisure in Fascist Italy* (New York: Cambridge University Press).
D'Emilio, J. (1983), *Sexual Politics, Sexual Communities* (Chicago: University of Chicago Press).
Dixon, D. (1980), 'Gambling and the law: the Street Betting Act, 1906 as an attack on working class culture,' in A. Tomlinson (ed.), *Leisure and Social Control* (London: Leisure Studies Association), pp. 1–34.
Dobbs, B. (1973), *Edwardians at Play* (London: Pelham Books).
Donajgrodzki, A. (1977), 'Introduction,' in A. Donajgrodzki (ed.), *Social Control in Nineteenth Century Britain* (London: Croom Helm), pp. 9–26.
Dubois, E., and Gordon, L. (1984), 'Seeking ecstasy on the battlefield: danger and pleasure in nineteenth century feminist sexual thought,' in C. Vance (ed.), *Pleasure and Danger* (London: Routledge & Kegan Paul), pp. 31–49.
Dunning, E., and Sheard, K. (1979), *Barbarians, Gentlemen and Players* (New York: New York University Press).
Espy, R. (1979), *The Politics of the Olympic Games* (Berkeley: University of California Press).
Evans, A. (1969), 'Work and leisure, 1919–1969,' *International Labour Review*, vol. 99, pp. 35–59.
Evans, H. (1974), *Service to Sport: The Story of the CCPR, 1935–1972* (London: Pelham Books).
Fogelson, R. (1971), *Violence as Protest* (New York: Doubleday).
Frey, J. (1985), 'Gambling, sport, and public policy,' in A. Johnson and J. Frey (eds.), *Government and Sport* (Totawa, NJ: Rowman & Allanheld), pp. 189–218.
Frith, S. (1983), 'The pleasure of the hearth: the making of BBC light entertainment,' in *Formations of Pleasure* (London: Routledge & Kegan Paul), pp. 101–23.
Gallagher, M. (1982), 'Negotiations of control in media organisations and occupations,' in M. Gurevitch, T. Bennett, J. Curran and J. Woollacott (eds.), *Culture, Society and the Media* (London: Methuen), pp. 151–73.
Gilbert, D. (1980), *The Miracle Machine* (New York: Coward, McCann & Geoghegan).
Goldman, R., and Dickens, D. (1984), 'Leisure and legitimation', *Society and Leisure*, vol. 7, pp. 299–326.
Goodman, G. (1979), *Choosing Sides: Playground and Street Life on the Lower East Side* (New York: Schocken Books).
Gottdiener, M. (1985), 'Hegemony and mass culture,' *American Journal of Sociology*, vol. 90, pp. 979–1001.
Groome, D, (1985), 'Increasing opportunities for enjoyment of rural recreation in Britain,' *Society and Leisure*, vol. 8, pp. 95–108.
Gruneau, R. (1984), 'Commercialism and the modern Olympics,' in A. Tomlinson and G. Whannel (eds.), *Five-Ring Circus: Money, Power and Politics in the Olympic Games* (London: Pluto Press), pp. 1–15.

Guttman, A. (1984), *The Games Must Go On: Avery Brundage and the Olympic Movement* (New York: Columbia University Press).
Hall, M., and Richardson, D. (1983), *Fair Ball: Toward Sex Equality in Canadian Sport* (Ottawa: Canadian Advisory Council on the Status of Women).
Hantrais, L. (1984), 'Leisure policy in France,' *Leisure Studies*, vol. 3, pp. 129–46.
Hardy, S. (1982), *How Boston Played* (Boston, Mass.: Northeastern University Press).
Hargreaves, J. (1982), 'Sport, culture and ideology,' in J. Hargreaves (ed.), *Sport, Culture and Ideology* (London: Routledge & Kegan Paul), pp. 30–62.
Hargreaves, J. (1984), 'Women and the Olympic phenomenon,' in Alan Tomlinson and Garry Whannel (eds.), *Five-Ring Circus: Money, Power and Politics at the Olympic Games* (London: Pluto Press), pp. 53–70.
Hargreaves, J. (1986), *Sport, Power and Culture* (New York: St Martin's Press).
Hazan, B. (1982), *Olympic Sports and Propaganda Games: Moscow, 1980* (New Brunswick, NJ: Transaction Books).
Hearn, F. (1976), 'Toward a critical theory of play,' *Telos*, vol. 30, pp. 145–60.
Hearn, F. (1978), 'Reply to Alt,' *Telos*, vol. 37, pp. 217–20.
Hebdige, D. (1979), *Subculture: The Meaning of Style* (London: Methuen).
Held, D., and Krieger, J. (1984), 'Theories of the state: some competing claims,' in S. Bornstein, D. Held and J. Krieger (eds.), *The State in Capitalist Europe* (London: Allen & Unwin), pp. 1–20.
Helmes, R. (1981), 'Ideology and social control in Canadian sport: a theoretical review,' in M. Hart and S. Birrell (eds.), *Sport in the Sociocultural Process* (Dubuque, Iowa: Wm C. Brown), pp. 207–32.
Hillman, M., and Whalley, A. (1977), *Fair Play for All* (London: Political and Economic Planning).
Hoberman, J. (1984), *Sport and Political Ideology* (Austin: University of Texas Press).
Hollander, P. (1966), 'Leisure as an American and Soviet value,' *Social Problems*, vol. 14, pp. 179–88.
Holt, R. (1981), *Sport and Society in Modern France* (Hamden, Conn.: Archon Books).
House of Lords, Select Committee on Sport and Leisure (1973), *Second Report* (London: HMSO).
Hunnicutt, B. (1980), 'Historical attitudes toward the increase of free time in the twentieth century,' *Society and Leisure*, vol. 3, pp. 195–218.
Ingham, A., and Hardy, S. (1984), 'Sport: structuration, subjugation and hegemony,' *Theory, Culture and Society*, vol. 2, pp. 85–103.
Iovchuk, M. T., and Kogan, L. N. (1975), *The Cultural Life of the Soviet Worker* (Moscow: Progress Publishers).
James, C. (1963), *Beyond a Boundary* (London: Hutchinson).
Jeffries, S. (1986), 'An analysis of the organizational structure of the Soviet youth sports system,' in Gerald Redmond (ed.), *Sport and Politics* (Champaign, Ill.: Human Kinetics Publishers), pp. 51–8.

Jessop, B. (1980), 'The transformation of the state in post-war Britain,' in R. Scase (ed.), *The State in Western Europe* (New York: St Martin's Press), pp. 23–93.

Johnson, A. (1982), 'The uneasy partnership of cities and professional sports,' in N. Theberge and P. Donnelly (eds.), *Sport and the Sociological Imagination* (Fort Worth: Texas Christian University Press), pp. 210–27.

Kanin, D. (1978), 'Superpower sport in cold war and detente,' in B. Lowe (ed.), *Sport and International Relations* (Champaign, Ill.: Stipes), pp. 249–62.

Kanin, D. (1981), *A Political History of the Olympic Games* (Boulder, Colo.: Westview Press).

Kaplan, M. (1975), *Leisure: Theory and Policy* (New York: John Wiley).

Kellner, D. (1982), 'TV, ideology and emancipatory culture,' in H. Newcombe (ed.), *Television: The Critical View* (New York: Oxford University Press), pp. 386–423.

Kellner, D. (1984), 'Critical theory and the culture industries,' *Telos*, vol. 62, pp. 196–206.

Kelly, J. (1982), *Leisure* (Englewood Cliffs, NJ: Prentice-Hall).

Killanin, M. (1983), *My Olympic Years* (London: Secker & Warburg).

Kolatch, J. (1972), *Sport, Politics and Ideology in China* (New York: Jonathan David).

Kostka, V. (1978), 'Czechoslovakia,' in J. Riordan (ed.), *Sport under Communism* (London: C. Hurst & Co), pp. 55–66.

Kraus, R. (1978), *Recreation and Leisure in Modern Society* (Santa Monica, Calif.: Goodyear).

Lane, R. (1978), 'The regulation of experience: leisure in a market society,' *Social Science Information*, vol. 17, pp. 147–84.

Lasch, C. (1977), *Haven in a Heartless World* (New York: Basic Books).

Levitan, S., and Belous, R. (1977), *Shorter Hours, Shorter Weeks: Spreading the Work to Reduce Unemployment* (Baltimore, Md: Johns Hopkins University Press).

MacAloon, J. (1981), *This Great Symbol: Pierre Coubertin and the Origins of the Modern Olympic Games* (University of Chicago Press).

McIntosh, P., and Charlton, V. (1985), *The Impact of Sport for All Policy* (London: Sports Council).

McLellan, G. (1986), 'What the trends tell us,' *Parks and Recreations*, vol. 21, pp. 45–8.

Maltby, R. (1983), *Harmless Entertainment: Hollywood and the Ideology of Consensus* (Metuchen, NJ: Scarecrow Press).

Mandell, R. (1971), *The Nazi Olympics* (New York: Macmillan).

Mandell, R. (1984), *Sport: A Cultural Heritage* (New York: Columbia University Press).

Marsh, P., Rosser, E., and Harre, R. (1978), *Rules of Disorder* (London: Routledge & Kegan Paul).

Marshall, T. H. (1950), *Citizenship and Social Class* (Oxford University Press).

Meller, H. (1976), *Leisure and the Changing City, 1870–1914* (London: Routledge & Kegan Paul).

Mercer, C. (1983), 'A poverty of desire: pleasure and popular politics,' in

*Formations of Pleasure* (London: Routledge & Kegan Paul), pp. 84–100.
Mickiewicz, E. (1981), *Media and the Russian Public* (New York: Praeger).
Morgan, K. (1981), *Rebirth of a Nation: Wales 1880–1980* (Oxford University Press).
Moskoff, W. (1984), *Labour and Leisure in the Soviet Union* (New York: St Martin's Press).
Mosse, G. (1966), 'Introduction,' in G. Mosse (ed.), *Nazi Culture* (New York: Grossett & Dunlap), pp. xix–xli.
Mrozek, D. (1983), *Sport and American Mentality, 1880–1910* (Knoxville: University of Tennessee Press).
Myerscough, J. (1974), 'The recent history of the use of leisure time,' in I. Appleton (ed.), *Leisure Research and Policy* (Edinburgh: Scottish Academic Press), pp. 3–16.
Nafziger, J. (1983), 'The Amateur Sports Act of 1978,' *Brigham Young University Law Review*, pp. 86–94.
Naison, M. (1985), 'Lefties and Righties: the Communist Party and sports during the Great Depression,' in D. Spivey (ed.), *Sport in America* (Westport, Conn.: Greenwood Press), pp. 129–44.
Owen, J. (1986), *Working Lives: The American Work Force since 1920* (Lexington, Ky: Lexington Books).
Patten, S. (1912), *The New Basis of Civilization* (New York: Macmillan).
Paxson, F. (1917), 'The rise of sport,' *Mississippi Valley Historical Review*, vol. 4, pp. 143–68.
Peiss, K. (1986), *Cheap Amusements: Working Women and Leisure in New York City, 1880–1920* (Philadelphia, Pa.: Temple University Press).
Ponomaryov, N. (1981), *Sport and Society* (Moscow: Progress Publishers).
President's Commission on Olympic Sports (1977), *Final Report* (Washington, DC: GPO).
Rader, B. (1983), *American Sports* (Englewood Cliffs, NJ: Prentice-Hall).
Richards, J. (1983), 'The cinema and cinema-going in Birmingham in the 1930s,' in J. Walton and J. Walvin (eds.), *Leisure in Britain, 1780–1939* (Manchester University Press), pp. 31–52.
Richards, J. (1984), *The Age of the Dream Palace: Cinema and Society in Britain, 1930–1939* (London: Routledge & Kegan Paul).
Riess, S. (1980), *Touching Base: Professional Baseball and American Culture in the Progressive Era* (Westport, Conn.: Greenwood Press).
Riordan, J. (1978), 'The USSR,' in J. Riordan (ed.), *Sport under Communism* (London: C. Hurst & Co), pp. 13–54.
Riordan, J. (1980), *Soviet Sport: Background to the Olympics* (New York University Press).
Riordan, J. (1984a), 'The workers' Olympics,' in A. Tomlinson and G. Whannel (eds.), *Five-Ring Circus: Money, Power and Politics in the Olympic Games* (London: Pluto Press), pp. 98–112.
Riordan, J. (1984b), 'Great Britain and the 1980 Olympics,' in M. Ilmarinen (ed.), *Sport and International Understanding* (Berlin: Springer-Verlag), pp. 138–44.
Robins, D. (1982), 'Sport and youth culture,' in J. Hargreaves (ed.), *Sport, Culture and Ideology* (London: Routledge & Kegan Paul).

Rojek, C. (1985), *Capitalism and Leisure Theory* (New York: Tavistock).
Rosenzweig, R. (1983), *Eight Hours for What We Will: Work and Leisure in an Industrial City, 1870–1920* (Cambridge University Press).
Rubin, G. (1984), 'Thinking sex: notes for a radical theory of the politics of sexuality,' in C. Vance (ed.), *Pleasure and Danger* (London: Routledge & Kegan Paul), pp. 267–319.
Russell, D. (1983), 'Popular musical culture and popular politics in the Yorkshire textile districts, 1880–1914,' in J. Walton and J. Walvin (eds.), *Leisure in Britain, 1780–1939* (Manchester University Press), pp. 99–116.
Sapora, A. (1981), *Leisure Services in Hungary and Illinois* (Champaign, Ill.: Stipes).
Scase, R. (1980), 'Introduction,' in R. Scase (ed.), *The State in Western Europe* (New York: St Martin's Press), pp. 11–22.
Shaw, D. (1980), 'Achievements and problems in Soviet recreational planning,' in J. Brine, M. Perrie and A. Sutton (eds.), *Home, School and Leisure in the Soviet Union* (London: Allen & Unwin), pp. 195–214.
Spivey, D. (1985), 'Black consciousness and the Olympic protest movement, 1964–1980,' in D. Spivey (ed.), *Sport in America* (Westport, Conn.: Greenwood Press), pp. 239–62.
Stachura, P. (1981), *The German Youth Movement, 1900–1945* (London: Macmillan).
Stedman-Jones, G. (1983), 'Class expression versus social control: a critique of recent trends in the social history of leisure,' in S. Cohen and A. Scull (eds.), *Social Control and the State* (New York: St Martin's Press), pp. 39–49.
Stokvis, R. 1982;, 'Conservative and progressive alternatives in the organization of sport,' *International Social Science Journal*, vol. 34, pp. 197–208.
Stollman, R. (1978), 'Fascist politics as a total work of art,' *New German Critique*, vol. 14, pp. 41–60.
Summerfield, P. (1981), 'The Effingham Arms and the Empire: deliberate selection in the evolution of music hall in London,' in E. Yeo and S. Yeo (eds.), *Popular Culture and Class Conflict, 1590–1914* (Brighton: Harvester Press), pp. 209–39.
Sutton-Smith, B. (1986), 'The idealization of play,' in C. Rees and A. Miracle (eds.), *Sport and Social Theory* (Champaign, Ill.: Human Kinetics Publishers), pp. 85–102.
Taylor, I. (1982), 'On the sport violence question: soccer hooliganism revisited,' in J. Hargreaves (ed.), *Sport, Culture and Ideology* (London: Routledge & Kegan Paul), pp. 152–96.
Taylor, J. (1972), *From Self-Help to Glamour: The Working Men's Club, 1860–1972* (Oxford: Ruskin College History Workshop).
Thorburn, A. (1984), 'Planning—the people business,' in A. Tomlinson (ed.), *Leisure: Politics, Planning and People* (London: Leisure Studies Association), pp. 14–19.
Tomkins, A. (1984), 'Cultural policy, the market and the local state,' in A. Tomlinson (ed.), *Leisure: Politics, Planning and People* (London: Leisure Studies Association), pp. 140–4.

United States Congress, House Committee on Energy and Commerce (1985), *The Professional Sports Team Community Protection Act* (Washington, DC: GPO).
United States Congress, House Select Committee on Professional Sports (1976), *Inquiry into Professional Sports* (Washington, DC: GPO).
United States Congress, Senate Committee on Commerce, Science and Transportation (1977), *Amateur Sports Act* (Washington, DC: GPO).
United States Congress, Senate Committee on Commerce, Science and Transportation (1985), *The Professional Sports Community Protection Act of 1985* (Washington, DC: GPO).
United States Congress, Senate Committee on Interior and Insular Affairs (1974), *The Recreational Imperative* (Washington, DC: GPO).
United States Congress, Senate Committee on the Judiciary (1983), *Professional Sports Antitrust Immunity* (Washington, DC: GPO).
Uwechue, R. (1978), 'Nation building and sport in Africa,' in B. Lowe (ed.), *Sport and International Relations* (Champaign, Ill.: Stipes), pp. 538–50.
Vamplew, W. (1983), 'Unsporting behaviour: the control of football and horse-racing crowds in England, 1875–1914,' in J. Goldstein (ed.), *Sports Violence* (Berlin: Springer-Verlag), pp. 21–32.
Walkowitz, J. (1980), *Prostitution and Victorian Society* (Cambridge University Press).
Walton, J. (1983), 'Municipal government and the holiday industry in Blackpool, 1876–1914,' in J. Walton and J. Walvin (eds.), *Leisure in Britain, 1780–1939* (Manchester University Press), pp. 159–86.
Walvin, J. (1975), *The People's Game: A Social History of British Football* (London: Allen Lane).
Walvin, J. (1978), *Leisure and Society: 1830–1950* (London: Longman).
Walvin, J. (1986), *Football and the Decline of Britain* (London: Macmillan).
Watson, I. (1983), *Song and Democratic Culture in Britain* (New York: St Martin's Press).
Weeks, J. (1981), *Sex, Politics and Society* (London: Longman).
Whannel, G. (1983), *Blowing the Whistle* (London: Pluto Press).
Wheeler, R. (1978), 'Organised sport and organised labor: the workers' sports movement,' *Journal of Contemporary History*, vol. 13, pp. 191–210.
White, M. (1980), *Shorter Working Time* (London: Policy Studies Institute).
Willener, A. (1970), *The Action Image of Society* (New York: Pantheon Books).

# Index

Alford, R. 8, 11
Amateur Athletic Union 16, 44, 72, 85–8, 167, 173
Amateur Sports Act (1978) 87–8, 158
amateurism 11, 43, 85, 99, 115, 134–5, 161–2, 171, 188
Andrew, E. 187
apartheid 74–6
Archer, R. 75
Aronowitz, S. 39, 67
Asian Games 161, 164
Association for Intercollegiate Athletics for Women 71–2

Badie, B. 6
Bailey, P. 22–4, 55
Baka, R. 172
baseball 62, 90, 165–6
basketball 63, 72, 86, 91
Baughman, J. 40
BBC 37, 40, 109–10, 118
Becker, H. 143–4
Bell, D. 101
Belous, R. 80
Bland, L. 48
Bouillon, A. 75
Boyer, P. 28, 30
Brake, M. 65
Bramham, P. 118
brass bands 28, 56
Burch, W. 98

Caldwell, G. 155, 167
Cantelon, H. 159
Carpenter, L. 71–2
Carr, S. 157
Castells, M. 60, 186
Cavallo, D. 32

Central Council for Physical Recreation 108, 111–15
Central Council for Recreative Physical Training 16
Chandler, J. 72
Charlton, V. 26, 102, 116–17
Cherry, G. 112
Childs, D. 135, 140
choral societies 28, 56, 106
cinemas 36–8, 52, 55, 82
Clarke, J. 26, 52, 57, 59, 64–5, 109, 117
Clumpner, R. 126, 171
Coalter, F. 109, 183
Cohen, A. 59
Commonwealth Games 156, 160, 171
Countryside Commission 107, 112, 114, 116
Cranz, G. 29, 31–3
cricket 19, 41, 43, 76, 106, 155
Critcher, C. 26, 52, 109, 117
Cunningham, H. 24, 28–9, 104

dance halls 69, 82
Dawson, D. 177
De Grazia, V. 146–8
D'Emilio, J. 47, 71
Deem, R. 6, 51, 73
Dickens, D. 39
Dobbs, B. 167
Donajarodzki, A. 27
*dopolavoro* 145–8
DuBois, E. 70
Dunning, E. 43

Espy, R. 152–3, 156, 162–3
European Games 156
Evans 103–4, 113–14
expenditures 84, 107, 117, 130, 136

# INDEX

Fair Labor Standards Act 81
Federal Communications Commission 40
FIFA 17, 138, 154, 156, 170
Fogelson, R. 27
football 63, 72, 90–4, 96
Frey, J. 54
friendly societies 28
Frith, S. 110

Gallagher, M. 40
gambling 12, 18, 25, 29, 41, 53–4, 83
Games of the Newly Emerging Forces 164–5
Gilbert, D. 126, 130
Gleneagles Agreement 76
Goldman, R. 39
Goodman, G. 24
Gordon, L. 70
Gottdiener, M. 66
Groome, D. 108, 118
Gruneau, R. 172
Guttman, A. 144, 157, 162–3
gymnastics 141, 168

Hantrais, L. 106
Hardy, S. 32
Hargreaves, J. 59, 115, 125, 159
Hazan, B. 129, 132, 137
Hearn, F. 18, 66
Hebdige, D. 65–6
Held, D. 7
Helmes, R. 168
Henry, I. 118
Hillman, M. 108
Hoberman, J. 123–5, 136, 138, 141–2
Hollander, P. 140
Holt, R. 107, 168–9
homosexuality 46–9, 71
Hunnicutt, B. 81

Independent Television Authority 111
Ingham, A. 12
International Olympic Committee 75
Iovchuk, M. 137

James, C. 155
Jeffries, S. 129
Jessop, B. 114
Johnson, A. 97

Kanin, D. 125, 139, 151–3
Kaplan, M. 52
Kellner, D. 38, 64
Kelly, J. 35, 84

Killanin, M. 158, 160
Kolatch, J. 127, 129, 133
Kostka, V. 128, 131, 136, 138
Kraus, R. 34–6, 82–3, 107

Lasch, C. 68
Levitan, S. 80

MacAloon, J. 156, 166
McIntosh, P. 26, 116–17, 182
McLellan, G. 84
Maltby, R. 37–8, 64
Mandell, R. 143–4, 168
Marsh, P. 60
Marshall, T. 10, 101
Marylebone Cricket Club 17, 112
Meller, H. 30–1
Mercer, C. 25
Mickiewicz, E. 132
Minister for Sport 108, 113, 116, 128–9, 137, 160–2, 181
Morgan, K. 169
Moskoff, W. 124, 127, 130–2
Mosse, G. 140, 141
Mrozek, D. 165–6
music hall 54–7, 105–6
Myerscough, J. 29

Nafziger, J. 88
Naison, M. 62
National Collegiate Athletic Association 16, 44, 71–2, 85, 88–9, 167, 170
National Football League Players' Association 91
National Park Service 83
National Recreation and Park Association 34
New Games Foundation 68
Notting Hill Carnival 58

Olympic boycott 62, 73, 115, 138–9, 157–61, 172–3
Olympic Games 43, 62–3, 72, 86, 88, 125, 128, 134–6, 138, 144, 150–7, 166, 172
Olympic movement 17, 75, 150–1, 153, 161–3, 170
Olympic Project for Human Rights 73
Outdoor Recreation Resources Review Commission 83
Owen, J. 81, 104

Pan-American Games 88, 156
parks 15, 19, 29–33, 106, 112

parks management 15, 33
patriarchy 50
Paxson, F. 43
Peiss, K. 57, 69
physical culture 122–3, 129, 131, 133, 137
playground movement 15, 18, 24, 30–1, 34, 82
Ponomaryov, N. 131, 137
pornography 49
President's Commission on Olympic Sports 85–7, 171
President's Council on Physical Fitness and Sport 85
private sphere 8–11, 13, 19–20, 78, 99, 121
Professional Sports Team Community Protection Bill 94
Progressives 28, 31, 34
prostitution 24, 45–6, 48–9, 70
public sphere 9, 39, 69, 120

racial discrimination 73
Rader, B. 30–1
radio 109–10
recreation 13, 15–16, 23–4, 26, 28, 31, 34–5, 52, 68, 79, 82, 105, 108–9, 111, 117
reserve system 89, 92
Richards, J. 29, 36–7
Riess, S. 165–6
Riordan, J. 61–3, 122–4, 129, 131, 133, 136–7, 159, 162
Robins, D. 59
Rojek, C. 21
Rosenzweig, R. 23, 52
Rubin, G. 47
rugby 75, 169
Russell, D. 28, 56

saloons 57
Sapora, A. 123, 126, 128, 131
Scase, R. 7
Select Committee on Professional Sports 89
Shaw, D. 130–1
Sheard, K. 43

soccer 12, 41–3, 56, 59, 63, 106, 124, 152, 169
Spivey, D. 74
sports centers 108–9, 114, 129
Sports Council 108–10, 113–18, 182
Stachura, P. 143
Stedman-Jones, G. 28, 102
Stokvis, R. 161
Stollman, R. 144
subcultures 64–6
Summerfield, P. 54
Supreme Council for Sport in Africa 75
Sutton-Smith, B. 34
swimming 19, 30, 109

Taylor, I. 42, 60
Taylor, J. 57
television 38–9, 64, 90–1, 111, 132
Thorburn, A. 119
Title IX 71–2
Tomkins, A. 119
track & field 19, 86, 153
trade unions 43, 62, 80, 103, 126, 129, 175

United States Olympic Committee 85–7, 158, 170
Uwechue, R. 154

vacations 103–4
Vamplew, W. 41
violence 41–2

Walkowitz, J. 46
Walton, J. 105
Walvin, J. 41, 43, 104, 106, 112, 152, 168
Watson, I. 57
Weeks, J. 45–6, 48
Whalley, A. 108
Whannel, G. 41, 108, 111, 114, 167
Wheeler, R. 61
White, M. 104
Willener, A. 67
Wolfenden Committee 113
workers' sports 61–3
working hours 81, 103–4, 130, 174–5